Anthropological World

An Introduction to Cultural Anthropology

Second Edition

Linda Amy Kimball
Western Washington University

Dale McGinnis
Pierce College, Tacoma, Washington

Shawna Craig
University of Texas at Austin

with a chapter by
Edward J. Vajda
Western Washington University

with illustrations by
David Flemming
Pierce College, Tacoma, Washington

KENDALL/HUNT PUBLISHING COMPANY
2460 Kerper Boulevard   P.O. Box 539   Dubuque, Iowa 52004-0539

Cover photo by Harry Teller

Courtesy of Patricia Adams

Contents

Preface to the Second Edition

Anthropological World makes students aware of the vital and exciting field of anthropology as an area of both intellectual importance and practical value.

Our basic aims and purposes remain the same as was stated in the Preface to the first edition; the book still provides enough flexibility for the instructor to use supplemental materials of his or her choice. But we feel that the changes in this second edition make it an improvement over the first.

Two new chapters enlarge the scope of the work. Edward J. Vajda's thought-provoking chapter 6 on "A Critique of the Notion that Language Imprisons the Mind" deals specifically with language, but has implications for other areas of anthropology as well. Chapter 3, "Overview of World Time Areas," complements chapter 2, "Overview of World Culture Areas," and has been added so that students can obtain a perspective on the past, and thus understand where they are in the present.

The addition of photographs and new drawings throughout the book provide a supplement to the written material, and these pictures will engage the students' attention.

New graphics in chapter 9, "Kinship," improve the presentation of the topic. A unique feature of the kinship graphics is that the Crow, Omaha, and Iroquois terminologies are diagrammed separately for male and female Ego; this makes it easy for students to begin studying each of these kinship terminologies in terms of an Ego of their own gender, and then to see how the system is different for Ego of the opposite gender. We have used this presentation in our classes, and find that students respond favorably to it.

A number of cultures are cited repeatedly in the text. So that these cultures will be more than mere names to the students, we have added a "Glossary of Cultures."

No one book can cover the entirety of the constantly growing and changing field of Anthropology. We have focused on what we feel are some of the core aspects of the subject. We have introduced students to the grand and marvellous river of anthropology, and hope that they will go on to explore much further.

Preface to the First Edition

This work is not written with the intent of replacing the instructor, as the professor should and must profess. A text is not a teacher, but merely a teacher's aid. A good aid is one that imparts fundamental concepts in a clear and concise manner. We have (we believe) presented the basic concepts in a relevant and interesting fashion. The book does not contain a great deal of theoretical sophistication nor has any attempt been made to challenge the professional anthropologist. Instead the emphasis has been on presenting anthropology in a fashion that we believe will interest and excite the non-professional, the beginning student.

Throughout this text we have attempted to maintain a harmonious balance in our descriptions and analyses of culture using three perspectives. First, the feminine and masculine perspectives shine throughout this work. Second, the temporal perspective is presented here. Culture is looked at along the temporal vectors of past, present, and future. Third, and finally, the ethnographic descriptions have been taken from anthropological readings and from the authors' fieldwork, respectively in Brunei Malay, among the Crow, and in Mexico and the United States. The combination of our three cultural areas of expertise, and our diversity of anthropological interests, allow us to weave an interesting ethnographic perspective throughout each chapter of the book.

Acknowledgments to the Second Edition

In revising a book, one strives to better the path trodden before. Many have helped us in this endeavor.

Many thanks go, once again, to all those mentioned in the Acknowledgments of the first edition. And to all those who are unnamed, but who helped us or inspired us in some way, thanks are due. Certain people have provided special help as we wandered through the revisions, and we would like to thank them specifically here.

Despite a busy schedule, Edward J. Vajda graciously wrote a valuable chapter for the book.

The Navajo photographs were taken by the late Harry Teller who wanted to see them published, now his wish has been fulfilled. Ms. Patricia Adams made the negatives available, and printed them for us.

David Flemming of the graphics section at Pierce Community College drew the original cartoons and illustrations used here. Ken Murphy of the graphics section did the kinship charts, and Linda Longmire did the timelines.

Small details can mount up in completing a task. Margie McGinnis provided essential help, particularly in the final stages of manuscript preparation. Gary Ward compiled the "Glossary of Cultures." Polly Campbell indexed the book. Richard Vanderway provided valuable help with the mechanics of final manuscript assembly. Robert Fong of the Pacific Cafe put up with noisy authors' conferences and kept the food and coffee well-supplied.

Our colleagues supported us in many ways. Joyce Hammond, Chairman, and all the members of the Anthropology Department at Western Washington University good-humoredly put up with glazed-eyed co-authors who managed to have books and papers scattered all over three rooms for several weekends. Members of the Anthropology Department at Pierce Community College managed to carry on despite a somewhat distracted chairman who had his head deep in revisions. Bud Taylor's reading of the history chapter finally bore fruit, though he may find it strangely metamorphosed; the chapter is included in this edition.

Special thanks and acknowledgment go to our students who used the first edition, commented upon it, and have put up with professors busily doing a revision. Thanks go to all those students and anthropologists who took the time to comment upon the first edition.

Without the help and support of our families and friends, this revision would not have been possible. Special thanks go to Marge and Megan McGinnis, Jeff Todd, Jean Lawson, Paul M. Hodgson, Arthur Kimball, the Haji Yussof family, and the Pasaribu family.

Any errors of commission or omission, and any opinions expressed herein, are those of the authors alone, and in no way reflect upon anyone else.

In the end, this book is built upon the work of those who have gone before us, is about those who share the world with us now, and is for those who will follow us in the future. We acknowledge them all.

Acknowledgments to the First Edition

Writing a book is a wandering adventure onto highways and byways of thought and endeavor. Some fellow travelers through the journey of life provided special help and encouragement on the adventure of writing this book, and we would like to thank them here.

Fieldwork is the heart of cultural anthropology, and the people among whom one lives during fieldwork become a very special part of life. A heartfelt "thank you" far beyond what mere words can convey goes to the Brunei Malays, the Crow Nation, and the Fidencistas of Northeastern Mexico and Northwest Washington State.

Inspiration and insight come but rarely. Mr. T. Y. Pang is a profound teacher who has given both. Mr. Pang also graciously did the Chinese calligraphy for this book.

Daily life goes on despite all. Our colleagues, students and friends have been especially helpful. Department Chair Joan Stevenson put up with a wild-eyed writing crew, Eileen Smith kept the authors organized and let them invade the office on the weekends. Carson Riley and Sandra Labyris provided an invaluable service with their first-rate editing and final manuscript preparation. Marie Timmons and Jim Sterling did the drawings, maps, and diagrams. Zhijian Yang did the index. Bud Taylor kindly performed the quixotic task of reading critically a history chapter which space limitations forced us to omit. Reference librarian Ray McInnis found answers to impossible questions. Colin E. Tweddell loaned office and books, and provided encouragement. Angelo Anastasio told us we were crazy and let us raid his book collection. Our anthropological colleagues indulged authors' temperaments, and the "officepoids" provided help and tolerated wild forays. Martha Grey typed many rough drafts, and provided culinary support. Vada Campbell typed rough drafts and provided a place to hibernate when noisy neighbors made work impossible elsewhere. Lynn Stagg ran vital last minute errands. We owe special thanks to our students for their ideas and energy. It was they who motivated us to write. Special gratitude goes to our students in the winter of 1986 who put up with harried, preoccupied professors.

Book writing spills over into daily life and can trouble sleep. Many helped make things bearable. Robert Fong provided humorous support and gourmet meals. Richard Vanderway read parts of the manuscript and provided encouragement. The staffs of the Pacific Cafe and the Oriental Star put up with noisy authors' conferences and kept the coffee cups filled. Erika Bourguignon has long been the mentor and inspiration for one of the authors, as she has been for many other anthropologists. Last but not least, we owe a debt to our families who showed great forbearance. Marge and Megan McGinnis were consistently patient and understanding. Sheelagh and Anna Craig were patient for their age, and provided lively evening company. Arthur Kimball went without cards and letters.

Other people, too numerous to mention by name, provided little helps and encouragements on the way. We thank them all.

However, any errors of commission or omission, and any opinions expressed herein, are those of the authors alone, and in no way reflect upon anyone else.

Anthropology Today 1

*How vast are the oceans, and deep the forest.
What are the lives of people, then and now?*
(Malay)

Sky, and Earth, and I. (Chinese)

Why? (American)

Human beings in all times and places think about their world and wonder at their place in it. Humans are thoughtful and creative, possessed of insatiable curiosity. Furthermore, humans have the ability to modify the environment in which they live, thus subjecting all other life forms to their whims and fancies. Therefore, it is important to study humans in all their richness and diversity in a calm and systematic manner, with the hope that the knowledge resulting from such studies can lead humans to a more harmonious way of living with themselves and with all other life forms on this planet Earth.

"Anthropology" derives from the Greek words *anthropos* "human" and *logos,* "the study of." By its very name, anthropology encompasses the study of all humankind.

Anthropology is one of the social sciences. *Social science* is that branch of intellectual enquiry which seeks to study humans and their endeavors in the same reasoned, orderly, systematic, and dispassioned manner that natural scientists use for the study of natural phenomena.

Social science disciplines include geography, economics, political science, psychology, and sociology. Each of these social sciences has a subfield or specialization which lies particularly close to anthropology. Geography maps and studies the earth's surface. Human geography focuses closely upon how humans interact with their physical surroundings. Economics studies how humans produce, distribute, and consume goods. Microeconomics focuses on small-scale economic phenomena, and upon economics in small-scale societies or in particular local regions. Political science studies the government of societies. Non-Western government focuses on traditional Asian, African, and indigenous American governmental systems. Psychology studies how the human psyche functions. (*Psyche* is the Greek word for "soul.") Cross-cultural psychology seeks to study the human psyche in non-Western cultures. Sociology studies human societies. Ethno-sociology focuses on the societal patterns of small groups and of non-Western cultural groups.

All the social sciences focus upon the study of humanity. Anthropology is a field-study oriented discipline which makes extensive use of the comparative method in analysis. The emphasis on data gathered first-hand, combined with a cross-cultural perspective brought to the analysis of cultures past and present, makes anthropology a unique and distinctly important social science.

Anthropological analyses rest heavily upon the concept of *culture.* Sir Edward Tylor's (1852–1917) formulation of the concept of culture was one of the great intellectual achievements of 19th century science. Tylor

(1871:1) defined culture as ". . . that complex whole which includes belief, art, morals, law, custom, and any other capabilities and habits acquired by man as a member of society." This insight, so profound in its simplicity, opened up an entirely new way of perceiving and understanding human life. Implicit within Tylor's definition is the concept that culture is learned, shared, and patterned behavior.

Thus, the anthropological concept of *culture,* like the concept of "set" in mathematics, is an abstract concept which makes possible immense amounts of concrete research and understanding. The different ways in which anthropologists use and interpret the concept of culture will become apparent throughout this book.

Culture is an integrative concept. Anthropologists maintain that no part of human life can be fully understood apart from the whole. Each individual human on earth lives in a particular culture. This culture includes a spoken language, accepted modes of dress and behavior, religion and a distinct way of determining who is a relative and how one should interact with relatives. The culture is situated in a particular geographic location and geographic setting, and has a particular technology, economy, political and social patterning. The culture forms an individual's food habits, dreams and imagination, and influences all aspects of life for each member of that culture.

An anthropological study of the Kwakiutl of the Pacific Northwest coast would include a discussion and analysis of all aspects of Kwakiutl life. This is the *holistic* approach.

Anthropologists also study the parts of culture. An acute and specialized knowledge of the components of culture is essential to understanding culture as an entity. Many anthropologists focus heavily upon one of the components of culture such as folktales, tool technology, economic exchanges, or religious symbolism. The purpose of studying the parts is to better understand the whole. Concentration on the holistic character of humans and their cultures maintains the unity of anthropology as a discipline.

The basic data of anthropology are gathered through first-hand field research. Cultural anthropology uses *participant observation* to obtain data. The anthropologist goes to live with a particular group of people, participates by sharing in their daily life, and at the same time observes daily life and writes down those observations. Anthropologists study the near and far, the exotic and the familiar. Recent anthropological studies have been done with Arctic hunter-gatherers, among desert tribes of Northern Africa, in village India and in New York City. Wherever it may be, "the field" is the source of anthropological data.

Anthropology is a social science. In the social sciences, as in the natural sciences, data collection is only the first step. The second step is the organization and analysis of the data, which also involves comparing them with other relevant studies. Third, and finally, the researcher summarizes the work in a book or article, so that the results of the research project are available for others to use in their own work.

An *ethnography* describes in detail the culture of a particular people. The anthropologist describes the separate components of the culture and analyzes the manner in which they inter-connect to form a unique and coherent whole. The descriptive ethnography also compares the group under study to other groups.

The prime focus of analytical studies in cultural anthropology is *cross-cultural comparison.* Cross-cultural comparison means comparing something, such as tool technology, in two or more cultures.

2

Anthropologists refuse to make or accept generalizations based on one study or on a single cultural group. They frequently compare people widely separated in space, such as peasant farmers in Meso-America and in Southeast Asia, or compare people widely separated in time, such as Nile Valley farmers in Egypt today and 4000 years ago. Anthropologists often select a few of the components of culture and compare their occurrence in a wide variety of cultures. Types of agriculture, kinship terminology, and spirit possession beliefs are a few of the components which have been the subject of major analytical cross-cultural comparisons. Such studies can lead to broad and valuable insights about humans and their culture. Agricultural experts, for example, find it vital to know what cultural factors are likely to help or hinder the implementation of new farming methods in a region where food is in short supply.

Anthropology studies human cultures today and in the past. Cultural anthropology, with its subfields of ethnography, ethnology, and linguistics, focuses on cultures which exist today. Archaeology, which is often considered another subfield of cultural anthropology, is the study of past cultures. And physical anthropology is the study of both the evolution of the human species and physical differences among human populations.

Major Divisions of Anthropology

Anthropology has two major divisions, physical and cultural. The two divisions are uniquely different, but are at the same time integrated.

Physical Anthropology

Human biology or physical anthropology is that division of anthropology which deals with humans as biological organisms. Some of the subdivisions of physical anthropology are primatology, paleontology, and human variation. *Primatology* is the study of primates such as monkeys and apes, with a focus on social behavior. *Paleontology* studies fossil humans and fossil primates in order to reconstruct their biological evolution. *Human variation* studies variations in the physical body size and characteristics of modern humans world-wide, in order to see how varied humans are as a biological species. Physical anthropology is important because it is *Homo sapiens* (modern humans) who form, carry and transmit culture.

Medical anthropology studies health and healing world-wide, combining elements of physical and cultural anthropology.

Cultural Anthropology

Cultural anthropology is concerned with humans as cultural organisms. The cultural anthropologist is interested in the learned behavioral characteristics of human beings in different cultures, including how people eat, make love, shelter from the elements and marry. The four main subfields of cultural anthropology are ethnography, ethnology, linguistics, and archaeology.

Ethnography

An *ethnography* is a written description of a living culture or sub-culture. A *subculture* is a small segment of a larger culture. Thus, dairy farmers, plumbers, astronauts, Chicanas, and Harlem Blacks are all subcultures within North America.

Unlike many other disciplines, anthropology does not depend on laboratory experiments. Because the behavior of humans is the focus of anthropology, the ethnographer's laboratory is the world, whether it be a Mayan village, a Black ghetto in Chicago, a harem in Saudi Arabia or a steel mill in Pennsylvania.

Ethnography, like much of geology and biology, depends upon field studies for data.

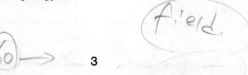

Figure 1.1 Rivers are the main transportation arteries for much of Southeast Asia. These men and women are leaving for home after a day of harvesting rice. Note the dugout canoe in the background. (Photograph by L. A. Kimball)

Ethnographic *fieldwork* is the careful and systematic collection of data which are obtained by living with the people of a particular culture and sharing in their life. The data gathered from fieldwork are the information basis, and also the vibrant life, of cultural anthropology.

Ethnology

Ethnology uses data to make analyses and comparisons, to build and test models of how particular cultural components work under different circumstances. An ethnological study might compare the differences between rice farmers of southern India and southern China. Ethnologists very often do not do fieldwork. Rather, they depend upon the work of ethnographers and historical records for their data.

Anthropological Linguistics

Anthropological linguistics studies people as speakers of language, and analyzes the structures of speech and other forms of communication, including body language and the use of personal space. It also includes the study of animal communication, such as chimpanzees learning sign language.

Language is an essential part of being human. Language is a sophisticated process of communicating through the use of symbols. Language is symbolic because there is no inherent relationship between a word and the object it stands for. A new branch of anthropological linguistics is *anthropological semiotics*. Semiotics is the study of signs and meanings.

A sign is anything that stands for or represents something to someone. Signs have an arbitrary nature; they can be interpreted differently by different people in various contexts. During World War II, Hitler's political regime used the swastika as a sign representing the Nazi movement and ideology. A Nazi would say that the swastika represented a good and righteous cause; a Jew's interpretation of the same sign would stress evil and cruelty. But in early Japanese history the swastika was a sign of good fortune. Thus, different cultures, and different people in the same culture, may have a sign in common. Yet the meanings attached to that sign may be quite diverse. Semiotics is the analysis of the signs and meaning of cultural systems.

Archaeology

Archaeology is the anthropological study of past cultures. Just as ethnographers use participant observation in field studies to learn about living cultures, so do archaeologists use special research techniques to learn about people who lived in prehistoric and historic cultures.

An archaeologist may be working 15,000 feet high in the Andes mountains of Peru, finding out about the daily life of people who lived in a city there 2,000 years ago. Or the archaeologist may be on the grounds of a state mental hospital, locating the site of buildings of an army fort that stood there a century ago.

Archaeologists have only the physical remains of the past to study. The jokes, songs, tales, and all the other richness of language have vanished. Perishable materials also are gone. What remains for the archaeologist to study are the material remains of culture. *Artifacts* are those physical objects modified by humans, such as pottery, and stone and bone tools. Domestic garbage, such as shell, fruit seeds, and animal bones also receive archaeological study.

Archaeologists perform careful, systematic, scientifically skilled and fully recorded excavations. The most important information in an archaeological site is the total context. A pot found beside a fireplace has a very different meaning from a pot found with a burial, or in a refuse heap. It takes long years of supervised training to become a skilled archaeologist. Subtle hints in the soil, for example, can indicate the location and shape of a dwelling or other building.

A vital part of archaeology is laboratory analysis. Study of earth samples, taken from a known place in the site and carefully labeled, may reveal pollen or other clues to past dietary habits of the people, or to the season of the year that an event, such as a burial, occurred.

Archaeological studies have opened large vistas in the human past. But much remains to be learned about the rich and varied course of past human lives. In this book we will occasionally mention archaeology and archaeological findings where they present relevant and useful insights to aspects of cultural anthropology.

The Concept of Culture and Its Uses

Culture has already been defined as learned, shared, patterned behavior. Seen from another perspective, culture is those things and events that are the result of the human ability to symbol.

Cultural Group

A *cultural group* is a group of people sharing the same culture. Thus the !Kung Bushmen gatherer-hunters of the Kalahari Desert are a single culture, and the Crow of the Great Plains are another. Large cultural groups often have several subcultures within them. Thus, the French of Brittany, Provence, and Normandy differ significantly in spoken

5

Figure 1.2 Around 1450 B.C. these Minoan amphoras were used as storage-jars on the Island of Thera (Santorini) in the Aegean Sea. (Photograph by Megan McGinnis)

French, traditional costume and cuisine; but all are parts of the larger "French" culture. French Canadians, on the other hand are part of Canadian culture, but share many characteristics of French culture, including the French language and the Roman Catholic religion.

Material and Non-Material Culture

The term _material culture_ refers to all tangible items of culture. Tangible items are ones which can be touched physically. This includes clothes, food, houses, pottery, tools, baskets, and all other material goods. _Non-material culture_ refers to all the intangible aspects of culture which cannot be touched

physically. Speech, thought, language and ideology are all non-material cultural items.

In the game of baseball the uniforms, bases, bats, balls and dugouts are material culture. However, the rules of the game, the signals between pitcher and catcher, base stealing, and winning or losing are non-material culture.

Real and Ideal Culture

Ideal culture is the way that people would like things to be. _Real culture_ is the way things actually are. In ideal American culture everyone has a home and three square meals a day. But in real American culture many people are homeless and do not have enough to eat. However, the idealistic belief that no

anth

6

Figure 1.3 The physical objects people use often make statements about life. This Eskimo wooden toolbox has a utilitarian function, but the decorations showing important animals both delight the eye and also link the toolbox owner to the world of animal beings.

one in America goes to bed hungry or cold is prevalent in American politics. It colors and affects the policy-making decisions of politicians who do not want to believe that there are such things as hungry children and the feminization of poverty in America—in Ethiopia perhaps, but not in the United States. It just isn't "American."

The concepts of real and ideal culture have practical application to success in the working world. The ideal work ethic is that most people put in a full day's work. But the reality is that often an unspoken worker's consensus limits the amount and time of work. The ideal office organization is the formal one indicated by titles and lines on organizational charts. The real office organization is the one that actually operates. Officially, one person may be the decision maker, but in reality another person may make all the decisions and the first merely puts the formal seal of approval on them. Knowing who really wields the power and influence in an office or workplace has obvious advantages for anyone working there.

The military has a metaphorical expression of ideal versus real culture. Ideal culture is doing everything "according to the book," that is, strictly following regulations. But everyone knows that senior sergeants are masters of real culture. They know how to circumvent regulations.

Three Basic Aspects of Culture

Any study of culture must follow a scheme. Many anthropologists use the scheme which analyzes culture into three basic aspects, technological, sociological, and ideological.

Humans make and use tools. Thus, the *technological* aspect studies how individuals and society use tools to modify, exploit, and protect their environment. The hoe as an instrument of technology modifies the environment when used to make gardens, exploits it when used on a field which should have been left fallow, and protects the environment when used to hoe a firebreak to halt the spread of fire.

Humans are social beings who have organized themselves into various social groups. The *sociological* aspect studies the relationships between individuals and society as a whole. The ordinary North American belongs to a small family group, belongs to a political party, and is under the governance of the Canadian or United States national government.

All humans must cope with all the wonders and trials of living. *Ideologies* are belief systems which explain why things are the way they are and how things should be done in order to maintain a balance. The ideological aspect covers religion, magic, philosophy, and law. Hanging a horseshoe over a barn door so that the open end points upward is an expression of ideology in rural America. The hanging of the horseshoe is to ensure that all within the barn prospers, and the open end is pointed upward "to keep the luck from running out."

The Discipline of Anthropology

History

Anthropology, like every other academic discipline, has its own history. Anthropology as an intellectual field of inquiry grew out of the humanistic thought of the eighteenth century, when European exploration yielded a flood of information about peoples of the world. In the nineteenth century the tide of information increased. By the latter nineteenth century scholars from such disciplines as physics, mathematics, biology, and geology had greatly increased knowledge and understanding of the physical and natural world. Scholars sought to apply equally rigorous and productive intellectual analysis to the human world.

Concurrently, people in industrialized Europe and North America became aware that unique cultures were vanishing under the impact of the standardization and homogenization of the machine age. Scholars sought to describe and record the vanishing cultures of the world, such as the North American Native Indian cultures.

Both trends of anthropological development continued into the twentieth century. Analytical techniques and field study methods were developed and refined. Franz Boas trained many important anthropologists in America and has been called the "father" of American anthropology.

Today anthropologists come from many cultural regions of the world, bringing their own analytical and conceptual perspectives to the discipline. Urban anthropology, the anthropology of complex societies, mathematical anthropology and applied anthropology are some of the newer rapidly growing areas of study. The 1960s saw the emergence of over 40 subfields of anthropology as specialization became necessary. Within this trend toward specialization anthropologists concentrate on certain cultural areas and topics to study. Thus, the culture area of an anthropologist could be South Asia, specifically India, and the subfield of anthropological study might be folklore and medical anthropology with an emphasis on ethnosemantics (the study of meanings) and ethnohistory (study of a culture's past through an analysis of its historical documents).

Temporal Perspective

A time perspective is important for anthropology. Each person is in a particular place on earth as a result of events that happened in the past.

Everyone dwelling in the Americas is an immigrant. Some entered on a jumbo jet yesterday, many are descended from immigrants who arrived by ship sometime during the past five centuries. The ancestors of the Native Americans entered the continent by an overland route more than 10,000 years ago.

8

Figure 1.4 Archaeology provides a window on the past. This 1986 archaeological excavation on the grounds of the State Hospital, Tacoma, Washington, provided information about an Army Fort that stood on the site a century before. (Photograph by Michael Avey)

American culture today tends to isolate the individual. One aspect of this isolation is temporal isolation, or severance from the past. But humans are not isolated either in time or space. Each individual is part of the grand saga of humankind here on earth. Cultural anthropology looks at this global saga now, and in the past.

Anthropology Today

Anthropology is truly an international discipline. Anthropologists come from all continents on the globe, and are bringing to bear the concepts of many different cultures on the problem of human understanding. Like all field scientists, anthropologists experience both hardship and fulfillment in their pursuit of knowledge. Like all scientists, they rejoice in new knowledge and understanding. Anthropology is also a humanistic discipline, delving deep into the richness and profoundness of being human.

Humans have always sought knowledge and understanding, often with a view toward practical application. And anthropology does have practical applications in fields ranging from international banking, medicine, and agriculture, to the daily concerns of business and domestic life. Anthropology also reaches far

1740s	Comparative Philogists and Indianists (History and origin of language)
1820s	Comparative Mythologists (Ideas of degeneration and evolution)
1850s	Romantic Movement in Anthropology (Evolution and transmission of language and folklore)
1870s	Classical Evolutionists / English Anthropological School (Savage Folklorists—Tylor, Frazer)
1900s	Historical Particularist / Diffusionist American Anthropological School (Boasian anthropology)
1920s	Anthropological Linguistics (Sapir, Whorf)
1930s	Functionalism (Reaction against historical particularism . . . Radcliffe-Browne: Structural functionalism Malinowski: Psychological functionalism) Peasant and Urban Studies (Redfield) Personality and Culture (Cultural relativity—Mead, Sapir, Benedict)
1950s	Structuralism (Levi-Strauss, Propp, Leach) Comparative Symbology (Turner, Geertz, Douglas) Culture Change (White, Steward, Shalins)
1960s	Over 40 subfields of anthropology developed Urban anthropology Advocacy / Interventionist anthropology Anthropology of complex societies Marxist anthropology
1980s	Third World anthropology Cultural semiotics

Figure 1.5. Outline of major anthropological developments

into other aspirations, the search for wisdom and knowledge. Humans have always sought knowledge and understanding from the sheer interest and fascination of expanding horizons. To be human is to question and wonder, to dream of horizons unknown, and then to seek more horizons. Anthropologists seek to know and understand the horizons of humans and their culture.

SUGGESTED READINGS

Fried, Morton H. *The Study of Anthropology.* New York: Crowell, 1972.
This work discusses anthropology as a chosen profession and is directed to the undergraduate.

Golde, Peggy, ed. *Women in the Field: Anthropological Experiences.* Chicago: Aldine, 1970.
An interesting collection of papers that reveal the woman's experience in anthropological fieldwork.

Kardiner, A. and E. Prebie. *They Studied Men.* Cleveland: World Publishing, 1961.
Written from a psychological perspective, this important survey of the leading social scientists of our century familiarizes the student with the history of anthropological thought and theory.

Oliver, Douglas Z. *Invitation to Anthropology.* Garden City, New York: Natural History Press, 1964.
This book deals with the basic concepts of anthropology and is designed for the beginning anthropological student.

Overview of World Culture Areas 2

All people who now live on the earth, or who have ever lived 'there, share life upon a living jewel floating in the harsh vastness of the universe. Human society today forms a globally interconnected community. Thus, a conception of the world as a whole is crucial to anthropology.

Habitability

The survival problems in each local region demand responses. All humans need (1) adequate food, (2) sufficient shelter, (3) clothing or bodily adornment, (4) protection from danger and the extremes of the elements, and (5) a certain satisfaction with life.

The most obvious problems are those concerned with sheer physical survival. In drought-ridden Africa, encroaching deserts, lack of water, and the consequent starvation represent a prolonged survival crisis today. Survival in the Arctic and in the desert hinges on constant battle with conditions at the limit of habitability for human life. A hurricane ripping through the Caribbean or war breaking out in the Eastern Mediterranean are uncontrollable violences. The street dwellers of Calcutta and the dispossessed Indians of Amazonia face the desperation of utter poverty and want. But humans need more than sheer physical survival. A certain satisfaction in life is also important.

Political situations form a key feature of habitability and survival potential. Peaceful stability and civil war are both political situations. Political boundaries override all other features, often in arbitrary fashion. The boundary between North and South Korea severs lush farmlands and rugged mountain terrain in one hostile slash drawn along an arbitrary straight line. The current turmoil in Central America and Southwest Asia demonstrates how political factors can become threats to survival far harsher and more implacable than all but the most severe "natural" factors.

The Global Entity

Pictures taken from the moon show the Earth as a single beautiful planet with blue seas, dark continents, and ever-shifting patterns of white clouds. Photographs from Earth-circling satellites depict Earth's large continental masses, the Americas, Eurasia, Africa, and Australia, surrounded by island-dotted oceans.

The world is a rich and varied geography of lands and seas. Terrain and climate taken together form the basic physical habitability of the Earth's land surface. Political boundaries cross the Earth, sometimes following natural terrain, sometimes drawn as arbitrary lines.

The world is also a rich and varied geography of human habitation. Anthropologists divide the world into culture areas, mapping the human terrain of the globe (Fig. 2.1).

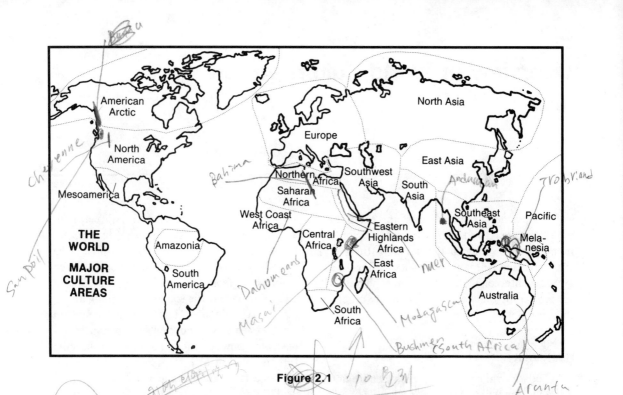

Figure 2.1

Culture Area

A *culture area* is a contiguous geographic area containing several cultures which show considerable internal similarities of patterns. Each culture area contrasts with neighboring culture areas.

The concept of culture area began as a classification system for ethnographic museum collections. These collections included numerous items of *material culture,* the physical manifestations of culture which can be touched or seen, such as clothing, houses, ornaments, tools, and the like. But the concept of culture area has proven useful in classifying living cultures, taking into consideration also the *non-material culture,* including language, religion, kinship, music, and all aspects of the culture which cannot directly be seen or touched.

Most large culture areas have several smaller divisions and sub-divisions. The small

Northern Puget Sound culture area is part of the larger Pacific Northwest region, a subdivision of the Pacific Coast region, which in turn is a division of the large North America culture area.

Culture Time

Cultures change over time and space. They do not remain static. So time must also be considered in relation to culture areas. Archaeologists, because they study the total depth of human life on earth, deal with culture areas which have altered and shifted over the centuries. (The Earth's *time areas* will be described in chapter 3.) But cultural anthropologists concentrate on culture areas at specific locales in time. Most cultural anthropologists focus on one of the following three time periods. First is the *ethnographic present,* which consists of the world and its cultures as they were before the massive change and disruption caused by European exploration and colonization, and the subsequent advent of industrialized technology. For much of the world the ethnographic present is around 1500 A.D., but in other areas it is later. On the East Coast of North America, the ethnographic present is at around 1650 A.D., and in the interior of Borneo around 1850. The second specific time is the *chronological present,* the time at which the anthropologist is writing. Clearly, an anthropologist writing in the 1930s had a perspective quite different from that of an anthropologist writing in the 1980s. The third specific time is the *ethno-historical present,* a particular span of time in the past for which there exist historical records which describe the contact between two different cultural groups, or between two major groups within a particular culture. The influence of Etruscan culture on Rome from 800–400 B.C., the plantation-slave culture of the south from 1800–1860, and the white contact with Indians in the Pacific Northwest from 1800–1900 are all studies written in ethno-historical present.

When the first Europeans arrived in North America they came to a land which had a rich cultural heritage extending back more than 10,000 years, a land which was filled with many widely-varying cultures. Each culture had its own distinctive language and adaptations to the problems of survival. Today, Euro-American culture dominates the region, with an industrial and grain-based agricultural approach to the problems of survival. English, Spanish and French are the dominant languages. The North American case is a striking example of the worldwide trend toward increasing linguistic and cultural homogeneity. The following overview of the world culture areas ranges through time and space, and suggests some of the problems and grandeur of the immense human panorama.

Overview of World Cultures

Eurasia

The Eurasian continent consists of two main culture areas, Europe and Asia. Europe is the region west of a line reaching southward down through the Ural Mountains and continuing to the Caspian Sea. The Bosporus Straits and the islands of the Mediterranean form the southernmost portion of Europe; the Arctic Ocean is the northern border. Iceland forms the westernmost extension of Europe. Asia comprises the remainder of the continent and also includes the Japanese and Philippine island arcs as well as the Indonesian archipelago up to, but not including, New Guinea.

Europe

Many peoples have fought and moved across the stage of Europe from long before the Roman Empire to the present. During the past two thousand years Christianity spread and flourished in Europe, providing a unifying intellectual tradition which differences of language and politics have modified but not broken. In counterpoint the forces of Islam surged out of Arabia, across Northern Africa, and into Spain, held the Balkans, and twice were barely prevented from dominating the continent. From the 1300s until World War I the Moslem Turkish Empire was a strong power block which controlled Greece and the Balkans as well as much of southwest Asia. Vikings traded from the Arctic to the Mediterranean. Mongols subjugated the eastern half of the continent in the 1300s. Gradually, the Renaissance, the "rebirth," brought an intellectual growth and awakening to Europe.

During the Late Middle Ages and the Renaissance, the growth of mercantilism and persistent emphasis on wealth and trading by independent cities laid the groundwork of

Figure 2.2 *Kampong Ayer,* the Water Village, is the traditional home of the Brunei Malays. (Photograph by L. A. Kimball)

social and economic forces which eventually led to the demise of absolute monarchy and to the severing of the connection between wealth and hereditary status.

The eighteenth century Industrial Revolution harnessing of steam power, and the late nineteenth century petroleum-powered internal combustion engine made available large amounts of manufacturing and transportation power. This power, combined with improved communications and transportation, sophisticated technology, scientific knowledge, population increase, and social ferment, resulted in a worldwide expansion of European trade and economic power.

Under the guise of capitalism, socialism, and communism the European worldview and industrial technological pattern have altered indigenous traditions in all areas of the globe.

The European worldview, economic pattern, and nuclear confrontation are dominant factors forming the world as we know it today.

Asia

Humans have lived in Asia for over half a million years, and two thirds of the Earth's people live there today. The five main culture areas of Asia are Southwest, South, North, East and Southeast Asia. The following descriptive highlights will show some key features of each area.

Southwest Asia

The basic traditional Southwest Asian economic adaptations use all available ecological niches. Fishing and trading sustain the coasts, irrigated farming supports high populations in fertile valleys, herding uses the hills, and specialized herding and oasis farming provide precarious subsistence for sparse desert populations.

16

Life is precarious for the people who live there. War and natural disaster threaten constantly. Nations may push toward industrialization, as Turkey does, or seek to revert to an idealized past, as Iran does. Only the family can provide any security. Honor, patrilineal kinship groups, and deep ties to language, locale, and religion form the core of cultural life.

Zoroastrianism, Judaism, Christianity, and Islam all arose in the burning deserts and verdant valleys of Southwest Asia. Each of these religions looks to some part of Southwest Asia as the "Holy Land." Thus, fires of religious fanaticism add to the social and economic factors of strife.

Daily newspaper headlines and radio bulletins scream of the latest fighting and injustices in Southwest Asia. The media call this region the "Middle East," but that name has a strong European bias which correspondingly titled East Asia as the "Far East." For over four thousand years, Southwest Asia has formed the crossroads of trade from Europe to the rest of Asia. Today the strategic importance of the area, and the oil deposits there, have put Southwest Asia in the center of power struggles for energy and political control.

South Asia

South Asia juts into the Indian Ocean and rises up into the great Himalayas and Hindu Kush Mountains in the north. Farmers of the ancient Indus Valley Culture used bullock carts and farming implements in 2500 B.C. which are similar to those still found in South Asian villages today. Farmers use all available flat land and terrace some of the mountains. Cities dot the lower reaches of the major rivers.

The principle religion of South Asia is Hinduism, which sees this present life as but one of many. The ultimate goal of every Hindu is to escape from the endless round of rebirth. Although Buddhism originated in South Asia around 600 B.C., Hinduism subsequently reabsorbed it. Buddhism remains the major religion of Sri Lanka. The Mughul invasions of South Asia brought massive forced conversions to Islam, particularly in the northern region. The beautiful Taj Mahal stands as a Mughul emperor's poem to his beloved Queen who died after bearing her fourteenth child. Pakistan and Bangladesh are officially Islamic.

Problems of overpopulation, internal hostility, and external political and economic threats confront South Asia. Yet amid the modern turmoil, individuals find comfort in an ancient cultural heritage.

North Asia

The vast area of North Asia begins at the towering slopes of the Himalaya Mountains. Three different realms comprise North Asia: the high plateau of Tibet, the desert and steppe central corridor, and the Siberian reaches.

Tibet long remained a world unto itself. Here Buddhism mixed with indigenous beliefs to produce a unique religion, one well suited to the howling frozen winters and the precipitous mountain trails. Valley farmers grew barley and other crops. Herders raised yak and sheep in high mountain pastures.

China colonized Tibet in the 1950s, destroyed much of the traditional culture, and introduced industries. But the basic economic adaptations remain as before. The Dalai Lama, the political and religious leader of Tibet, now heads the government in exile and Tibetan Buddhism has spread to Europe and America.

For more than 2000 years the desert and steppe areas of North Asia formed a corridor of communication which linked East Asia to Southwest Asia and Europe. Here foods and ideas flowed along the fabled Silk Road. Oasis towns were vital way-stations, and centers of sophisticated literate culture.

Across the steppe wandered pastoral nomads who herded cattle, horses, sheep, and goats. United under the leader Ghengis Khan they became the fierce Mongol horde which conquered Eastern Europe, China, and much of Southwest Asia.

In 1498 Europeans found the direct sea route to eastern Asia, and the Silk Road ceased to be a key communications corridor. Today China and the U.S.S.R. have their nuclear test-grounds and space-rocket launching facilities in central Asia.

The Siberian reaches of North Asia belong to the large circumpolar culture area which extends across northernmost Eurasia and North America. All peoples in the circumpolar region must cope with long dark winters and short summers. In North Asia the taiga or coniferous forest region houses reindeer herders. Arctic hunter-gatherers survive in the tundra, the treeless northernmost barrens. The Pacific shore of North Asia shows fascinating cultural and ecological parallels with the Pacific shore of northern North America. In both areas, the abundant marine resources enable groups to have permanent winter settlements, moving out in other seasons to follow the fish runs and to gather certain plant foods.

East Asia

China towers above the other regions of East Asia. The emperor ruled, by the Mandate of Heaven, from the center. He was the symbol and focus of the land that called itself the "Middle Land." A dense population farming and overfarming every available inch of ground provided the economic base which supported the fabled arts and luxuries of the Court. The Chinese classified all non-Chinese as barbarians.

Fundamental to Chinese society is the extended patrilineal family. Saving "face" and preserving the good name of the family were and remain central values. The welfare of the individual was secondary to the welfare of the family. Women became part of their husband's families at marriage, and paid homage to their husband's ancestors. By analogy, the state was seen as a gigantic extended family, with the emperor as the central paternal figure.

A complex and thorough bureaucracy controlled all the population, from the smallest village to the largest city. The District Magistrate was the lowest-level official in the hierarchy, and the Emperor was the highest, reigning over the entire Chinese Empire. The present Communist bureaucracy is in some respects a reformulation and intensification of the traditional one.

Protected by insularity, Japan developed a unique culture. Intensive agriculture, Shinto nature worship, and the *bushido* "Code of the Warrior" formed key bases of life. Elaborate politeness and detailed social conventions enable the population to live in overcrowded conditions. Since World War II Japan has become one of the world's leading economic powers.

As an extension of the mainland reaching south of the Yalu River, Korea lay vulnerable to numerous invasions. Long a tributary of China, Korea became a Japanese colony from 1913 until the end of World War II. Korea's traditional culture included a rich poetic heritage, often tinged with sadness, formal interpersonal etiquette, and the spicy kimchee pickle to accompany rice. Today the North and South share a common language and traditional culture heritage, but hold opposing political ideologies and face one another with hostility.

Chinese writing formed the basic means of communication within East Asia. The four countries traded extensively with one another. Paper, gunpowder and cannon, and movable type printing were invented in East Asia and spread from there to western Eurasia. Common usage of the Chinese script provided the region with a unique coherence and intercommunication. The resulting intellectual tradition went into temporary eclipse with the arrival of European science and technology. But now the East Asian intellectual tradition is resurging and spreading. Many recent advances in Western scientific thought and medical practice use traditional East Asian concepts.

Southeast Asia

The Southeast Asian culture area consists of two main regions, mainland and island. The Malay Peninsula and Taiwan share patterns of traditional culture with Island Southeast Asia, although in terms of the current national culture and language, Taiwan is part of East Asia. Monsoon and humid equatorial tropic climates dominate Southeast Asia. Thus, many plants grow lushly, but written records and other perishable materials vanish quickly.

Cultural opposition between hill dwellers and plains agriculturalists forms the dominant motif of mainland Southeast Asian life. Hill dwellers speak numerous different languages, each group has its own dress and customs, and each group lives at a certain range of altitudes and grows crops suited to that range. This pattern of multicultural hill dwellers set apart from the lowland dwellers also exists in large areas of Southwest China and in the Assam district of India.

Southeast Asian lowland dwellers farm irrigated rice using the karbau (water buffalo) to pull a plow. Large numbers of people speak one language and owe allegiance to a particular central power. In Thailand the traditional power was and remains the monarchy, today combined with a central nation state. Traditionally Buddhist, the lowland powers fought with one another and built the great architectural monuments associated with the area, including Angkor Wat in Cambodia and the temple city of Pagan in Burma. As in Southwest Asia, war and conquest fill the history of mainland Southeast Asia.

Figure 2.3 "Home is where the heart is." This Borneo house, since torn down, once housed a large extended family. The floor of the house was about five feet off the ground. Note the moored log which served as a quay. (Photograph by L. A. Kimball)

Islands dotted amid the sea provide a unique environmental setting for Island Southeast Asia. The basic division of the cultural world on each island is upstream, the mountainous interior, and downstream where kingdoms arose in the lowlands.

Headhunting and shifting agriculture formed basic lifeways for many interior peoples. The coastal people fished, traded overseas, and farmed rice and sago in the lowlands and swamps as they still do. Islam is the official religion of Indonesia, Brunei, and Malaysia. The magnificent, newly restored Borobudor temple mountain of Java and the temples of Bali are famous examples of Island Hindu-Buddhist architecture. Other architectural monuments include the megaliths of Borneo, the sturdy Batak multi-family houses of Sumatra, and the enormous Ifugao rice terraces of the Philippines.

Some three or four thousand years ago sailors from Island Southeast Asia set off and eventually populated the Micronesian and Polynesian islands of the Pacific. Southeast Asia today forms an important crossroads of trade, clearly seen in the flourishing city nation of Singapore. Southeast Asia also has metals and rare earths vital to modern technology, as well as significant oil reserves and consequent strategic importance.

Australia and Melanesia

Australia and Melanesia present examples of life in markedly contrasting environments. Long isolated from outside contacts, the region developed many unique cultures and languages. Lying east of the Wallace Line, Australia and Melanesia share a unique flora and fauna with the Eastern Indonesian archipelago.

Australia

The indigenous groups of interior Australia survived in a climate of hostile aridity. They had few material possessions, no more than could be carried along on their constant journeys. But a richness beyond compare characterized their world of thought, understanding, and complex kinship conceptions. Much of that culture is dying today, leaving the indigenous groups with difficult problems of adjustment to Western culture. Little is known about the indigenous groups who originally hunted and gathered in the lush coastal areas and in Tasmania. Today that land is prime agricultural territory, and the site of Australia's cities and industry.

Melanesia

The island of New Guinea and the surrounding smaller Melanesian islands contain an enormous diversity of languages and cultures. Each small section of a valley or portion of an island has its own distinctive culture and language.

Small-scale trade routes laced the area, so that obsidian from the interior of New Guinea would be traded to the coast, and certain valuable shells traded from the coast to the interior. Some ocean-going canoe trade occurred among coastal regions.

An elaborate cycle of feasting and gift exchange characterizes many of the cultures. In the past it was often associated with warfare and headhunting. The traditional power structure centered around the "Big Man." The position of Big Man was won through fierce competition in feast-giving and war leadership, and was easily lost. Modern national leadership takes Westernized forms. But tribal and linguistic affinities cause rivalries and difficulties in large-scale cooperation.

Oceania

The islands of the Pacific contain little land area but lie spread across nearly half the Earth. These islands form the Oceanic culture area. The sea dominates life. For two thousand years skilled sailors and sophisticated navigators roamed the vast Pacific. Large volcanic high islands, such as the Hawaiian chain, or close-grouped large atolls, such as the Carolines, provided substantial food and population bases, though poor soil and frequent hurricanes limited agriculture in much of Oceania. On many atolls the abundance or lack of drinking water provided stark limits to human habitation.

Taro, coconuts, and marine foods comprised staples of the diet. On the high islands, including Tahiti and Hawaii, as well as on the two large islands of New Zealand, agriculture was a mainstay. Elsewhere, as on atolls, its importance was less.

Most famous of all the monuments of Oceania are the large stone heads of Easter Island. Tantalizingly faint botanical and linguistic clues hint that Hawaii, Easter Island, and some other areas of Oceania may have had contact with the West Coast of the Americas before the Europeans arrived there.

During the past two centuries Oceania has become a pawn of external interests. But several areas are attempting to regain economic and social as well as political independence.

Africa

Africa today is a continent divided into two worlds. Throughout the continent the old confronts the new. The great cultural division between circum-Mediterranean Africa and Sub-Saharan Africa has ancient roots. Archaeological finds in the Sahara Desert, including rock paintings, indicate that some 10,000 years ago the region was a grassland supporting numerous cattle herders. Dessication pushed them into the Nile Valley, into the coastal areas of the north, and into the jungles to the south.

Circum-Mediterranean Africa

The circum-Mediterranean region which lies in the north of Africa occupies the area south of the Mediterranean Sea and north of the Sahara Desert. The 4,500 year old pyramids and inscriptions of Egypt mark the antiquity of literate cultures in the region. In Roman times North Africa produced much of the grain and other agricultural produce which

fed Rome. In the Middle Ages Islamic kingdoms preserved the knowledge lost to Europe, and Timbuktu housed one of the greatest universities in the world. Circum-Mediterranean Africa today has many cultural similarities to Southwest Asia, including the pattern of coastal trading cities, the importance of Islam as the dominant religion of the area, and the sharing of Arabic language and script.

Sub-Saharan Africa

Sub-Saharan Africa consists of all of Africa south of the Sahara Desert. Ancient kingdoms flourished on the West Coast, as the famous Benin bronzes attest. Linguistically and culturally the West Coast is highly complex. A major problem facing the region today is the rapid southward spread of the Sahara Desert, and the resultant famines and disruption of life.

South Africa

When the first Europeans arrived in South Africa they found Bushmen and Hottentot gatherer-hunters inhabiting the Kalahari Desert, and agriculturalists in the surrounding fertile regions. In the late 1700s the European farmers moving further northward into Africa met the fierce Zulu moving south, and from that encounter stemmed many of the problems confronting South Africa today.

Overpopulation, drought, and the dislocations of modernity pose problems for sub-Saharan Africa. But the tenacity, vitality, and adaptability of traditional cultures hold promise for the future.

America

The Americas range over all the climatic zones of the globe, from high Arctic to equatorial and sub-Antarctic. During pre-contact times, indigenous groups used all the available

Figure 2.4 These !Kung women are gathering edible roots and plants in the Kalahari Desert of South Africa.

ecological niches, which sustained rich and varied cultures basically in harmony with the environment. Conquering Europeans brought a new population and an exploitative world view whose modern consequences include severe environmental degradation, violent social unrest, and entrapment in the global economic network. Corn (maize), tomatoes, potatoes, chocolate, and peanuts are among the American foods which now feed much of the world. The American culture area consists of three main divisions: North, Central, and South.

North America

The high Arctic of North America presented extreme survival conditions successfully met by the Eskimo. Through hunting and gathering based on intimate knowledge and skilled usage of terrain and all available animals and plants, land and marine, the Eskimo survived and flourished. At one time they inhabited the far north of Greenland, but the same increasing cold of the environment which finally killed off the last Viking farmers in southern Greenland forced many Eskimos to move southward in Greenland. Eskimo occupation of northern Canada and the Alaskan shore has been continuous for millenia.

The vast boreal forest, corresponding to the taiga of Eurasia, housed caribou hunters who moved to follow the herds. In the Pacific Coast region hunter-gatherers lived in permanent plank-built wooden houses and erected large wooden totem poles. Peoples of the Pacific Coast region obtained a steady food supply from the regular and abundant salmon runs, gleaning the intertidal zone at low tide, hunting and fishing at sea, and hunting and gathering on land. Many interior groups in the mountain region moved about hunting and gathering.

The Great Plains of North America correspond to the steppe of Eurasia. Horses reached the Great Plains some two centuries before European settlers. The Indians of the Plains learned to tame and ride horses, abandoned farming and adopted a lifestyle based on hunting buffalo.

Throughout the vast temperate reaches of North America many agricultural groups flourished on beans, maize, and squash, supplemented by hunting and gathering. Trade networks reached from the Rockies to the Atlantic. Groups as far apart as the Ohio Valley and Carolina erected large ceremonial earth-mounds, some in the form of truncated pyramids or cones, others in the form of animal effigies.

In the Southwest, arid conditions demanded special irrigated agricultural techniques and groups lived in large multi-family dwellings. The Carribean islands housed several cultures which combined agriculture with fishing. Some had trade links to Central America.

Central America

Maya pyramids and Aztec cities astounded the Spanish conquerers who first came to Central America. Aztec Tenochtitlan, on the site of present-day Mexico City, far exceeded the contemporary European cities in size and splendor. Central American Indian groups today retain the languages and much of the popular culture of pre-contact times. But the intellectual tradition, the intricate calendars, and the writing system, as well as the elaborate state organization, have vanished.

Farmers in Central America face different challenges in the mountainous regions, in the arid interior plateaus, and in the humid coastal lowlands. Warfare and inequitable distribution of wealth characterized the region in prehistoric times, and still mark it today.

Figure 2.5 In the early part of the twentieth century this Navajo woman in traditional dress paused on her horse beside the well where she often drew water. (Photograph by Harry Teller)

South America

The land area of South America presents enormous contrasts in topography. Best known is the Andean cordillera (mountain chain). Here adaptation to high altitude living presents a basic problem of life. The Inca empire once linked much of the region through roads and bridges, and joined it with some of the coastal lowlands and some of the Amazonian lowlands into a single state. The wheel was used in the Americas only on children's toys, not as a form of transportation. The "Inca Highway" and its bridges were designed for human and animal travel. Throughout the cordillera numerous varieties of potatoes still form the staple diet. The llama serves as a beast of burden and source of fur and meat in the Andes. The llama thus compares as a key high altitude domesticated animal with the yak of the Himalayas and the Tibetan Plateau.

The Amazon Basin provides a lowland tropical home to numerous hunting-gathering and agricultural groups who once roamed the jungle unmolested by outsiders. But road-building, agricultural settlement projects, and gem mining have caused major destruction of peoples and habitat. Coastal Brazilian farming techniques, based on those of Europe, are not suitable to the Amazon Basin.

The vast pampas is open grassland comparable to the steppe of Eurasia and the Great Plains of North America. At the time of European arrival hunting groups flourished on the abundant game of the pampas. Europeans introduced horses and cattle. In order to obtain the pampas for cattle grazing, the Europeans systematically killed off the Indians. The pampas today is a major beef-raising region; *gauchos* are the cowboys of the pampas.

Tierra del Fuego, "Land of Fires," the southern tip of South America, forms one of the world's more hostile environments; hardy enduring hunter-gatherers lived there, dining on marine resources. They died off from diseases acquired through European contact in the nineteenth century.

The Americas of today, like Australia, New Zealand, and the Siberian reaches, have become a large extension and development of European culture. This culture may find it necessary to adapt non-European concepts and attitudes in order to find a route to the future.

A Global Perspective

Above all else, the panorama of world culture areas shows the incredible human ability to adapt, survive, and endure. Adaptation involves skills, knowledge, and production of essential tools to provide adequate food, shelter, and warmth for survival. But tools and knowledge are not everything needed by humans. Art, religion, and a variety of social systems, though they cannot be seen or touched, play key roles in human survival throughout the world. But no matter what the special circumstances of environment, humans adapt in particular ways because they have been taught how to solve the problems of survival. These solutions and the world view that supports them and makes sense of them are provided by culture.

SUGGESTED READINGS

Bowen, Elenore Smith. *Return to Laughter.* New York: Doubleday, 1964.
   This anthropological novel is based on a great deal of fact and depicts the cultural life in a northwest African village as well as an anthropologist's attempt to study the culture within the village.

Hoebel, E. A. *The Cheyennes: Indians of the Great Plains.* 2nd edition. New York: Holt, Rinehart and Winston, 1978.
   An ethnography dealing with a Plains Indian tribe's culture which includes the technological, sociological, and ideological aspects.

Herskovits, M. J., ed. *Cultural Relativism: Perspectives in Cultural Pluralism*. New York: Random House, 1972.
This book contains a number of excellent articles on cultural relativism.

Turnbull, Colin M. *The Forest People*. New York: Simon and Schuster, 1961.
An ethnography illustrating the daily life of the Mbuti Pygmies who live in the Ituri rain forest of Zaire, Africa. The book illustrates how the Pygmies have adapted to a life in the rain forest.

Vandenbeld, John. *Nature of Australia; A Portrait of the Island Continent*. Facts on File, New York, 1988.
A vividly illustrated natural history account which describes how the Australian Aborigines managed their environment.

An Overview of World Time Areas

3

Human generations pass one after the other. Each generation is molded by the past, lives in the present, and forms the pattern of the future. Our modern world is but one more tumbling bend in the long-flowing stream of human culture. Archaeologists are anthropologists who specialize in the study of the rich and varied human past, and they have reconstructed much of humankind's epic saga upon the Earth.

An overview of world time areas will help to set the present time period in perspective, just as an overview of world culture areas helped to set the present place in perspective.

In looking at the past, it is necessary to have a way of indicating dates. The dates given will be in terms of B.P., Before the Present, or in terms of the era we are in now. The traditional dates relating to our present era were B.C., Before Christ, and A.D. (Anno Domini), the Year of Our Lord. But many scholars of various religious persuasions prefer to use alternative terms which lack religious bias; these terms are: B.C.E.; Before the Current Era, and C.E., Current Era; years B.C.E. = years B.C., and years C.E. = years A.D. The following account will use various of these terms as seems appropriate.

Now let us stand in the year 2000 C.E. and take a look back at the past.

The Long Hunting-Gathering Era

The earliest period of humankind's stay on Earth reaches far back into time. By 100,000 years ago, humans hunted and gath-

ered in Eurasia and Africa; they spoke, sang, made tools, and used fire for cooking. One hundred thousand years ago, Australia and New Guinea, the New World (the Americas) and the Pacific Islands had no population of humans. If one allows that twenty-five years constitutes a human generation, then 100,000 years means 4,000 human lifetimes ago. During this long time, humans survived for tens of thousands of years as the Earth alternately warmed and cooled. During the cooler periods, glaciers expanded over much of the Earth's land surface, and the sea levels were lower than they are now; during the warmer periods, glaciers receded and the sea levels rose. Today we are living in one of the warmer periods with a relatively high sea level and small glaciers; but the climate could change, as it has done several times in the past, and humans will again have to adapt to new conditions.

Careful archaeological excavation, followed by sophisticated laboratory analysis, has revealed the sad event that happened one bright spring day 60,000 years B.P., 2040 generations ago. A respected medicine man lay dead in the hills of what is now Iraq, his medical knowledge surviving only in the memories of those whom he had taught. Grieving relatives dug a grave inside a cave high up in the hills; they laid the body of the medicine man in its final resting place, said their last farewells, and as a final tribute, placed the flowers of medicinal plants in the grave. Even today, traditional medical practitioners in Iraq still

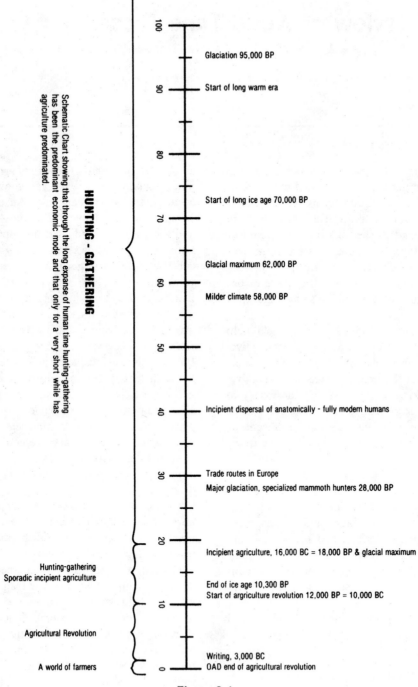

HUNTING - GATHERING

Schematic Chart showing that through the long expanse of human time hunting-gathering has been the predominant economic mode and that only for a very short while has agriculture predominated.

100

Glaciation 95,000 BP

90 — Start of long warm era

80

Start of long ice age 70,000 BP

70

Glacial maximum 62,000 BP

60 — Milder climate 58,000 BP

50

40 — Incipient dispersal of anatomically - fully modern humans

30 — Trade routes in Europe
Major glaciation, specialized mammoth hunters 28,000 BP

20 — Incipient agriculture, 16,000 BC = 18,000 BP & glacial maximum

Hunting-gathering
Sporadic incipient agriculture

End of ice age 10,300 BP
Start of argriculture revolution 12,000 BP = 10,000 BC

10

Agricultural Revolution

A world of farmers

Writing, 3,000 BC
0AD end of agricultural revolution

0

Figure 3.1

A BRIEF CHRONOLOGY OF THE LAST 50,000 YEARS

(All dates are in years before the present, with the present being the year 2,000 A.D.) ("Humans" means "modern humans")

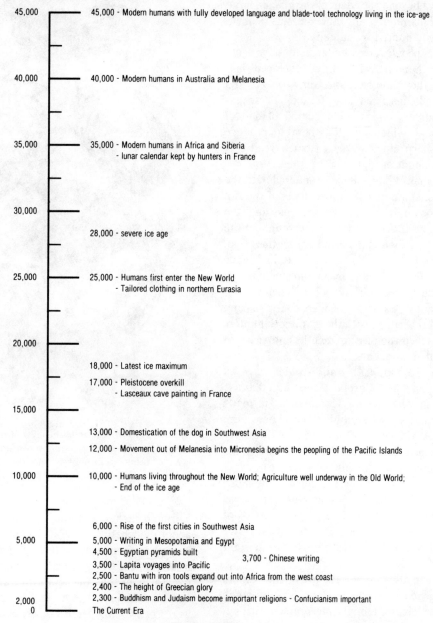

45,000	45,000 - Modern humans with fully developed language and blade-tool technology living in the ice-age
40,000	40,000 - Modern humans in Australia and Melanesia
35,000	35,000 - Modern humans in Africa and Siberia - lunar calendar kept by hunters in France
30,000	
	28,000 - severe ice age
25,000	25,000 - Humans first enter the New World - Tailored clothing in northern Eurasia
20,000	
	18,000 - Latest ice maximum
	17,000 - Pleistocene overkill - Lasceaux cave painting in France
15,000	
	13,000 - Domestication of the dog in Southwest Asia
	12,000 - Movement out of Melanesia into Micronesia begins the peopling of the Pacific Islands
10,000	10,000 - Humans living throughout the New World; Agriculture well underway in the Old World; - End of the ice age
	6,000 - Rise of the first cities in Southwest Asia
5,000	5,000 - Writing in Mesopotamia and Egypt 4,500 - Egyptian pyramids built 3,700 - Chinese writing 3,500 - Lapita voyages into Pacific 2,500 - Bantu with iron tools expand out into Africa from the west coast 2,400 - The height of Greecian glory
2,000 0	2,300 - Buddhism and Judaism become important religions - Confucianism important The Current Era

Figure 3.2

29

use those same plants (Solecki 1975). Our links with the past are many and deep.

Forty-five thousand years ago, large glaciers covered much of Eurasia. In the tundra and taiga beyond the edges of the glacier, large herds of mammoths and other animals roamed, vigorously hunted by humans.

The people of those ancient days were modern humans with fully developed language; they laughed and sang, joked and grumbled, discussed and argued. These ancient hunters had a sophisticated blade-tool technology which enabled them to produce many sharp efficient tools from a relatively small amount of high-quality stone.

Humans have long wondered at the heavens, and noted the movements of the sun and moon relative to the seasons, and the shifting patterns of day-length throughout the year. More than a thousand generations ago, large-game hunters of 35,000 B.P. in France kept a lunar calendar by making notches on ivory and bone (Marshak 1972). When writing important dates on a calendar, one is sharing a cultural heritage with the mammoth hunters who notched the passing months and years on their lunar calendars.

By 30,000 B.P. trade routes crossed through much of Europe. Around 29,000 B.P. people in what is now Czechoslovakia made the earliest known ceramic items. These were figurines of "Venuses" and animals. The Venuses depict fat women well able to survive the rigors of starvation while continuing to nurse their young, an important consideration for survival. The life of the hunter-gatherers was often one of feast, but interspersed periods of famine also occurred. The ability to live through the times of scarcity was important for survival.

When all was well, the life of the hunters was a good one, with abundant food and much time for leisure, though interspersed with periods of prolonged, intense activity. At night men and women sat around the fire exchanging tales and accounts of the day.

Figure 3.3 "Beauty is in the eye of the beholder." This Venus figurine represents one ideal of feminine beauty among ice-age hunter-gatherers of Europe.

Through such talk, adults shared information about the location of plants and other items to be gathered, and the haunts and habits of animals and the tricks of tracking and killing, as well as about their own cultural traditions and speculations on life. The few old people who were aged 40 to 50 were a repository of wisdom for the young who learned by listening to their elders as well as by practical experience.

Figure 3.4 Strong courage and deep purpose motivated the Central European hunter-gatherers who painted these pictures far inside a cave thousands of years ago. What meaning did these pictures and designs have for the artists who painted them by flickering torchlight? We can never know.

Volcanic explosions, earthquakes, storms and other violent forces remind us that humans are at the mercy of vast natural forces. So, too, were the ancient hunter-gatherers of the Old World. Around 28,000 B.P., the Ice Age grew severe; glaciers overran animals' grazing ground, humans huddled closer in the severe winters, and life continued. Artists from Russia to France drew realistic and abstract figures

on cave walls, ". . . but anyone who has not stalked a herd of woolly mammoths at the snout of a glacier may be unable to guess the meaning of this art" (Calder, 1983:159).

Tailors can trace their occupational heritage back to 25,000 B.P. near Moscow. There a group of large game hunters buried a man and two boys in tailored clothing ornamented with rows of sewn-on beads. The clothing soon rotted away, but the beads remained in ordered array for the archaeologists, who used these beads to reconstruct the shape and cut of the clothing to which they were once attached.

Sophisticated hunter-gatherers roamed throughout most of Africa, though little is known about them. In time, modern human peoples had spread out over almost all of the Old World, reaching Australia around 50,000 B.P. But the New World remained empty of people.

Stirrings of Change

During the last ice age maximum, around 18,000 B.P., the places where later would stand Seattle, Toronto, Montreal, Boston, Leningrad, and Copenhagen, lay buried deep beneath glacial ice. The Sahara Desert was more extensive than it is today, and dry land joined Florida to Cuba, Java to mainland Southeast Asia, Tasmania to Australia, and America to Asia.

Seeking to survive, humans moved and changed. Around 25,000 B.P., as glaciers locked up even more water, the sea levels fell and the Bering Strait became dry land which formed a "land bridge" between the Asian continent and the North American continent. This "land bridge" was a thousand miles wide in some places, and is referred to by archaeologists and geologists as Beringia.

Slowly, perhaps in different groups, at different times, hunter-gatherers wandered out of Northeast Asia, across Beringia, and into the New World. Their descendants would be the American Indians who by 17,000 B.P. had spread to the southernmost tip of the continent. The vast panorama of human life in the New World had begun.

I wish these critters would find their own condo.

Figure 3.5 (Cartoon by David Flemming)

Crisis

Fiction often depicts the past as an idyllic place, but humans ever and always have been beset by problems, and have caused them. Seventeen thousand years ago, in both the Old and New World, humans slaughtered too many of the large game animals which were also being pushed near the limits of survival by changing climate and environment; and the once-abundant herds diminished greatly or died out altogether. Mammoths became extinct in this "Pleistocene Overkill." (The "Pleistocene" is the name of the geologic epoch which began 1,800,000 years ago and continued until 10,300 B.P. Today we are living in the "Holocene" epoch.)

During the time of the Pleistocene overkill, hunters in Lasceaux, France, ventured far into underground caves. On the walls of these

Figure 3.6 Hunting mammoths 35,000 years ago required skill, knowledge, endurance and courage. The man on the ledge will throw his rock at the mammoth's head in an effort to stun or blind the animal.

caves, the hunters painted pictures of the animals important to their lives. Was this a paean of joy at abundance, or was it a desperate effort to make the faltering herds increase? We shall never know.

The Great Change

"A man's best friend is his dog." This commonplace statement of our culture shows the importance of dogs to humankind. The domestication of the dog in Southwest Asia around 12,000 B.P. was a first step in humankind's great change from a hunting-gathering lifestyle to one predominantly settled and agricultural.

The agricultural revolution took place over the ten thousand years from 12,000–2,000 B.P., that is, from 10,000 B.C.—1 A.D. In 10,000 B.C. agriculture occurred in only a few areas of the world; by 1 A.D. it was the predominant economic mode of life, and fed more people than all other economies combined, and continues to do so to the present.

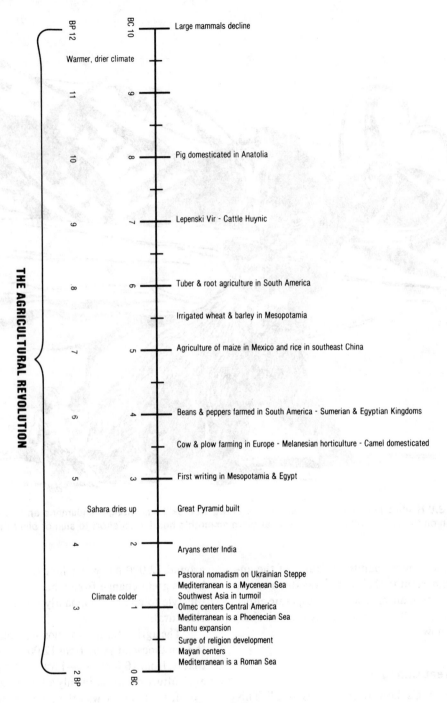

THE AGRICULTURAL REVOLUTION

BP	BC	
12	10	Large mammals decline
		Warmer, drier climate
11	9	
10	8	Pig domesticated in Anatolia
9	7	Lepenski Vir - Cattle Huynic
8	6	Tuber & root agriculture in South America
		Irrigated wheat & barley in Mesopotamia
7	5	Agriculture of maize in Mexico and rice in southeast China
6	4	Beans & peppers farmed in South America - Sumerian & Egyptian Kingdoms
		Cow & plow farming in Europe - Melanesian horticulture - Camel domesticated
5	3	First writing in Mesopotamia & Egypt
		Sahara dries up — Great Pyramid built
4	2	Aryans enter India
3	1	Pastoral nomadism on Ukrainian Steppe / Mediterranean is a Mycenean Sea / Southwest Asia in turmoil / Climate colder / Olmec centers Central America / Mediterranean is a Phoenecian Sea / Bantu expansion
2 BP	0 BC	Surge of religion development / Mayan centers / Mediterranean is a Roman Sea

Figure 3.7

34

Some of the main events in the agricultural revolution were as follows: 12,000 B.P. cereal grains in Southwest Asia; 10,000 B.P. reliance on tubers and roots in South America; 9000 B.P. rice in Southeast China and maize in Central America; 7000 B.P. beans and pepper in South America; and 7000 B.P. yams in Southeast Asia and horticulture in New Guinea as evidenced by irrigation ditches. Each of these was an independent domestication. The differing events in the world show up in the fact that 5000 B.P. saw large mammoth kills in Mexico, while farming villages were widespread in the Fertile Crescent.

Any change which spans ten millennia, 400 generations, is not a revolution in the sense of being a rapid change. But "revolution" also means "absolute drastic change, an overturning of all that has gone before." In this sense the agricultural revolution was indeed a revolution, comparable only to the tool-making revolution in which human ancestors first began to make and use tools, and the technological revolution which has altered the face of the globe in the past two centuries. The effects of the agricultural revolution permeate our life.

Our very culture and mode of thinking are linked inextricably to agriculture. We speak of sowing and reaping, of harvesting and storing. A difficult task is a "tough row to hoe"; someone overworked may feel like a "beast of burden." We conceptualize the seasons in terms of the growth cycle of plants, not in terms of the annual migration cycle of the mammoth. And we have the farmer's possessive attitude toward land as being something that one owns; a concept not found among hunter-gatherers. Hunter-gatherers have few possessions, for they must be mobile and able to shift with the game. But farmers stay put in one location; they build permanent houses and accumulate material goods. Concepts of religion and the "other beings" of the world changed dramatically with the gradual transformation from hunting-gathering to an agricultural way of life.

So embedded in the agricultural life way are we, that in a very real sense we cannot emotionally feel or understand the life-ways of hunter-gatherers. Hunter-gatherers live intimately with the element of chance. The game will either come where it always has or it will go elsewhere and the group will starve if the plant food also fails. The plants will either regenerate where they were harvested, or they will not and one has to seek elsewhere for them or try alternatives. Life alternates between periods of intensive prolonged labor and intervals of rest and leisure. The many hunter-gatherers of the long human past lived rich lives, following the abundant herds of game which roamed through favorable home territory.

Then, over the course of 10,000 years, humanity crossed a great divide. We today stand on the other side of that divide, separated forever from the numerous generations of hunter-gatherers who roamed over almost all the land surface of the Earth and who were our forebearers. It is in this sense, in the complete alteration of life and concept beyond recall, that the agricultural revolution was a revolution. The agricultural revolution had a profound effect on human cultures in most of the world.

America

Amerindians once hunted mammoth from Pennsylvania to the Pacific Coast, and from Alaska to the Valley of Mexico. But as a warmer drier climate set in around 8000 B.C. (= 10,000 B.P.) people had to hunt smaller animals and to depend more upon gathering. Localized hunting-gathering cultures developed in each region, and the climatic alteration fashioned a new pattern of habitat niches in the environment.

Maize agriculture began at least 7000 B.P. in Mesoamerica, and by 4000 B.P. had spread to most of Mesoamerica and also into North America. Agriculturalists developed distinctive ways of life and unique cultural patterns in different parts of the Americas.

In North America, the Eastern Woodland farmers gradually developed an economy based on mixed gardening of maize, beans, and squash, the classical North American crop triad, which they augmented by hunting, fishing and gathering, and by utilization of forest resources. In the Mississippi River Valley system the Hopewell Indians (100–400 A.D.) of the southeast United States built large ceremonial centers with earthen mounds over thirty feet high and ninety feet across at the base. In what is now the southwestern United States, the Anasazi of 1700–1500 years ago built large pueblos which were linked by an extensive system of developed trails. Throughout North America, the woods teemed with game, in a manner which has not been seen since the advent of Europeans and guns.

In Central America the Olmec, who lived on the Gulf Coast of Mexico, had a highly stratified society which built ceremonial centers by 1200 B.C. Monumental stone heads dominated these centers. Olmec jade figurines and other items were traded in most of Southern Mexico, suggesting strong cultural influence if not outright political and economic domination. Later the Zapotec culture developed the earliest known American writing, a hieroglyphic script which formed the pattern for the writing systems which remained in use in Mesoamerica up until the Spanish conquest. By 1 A.D., the Mayans were building ceremonial centers in the region of Yucatan. They had a sophisticated calendar and developed their own tradition of hieroglyphic writing.

The Mayan ceremonial centers were also large residential concentrations, in a word, small cities. Irrigation ditches, and roads, facilitated agriculture and transportation. They had specialized priests and a secular ruling hierarchy. Calendrical calculations served both the practical purposes of agriculture and the intellectual purposes of understanding the cosmos. The calendars were astonishingly accurate, had leap-years to keep the long-term solar-count correct, and had a means of correlating the lunar and solar years (Alvarado 1980). Evidence of trade with the southern United States and the Caribbean suggests that the Mesoamericans had sophisticated sailing and navigational skills.

Agriculture had spread through much of the highlands and the west coast of South America by 3000 B.C., a region where some of the western hemisphere's earliest ceramics occur. Copper smelting began in the Andes Mountains in 1200 B.C.

The Chavin religious cult and stylized animal art forms spread through much of the Andean area by 700 B.C. To what extent this was the spread of a religious cult, and to what extent it was a kingdom with widespread economic and political as well as religious ties, remains uncertain. Potatoes, maize, and other crops fed Chavin towns along the northern part of the west coast of South America.

The agriculturalists of the Americas used the wheel only for children's toys, and for designs; roads were trails designed for human walking and running. Only in the Andes was a pack animal, the llama, domesticated. Humans did all agricultural labor without draft animals, but this agriculture supported a dense population in many areas, and provided the food base which supported immense cultural achievements.

Pacific

The vast Pacific covers nearly half the Earth's surface, and entry into its habitable lands has always necessitated crossing open water. Melanesia and Australia were the first Pacific lands populated, around 50,000 B.P.;

Figure 3.8 A sophisticated and accurate solar and lunar calendar scheduled the religious ceremonies once held in the temple atop this Maya pyramid. Much of the temple decoration is Maya hieroglyphic writing which names the deities honored and records the ruler who sponsored the pyramid construction.

only much later (1500 B.C.–1000 A.D.) did the skilled navigators settle Micronesia and the Polynesia.

Little is known about the early hunter-gatherers of Melanesia, but by 5000 B.P. much of Melanesia had shifted from hunting-gathering to horticulture based on yams, taro, other root crops, and greens. Shifting "big man" (big men will be discussed in detail in chapter 11) alliances formed the political structure, and periodic warfare among groups was important in power shifts. There was no amalgamation into larger territorial units or into towns. A pattern of intensely localized cultures developed and remained substantially unchanged until the period of European contact in the 1800's. Around 1500 B.C.E. some Melanesians set sail to begin peopling the near-by Pacific Islands.

Figure 3.9 Melanesian traders made overseas voyages in double-hulled sailing canoes. They were skilled ship-handlers, and some developed very sophisticated navigational techniques.

Australian aborigines remained hunter-gatherers in all the different ecological settings of the continent. They carefully managed their environment and used selective burning to maintain habitats favorable for the animals they hunted (Vandenbeld 1988). In the lush east coast areas, life was comparatively easy; in the harsh inner desert areas, the survival margin was narrow. The aborigines never farmed; it was Europeans who brought agriculture to the continent.

Sailors brought the agricultural revolution to Micronesia and Polynesia. By 300 A.D. most of the habitable islands of the Pacific had been settled except for New Zealand and the Easter, Society, Marquesas and Hawaiian Islands. Navigator specialists used sophisticated techniques to guide double-hulled sailing canoes over wide expanses of open ocean. The settlers brought yam, taro, coconut and other crops with them, and utilized varied sea resources. Towns grew up on the larger more populous island groups, and a hierarchy of trade and social status marked the relationship among people and between the inhabitants of different islands and island groups.

Sub-Saharan Africa

Africa may be the original homeland of humankind. Certainly there have been modern humans living in Africa for 100,000 years. Hunter-gatherers ranged the African continent 8,000 years ago, including the green Sahara. As the Sahara dried up around 4000 B.C., cattle herders who once had grazed their herds on the grasslands moved southward into Central Africa seeking new and, literally, greener pastures.

Iron making came to West Africa circa 750 B.C. Iron tools keep a sharp edge and are comparatively durable, so that clearing the jungle is easier than with bronze or stone edges which dull quickly. Farmers cleared large areas with these new iron tools, and produced some surplus so that small local kingdoms began to appear. Armed with iron tools, Bantu-speaking peoples with a mixed economy of fishing, hunting, and farming expanded from the grasslands of the Cameroon region southward into equatorial forest and eastward along the margins of the forest. By 1 A.D. the Bantu-speakers had covered large areas of eastern and southern Africa, areas where once hunter-gatherers had roamed.

The Bantu expansion is a classic case of the "empty-land syndrome," people with a new exploitative technology perceive that an area of land is being under-utilized by an older technology and thus is "empty," available for the newer more intense use (Tweddell and Kimball 1985). Thus, the iron-armed Bantu perceived the forests of the hunter-gatherers as a vast expanse of empty land awaiting exploitation. In clearing the forests, the Bantu deprived the hunter-gatherers of their forest home. On the broad savannah grasslands of eastern Africa, some groups developed a pastoral nomadic way of life, centered around the raising of cattle. What remained for the hunter-gatherers were the deep jungle, where the pygmies of the Ituri Rainforest still live today, and the arid areas not suitable even for pastoral nomadism, such as the Kalahari Desert, where the Bushmen live, and the southern tip where Hottentots were still found when the Dutch settled in 1652.

East Asia

The East Asian part of Asia had long been a world unto itself. As climate changed during the melting of the glaciers at the end of the ice age, many regional hunting-gathering cultures developed in the region of East Asia. North Chinese agriculturalists of 6000 B.C.E. raised pigs and millet. The Yangshao people, who lived in the upper reaches (upstream portion) of the Yellow River raised millet as a staple crop and produced ceramics with colorful stylized designs.

Around 1800 B.C.E. the Shang Dynasty had become a major kingdom in northern China. The Shang made exquisite bronze vessels, produced fine silks, and had a well-developed written script which was the progenitor of the Chinese writing system still in use today. The Chinese writing system represents the longest continuous use of a script on Earth.

The subsequent Chinese history was a long tale of wars and feudal fighting between kingdoms. Near anarchy reigned over the land in the Warring States Period of the 470's B.C.E. Yet, it was during this time that Confucius taught, and his teachings were written down as the *Analects,* and Lao Tze wrote the *Dao De Jing,* which is the basic text of Taoism. The Confucian model formed the ideal pattern of life and society in the Chinese Empire until the beginning of the 20th century C.E.

The Warring States Period ended with the unification of China under the Ch'in emperor. He standardized weights and measures and unified the writing system. His great construction project was the tearing down of local defense walls built around the warring states, and the joining together of already existing walls in the north until they were unified as the Great Wall.

Rebellion overthrew the second emperor of Ch'in early in his reign and led to the foundation of the Han Dynasty, which lasted for 400 years. Han China was essentially North China, and did not yet include the fertile rice lands of the Yangtze region. But Han China extended far to the west, and the overland trade route known as the "Silk Road" linked China to Southwest Asian middlemen who traded with Rome. A literate bureaucracy administered China (discussed in more detail in chapter 11) of the Han Dynasty, and the Emperor ruled by the Mandate of Heaven as the supreme head of the nation, rather as a father was expected to rule his family; this pattern of the emperor and the bureaucracy remained the essential basic structure of Chinese government until the fall of the last dynasty in 1911.

South Asia

Rivers have long had an important cosmological, as well as economic, role in South Asia. "Mother Ganges" is an important spiritual focus, deity, and river of purification in the Hindu religion. Little is known about the coming of agriculture to South Asia, except that it seems to have begun earlier in the Indus Valley region than in the area of the Ganges River.

Around 2500 B.C., the Harrapan culture flourished in the Indus Valley region of South Asia. Harrapans traded by sea and land with Sumer in Mesopotamia. The Harrapan writing has not yet been deciphered. Harrapan cities were well-planned with orderly street layouts, water conduits and efficient sewerage. In this respect, Harrapan culture reminds one of the type of civil engineering which would be done by Rome nearly three millennia later. In time, Harrapan cities became overcrowded and finally were abandoned. Harrapan culture fell under the impact of a combination of circumstances, including overpopulation, climatic deterioration in the form of increasing aridity,

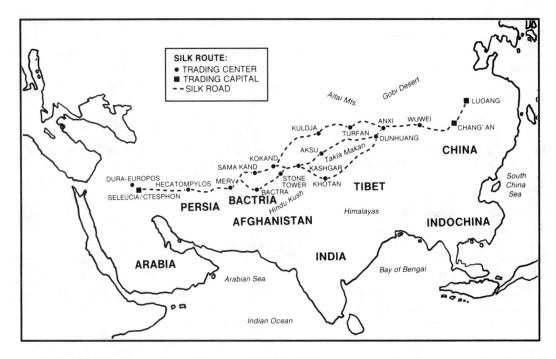

Figure 3.10

pressure from horse nomads on the frontier, and soil salinization because irrigated fields were inadequately drained.

Around 1800 B.C. horse and chariot people who spoke an Indo-European language, that is a language related to modern English, entered the northwest of South Asia. By the 1000's B.C., they had settled the Ganges Valley region and used iron tools to clear much of it for farming. These Indo-European speakers codified the earliest Hindu scriptures, the *Veddas* and *Puranas,* and transmitted them orally for hundreds of years.

These scriptures, which were written down in the Sanskrit language around 500 B.C.E., remain fundamental to the Hindu religion today, and have inspired much of the great literature of the Indian subcontinent.

From 324–185 B.C.E. the Mauryan kingdom controlled much of Northern India. The greatest Mauryan ruler, Ashoka, promoted Buddhism. He built roads and resting places for travellers throughout the kingdom, as well as many water storage tanks (ponds) and numerous temples. The Mauryan kingdom of Ashoka's time had the four castes and the lowly outcaste untouchables pattern of social structure still found in India today (discussed in chapter 10).

Southeast Asia

The basic geographic patterning of Southeast Asia is the contrast between hilly interior areas and flat alluvial plains, and the contrast between the solid land area of mainland Southeast Asia and the dispersed islands of Insular Southeast Asia. Hunter-gatherers once roamed over all of the region, but agriculturalists gradually took over the plains, pushing the hunter-gatherers into ever more remote areas.

By the 4000's B.C. inhabitants of lowland areas of Thailand raised "dry rice," rice grown in the fields which are not irrigated. Only around 900 B.C. did "wet rice," rice which is grown in fields that are irrigated, begin to be raised in the area. In wet rice agriculture, the same fields can be used year after year, and with proper care still retain their fertility; this makes possible a high population density.

In the region of Dong Son in the Red River Delta of Northern Vietnam, the Dong Son people of 500 B.C. made large twelve-foot diameter bronze drums with a deep resonating timbre. These Dong Son drums were traded to the Philippines, Borneo, and other parts of Island Asia. This trade implies established long-distance overseas trade routes and the port and harbor facilities to service them; these in turn would require reasonably large settlements and a stable political situation in the immediate area. Island Southeast Asia has few good ports for ocean-going ships, and the best ports were probably the centers of small states headed by a king whose power came from control of trade.

Southwest Asia and Egypt

Southwest Asia is a geographically complex area of widely varying climate and topography. Forests once covered most of the area but gradually vanished through a combination of climatic change and human activities. Agriculture first arose around 12,000 B.P. in the two great river-system regions of Southwest Asia, the Egyptian Nile, and the Mesopotamian Tigris and Euphrates. From then on, the general pattern in Southwest Asia was one of intensifying agriculturalization. The establishment of towns and cities, and the establishment of trade routes accompanied a pattern of perennial warfare. Kingdoms had marked status hierarchies, ranging from slaves to kings. The two primary foci of regional rivalry were Mesopotamia and Egypt; various client states allied themselves with each.

The pig was first domesticated in Southwest Asia, in Anatolia (the region of modern Turkey) by 8000 B.C., but later was prohibited as food by the Jewish and Islamic religions, both founded in Southwest Asia. The pig is an efficient meat animal because it is a scavenger, which can be fed on scraps and offal. But undercooked pork carries the risk of trichinosis, a debilitating and sometimes fatal disease.

Catal Huyuk in Anatolia was the world's first city in 6500–5700 B.C. The weavers who lived in dense-packed housing there obtained their food through trade with the surrounding area and worshipped at shrines decorated with cattle horns. The concentration of wealth in towns and cities brought widespread sporadic warfare to Southwest Asia by 6000 B.C.

Half a millennium later, in 5000 B.C., farmers in Central Mesopotamia irrigated wheat and barley fields. Mesopotamia means "between rivers" and refers to the alluvial plain in the vicinity of the Tigris and Euphrates Rivers, in the area of modern Iraq.

The most ancient large kingdom of Mesopotamia was Sumer, which flourished from 2700–2100 B.C.E. The Sumerians had plow agriculture, made pottery on the potter's wheel, which facilitated mass production of pots, smelted bronze, and traded with Eastern Arabia and with the Harrapan civilization of the Indus Valley in South Asia. Sumerians wrote on clay tablets and had the world's first extensive written history. Kings ruled Sumer, and slaves did much of the heavy work in the city. The priests and scribes were the elite of society, while most of the people were peasant farmers; a basic pattern of society still found in the region today. Domestication of the donkey and camel to serve as beasts of burden around 3000 B.C. made possible the transportation of large quantities of goods along overland trails.

Kingdoms rise and fall, and by 2400 B.C. the Akkadians, who spoke a language related to modern Arabic and Hebrew, held a tight rule over Mesopotamia and much of Southwest Asia. Hammurabi, king of Babylon, promulgated a code of laws based on the "an eye for an eye and a tooth for a tooth" principle of direct retribution for wrongs.

In Egypt a series of local kingdoms fought with one another for centuries. Sometime around 3000 B.C., the legendary king Narmer united the land into one country. Egypt had a unique situation. On either side of the Nile Valley the desert hemmed in life. Crops of wheat and barley depended upon the annual flood of the Nile which left a layer of silt that renewed the fertility of the soil. Nile water also provided irrigation. Egypt was an upstream-downstream culture. Upstream from Egypt lived Nubians and other Africans. Far downstream lay the Nile delta and the rich anchovy fisheries of the Mediterranean sea. By 3000 B.C. Egypt had a system of hieroglyphic writing which remained in use for the next three millenia. The king, or pharaoh, was the religious and secular ruler of the land. Different ruling dynasties came and went, and there were some major inter-dynastic periods of anarchy; but for nearly 2700 years the pharaoh remained the focus of the kingdom and the symbol of continuity, much as did the emperor in China from the Han dynasty until 1911.

The most famous architectural monuments of the Egyptians are the pyramids. The largest of these, the Great Pyramid of Cheops at Geza, was built around 2580 B.C., that is longer B.C. than we are A.D.

Metallurgy often turns to war. Bronze weapons were in general use in Southwest Asia by 2000 B.C., and by 1100 B.C. the first steel knives were forged on the Island of Cyprus.

For centuries, kingdoms and power-bases shifted in Southwest Asia. Persia was a major power centered on the Iranian Plateau. The Persian empire reached a height of splendor and power with Cyrus the Great's conquest of Babylonia in 539 B.C.

But in 331 B.C., Alexander the Great, King of Macedonian Greece, defeated the Persians under Darius III. Alexander continued his conquest into northeast India, and after he died, his generals divided up his empire, each general ruling a separate section of it, including Egypt, the Arabian Peninsula, Persia, and Northwest India.

Later events in Southwest Asia are associated with the Roman Empire. In 20 B.C., Herod the Great rebuilt the Temple in Jerusalem and in 7 B.C. was born Jesus Christ.

Europe

Reaching from the Urals to the Atlantic, and from the Arctic Sea to the Mediterranean, Europe is a region long criss-crossed by travelers, traders, invaders and raiders. After 8000 B.C. hunter-gatherer-fishers moved into Northern Europe in the wake of the receding glaciers.

By 6000 B.C. a small village sat at Lepenski Vir on a bend by the rapids of the Danube River in the Balkans. The carp, sturgeon and bream attracted by the rapids formed the protein basis of the villagers' diet. Plant food gathered from the surrounding areas provided additional food. At this same time, inhabitants of the British and Scandinavian coasts fished for cod. Meanwhile, agriculture had spread into Europe from Crete and Greece.

Around 4500 B.C. copper axe-heads were made in the Balkans; and another significant innovation occurred, the milking of cattle. Use of cattle milk as a food source meant that a given quantity of cattle could feed more people than if only the flesh were used. The taming of horses on the Ukrainian steppe around 4400 B.C. put a large work animal at human disposal.

By 3200 B.C. cow and plow agriculture, with cows drawing plows and pulling carts, had emerged as an efficient combination of cultivation and herding which had amalgamated into mixed farming. The energy provided by

Figure 3.11 For thousands of years, the slow steady plodding of oxen has been a way to move heavy loads overland. Ox transport is still important in much of the world.

the cow made it possible to farm lands not amenable to the hoe cultivation with only human muscle power, which had been the earliest pattern of European agriculture. Because efficient plowing requires large clear fields which are free of stumps and debris, the spread of plow agriculture caused significant deforestation of Europe. It also provided a food surplus which could be accumulated and used to feed non-agricultural laborers. The energy thus freed found various expressions, one of the most notable being the construction of megaliths such as Stonehenge in England and Carnac in France, around 2300 B.C.

The pastoral nomads on the Ukrainian steppes of 1500 B.C. herded cattle and horses. These nomads periodically invaded settled areas in search of plunder, then retreated back to the steppe. Around 1200 B.C., nomads spread out over the vast Central Asian steppe; from these early steppe pastoralists other groups, including the ancestors of the Mongols, acquired the steppe pastoral nomadic mode of life.

Trading and mixed farming continued in Europe. Power lay in the hands of leaders, who were perhaps not unlike the Melanesian "big

43

men" (discussed in Chapter 11), or there may have been a strong hereditary component of leadership. European history begins with the Greek and Roman empires.

The Mediterranean

The Mediterranean has long been a sea which both divides and unites. Touching upon Northern Africa, Southern Europe, and Western Asia, the Mediterranean became a link between those continents once adequate ship-building, sailing, and navigational skills had developed; but adverse political and economic conditions repeatedly shattered the ship-borne communications and trading links.

The Mediterranean assumed prominence as a hub of culture and commercial activity during the second millennium B.C. The Mediterranean of 1500 B.C. was a Minoan Sea. From their palace center at Knosos on the island of Crete, the Minoans ran a maritime trading empire whose records were written in a syllabic script in a very archaic form of Greek; this was more than half a millennium before the *Iliad* and the *Odyssey* were written down in Classical Greek.

By the 800's B.C., the Mediterranean was a Phonecian Sea. Phonecian trade routes criss-crossed the Mediterranean and extended to England for tin. The Phonecians used an alphabetic system of writing. In the 700's B.C. the Greeks adopted the Phonecian alphabet but modified it to suit the Greek language; they added signs to represent the vowel sounds, and altered the shape of the letters to be more easily cut with a straight-edge chisel.

Athens was a center of science, literature, drama, and democracy in Greece of the 400's B.C. Democratic rights were available only to the free males, not to females or to slaves. The cultural heritage of Athenian Greece is one of the foundations upon which Western culture has been built. Our expression "Spartan training" refers to the Greeks of Sparta who underwent severe military discipline and training in their youth. And the "Socratic method of teaching" refers to the use of question and answer dialogue, a method used by the Athenian philosopher Socrates. Even after he was condemned to death and forced to drink hemlock poison, Socrates continued talking to his pupils, adult men, until death overtook him.

Alexander of Macedonia grew up in the world of Greek culture and religion. He ruled from 336–323 B.C. and conquered much of the known world, including Persia, Egypt, and Southwest Asia. Alexander established Greek administration and brought in Greek settlers who introduced Greek culture everywhere he conquered, as far as Northwestern India. Alexander died at the age of 33; his generals divided up the empire and continued to administer it. The Greek name for "Greece" is "Hellas," hence the Greek culture introduced and spread by Alexander is referred to as "Hellenic Culture." It was this culture that the Romans admired, and it was this culture that shaped the tastes of the eastern Mediterranean.

The Mediterranean of 100 B.C. was a Roman sea. Rome consolidated control of all Italy by 250 B.C. and defeated the Punic (Phonecian) trading city of Carthage in the Punic Wars. The vengeful Romans razed Carthage to the ground in 146 B.C. and strew salt over the site so that no living thing could grow there. Yet the Roman classic, the *Aeneid,* written by Vergil, recounts how Aeneas, the ancestral hero credited with founding Rome, loved Dido who was the Queen of Carthage. Aeneas finally left Carthage and Dido to continue his voyage to found Rome. Dido then committed suicide in grief at the loss of her lover. Carthage had been a key Phonecian port; and after destroying the old city, the Romans built a new city nearby to utilize the same good harbor. The Romans became masters of the Mediterranean, and by 100 B.C. were able to call the Mediterranean Mare Nostrum ("Our Sea").

Roman hegemony reached north of the Alps into Europe with the expeditions of Julius Caesar into France, Switzerland, Germany and Britain. Caesar wrote his own history of the expedition, the *Gaulic Wars*.

Through Southwest Asian middlemen, Rome traded with China for fine silks. Egypt was the granary of Rome, for agriculture in Italy became depressed as Rome grew militarily powerful, and Italy could no longer feed the City of Rome. By 1 A.D. two major powers dominated Asia, Rome and Han China.

Some Patterns

The inhabitants of the world in 1 A.D. had no conception that a new era had begun. But we, who look back from two millennia further on, can see that there is a justification for the era division. By 1 A.D., two of the three major transitions which led to the world as we know it today had taken place. The first transition was the agricultural revolution. The second transition was the rise of literate city-states and literate religions as major foci of human life and international politics. The third revolution, the scientific and industrial revolution, would take place in the 17th–20th centuries A.D. In 1 A.D., signs of the second major transition, the rise of literate city-states and religions, abounded; and the circumstances which had given rise to them were history.

In the 1250's B.C., Southwest Asia was in turmoil. The Minoan and Hittite (Indo-European speaking kingdom in Anatolia) empires had collapsed. Egypt was weak, and this is the traditional time for the exodus of the Jews from Egypt. Anarchy, war, and piracy raged all over Southwest Asia. These may well be linked to the fact that the climate had cooled sharply, leading to diminished harvests which set desperate people on rampages that had repercussions in many places.

During the centuries of 500–300 B.C., the religions of Taoism and Confucianism in China, Jainism and Buddhism in India, Zoroastrianism in Persia, and Judaism in Mesopotamia and the eastern Mediterranean began or were formalized in writing in conjunction with an expansion of their activity. Each of these religions traces back to earlier traditions, for instance, Buddhism had roots in Hinduism, but each religion also was a new synthesis and understanding. It is not coincidental that by the time the cultures where these religions were formulated used iron, and were significantly altering the physical environment, and that large dominating kingdoms had an increasingly strong structure.

A New Era

To individuals living in the world, the year 1 A.D. was a year like any other. Local events and happenings marked the time. But it is interesting for us to step back and take a brief glance at the world as it was in that year.

The agricultural revolution had finished. Most of the good farming areas in the world were being farmed, except in Australia. Hunter-gatherers lived only in the far north, in the deep jungle, in some arid areas, and in other areas on the fringes of the best agricultural land. Trade routes criss-crossed many of the land areas of the world, and major sea lanes joined trading ports.

Bantu-speakers using iron tools lived in much of Africa. In the Pacific only the western islands and New Zealand remained unpopulated. In Mesoamerica powerful kingdoms ruled, and Teotihuacan was already a city. In the Yucatan, Mayan ceremonial centers reached pyramids to the sky. In the Mekong Delta of Vietnam, the Funan Kingdom flourished, building stone temples and trading with China and India. The Ganges region had become the center of city life in India. Across Central Asia, the Silk Road linked China and Rome in trade. Egypt was no longer a great power, merely a colony of Rome, but Egyptians looked with pride at the pyramids which had already been standing for more than 2500 years. On the eastern shore of the Mediterranean a little boy named Jesus played; and in Rome the emperor Augustus ruled.

The Roman Empire of the Mediterranean and the Han Empire of China were the two great Eurasian powers. Neither was aware of the Americas or of the vast reaches of the Pacific. Thus began the current era.

Formation of the Current Era

The era from 1 A.D. to the present time is a time of farmers because agriculture is the predominant global mode of economy and food production, and it is the era of literate nation-states and religions as centers of human life. The two millenia of the current era contain four major periods, when seen in broad cultural and historical perspective. The time of 0–1500 A.D. was the formation of the current era. The three centuries 1500–1800 were the age of European expansion and exploration. The period of 1800–1914 was the age of the machine. And the period from 1914 to present is the age of flight.

The period of the formation of the current era lasted from 0–1500 A.D./C.E. Various basic patterns characterized it in different areas of the world. In the Pacific the last islands were settled, including Hawaii and New Zealand. Urbanization developed in the Americas. Short-lived kingdoms rose and fell in sub-Saharan Africa, and in Eurasia, technological innovations, nomad raids, and religious movements altered the life of a continent.

Pacific

One of the greatest intellectual achievements of the current era was the perfection of sophisticated navigational techniques which made possible human sailing across the thousands of miles of open Pacific Ocean. Using

Figure 3.12 The stone heads of Easter Island seem mysterious, but may have been intended to protect the Island from harm. The organization of the labor, which was necessary to carve, transport, and erect the giant stone figures, both symbolized and actualized the elaborate ranked hierarchy of the island.

these techniques, Polynesian navigators completed the settlement of the Pacific Islands, and a few may have reached the coast of South America. Frequent warfare occurred both within large islands and between groups of islands, with whole war-fleets sailing hundreds of miles to do battle.

Pacific islanders raised monumental architecture, such as the famed stone heads of Easter Island, and the large stone forts of Palau. The islanders did not develop writing, but memorizing specialists retained and transmitted long royal genealogies and vast epic and ritual literary cycles.

North America

In North America many regional cultures continued their development. And the Eskimos moved into the last inhabitable niches in the far northern coastal region of Canada, Alaska, and Greenland.

The Hopewell of the Mississippi Valley built ceremonial mound complexes in the 300's A.D. Long trade routes linked Ohio with the Gulf coast, the Rockies, Wisconsin, and the Atlantic coast. Luxury goods such as fine polished stone figurines and delicate mica silhouette shapes were buried in the graves of the elite.

Northwest coast cultures in the 500's A.D. developed their characteristic pattern of reliance on salmon runs, elaborate material culture, and social prestige rankings. Although the northwest coast people were hunter-gatherers, and not agriculturalists, the salmon runs provided a steady and reliable food supply which enabled people to live in permanent villages with massive wooden plank multi-family houses. They built monumental wooden "totem poles." They also built large plank ocean-going canoes for long distance coastal trading and raiding, and for whale-hunting.

A warmer climatic period began around 930 A.D. and lasted for two centuries. During this time, European Vikings colonized Greenland and founded settlements on Newfoundland. When the climate cooled, settlements on Newfoundland were abandoned, and those on Greenland starved to death as agriculture became impossible and ice floes prevented Viking supply ships from arriving.

European presence returned to the Americas as Spanish, Portuguese and French explored, conquered, and settled in the half-century following 1493. The Europeans brought smallpox, measles, and influenza which decimated the American Indian population. By 1700 Europeans were dominant in the New World, and American cities were European cities. But such had not always been the case.

Central America

The first great city in the New World was Teotihuacan, which reached a height of power 300–750 A.D. By the 500's A.D., Teotihuacan was the sixth largest city in the world, with a population of about 200,000, and was influential over much of Mesoamerica, except for the Mayan areas.

Mayan power reached its height in the 600's A.D. The subsequent decline of the Maya may have resulted from a combination of factors, including: local climatic variations, war, disease incursions, or revolt in reaction to excess demands of the elite for labor and taxes to build monumental centers.

In the 1300's a wild group from the north, the Aztecs, entered the Valley of Mexico. They established their settlement at Tenochtitlan, the future Mexico City, and increased in strength. One impetus was that their deities demanded constant sacrifices. If human sacrifices were not provided, the sun would not shine and other natural disasters would befall, or so the Aztec believed. In one particularly crucial, and long-remembered, four day ceremony, 200,000 individuals lost their lives. At its height, Tenochtitlan had a population of close to a million. But the escalating demands for human sacrifices caused enmity among neighboring groups, many of whom willingly aided the Spanish to overthrow the Aztecs in the early 1500's. Cortez destroyed Tenochtitlan in 1521.

In South America, small states arose in the Andes and on the west coast. Elsewhere hunters and fishers and slash-and-burn farmers lived in the Amazon region, and big game hunters on the pampas grasslands of Argentina.

The Incas settled at Cuzco high in the Andes in the mid-1200's. In the 1470's, they completed the conquests that gave them an empire covering most of the Andes and reaching to the sea. Specialized foot messenger service carried messages to and from the Supreme Inca, the ruler, over an elaborate system of trails on which sophisticated rope suspension bridges spanned deep gorges. The Inca worshipped the sun at special temples. But Inca glory was short lived, for in 1532 the Spanish began to conquer the region.

Only the Incas and the Tibetans have ever had major kingdoms whose center was in a high mountainous area. An important study waiting to be done is one which examines the parallels and the differences between these two large mountain kingdoms.

Africa

During the current era, Africa has remained a continent divided. The northern portion, circum-Mediterranean Africa, has strong and ancient links to other circum-Mediterranean areas, while sub-Saharan Africa remains a world unto itself.

In the 700's C.E., Islam expanded southward across the Sahara in an overland movement following the established cross-desert trade routes, bringing the Arabic language and script as well as the Islamic religion into Northern Africa. At the same time, the Moslem movement extended overseas along the east coast of Africa. At favorable anchorages the Muslims set up coastal trading villages where they traded in gold and ivory, spices and silk, and slaves.

The 1100's–1300's saw the continuation and intensification of Moslem trans-Saharan trade. From the north came salt, textiles, swords, horses, copper, and various luxury goods. From the south came slaves, gold, and ivory. In the west coast region of Africa, many local kingdoms appeared, lasted a few generations, then vanished. The mechanism of trans-Saharan and west coast trade was sophisticated and intricate, constantly adapting to local difficulties and conditions.

The city of Timbuktu was the trading and intellectual center of the Songhai Empire of Sudan in the 1400's. The University at Timbuctu attracted scholars from all over the Old World, and the city had the best bookstore in all Western Eurasia. Yet today nothing remains of such brilliance but a few mud-brick walls crumbling into dust, and the expression, "Timbuctu," meaning "an unbelievably remote urban area."

Far in the southeast region, the Bantu built the great fort of Zimbabwe in stone during the 1200's. Zimbabwe served as the political, commercial, and religious center of the Shona Kingdom until the mid-1400's. Its location on the southern part of the east coast region put it at the hub of several important trade networks.

Numerous kingdoms rose and fell in West Africa. One of these was the kingdom of Benin, famed for its fine bronzes. Much of the history of this region has been reconstructed by ethnohistorians on the basis of information retained in the oral literature of the region today.

The Portuguese first contacted West Coast Africa in the late 1400's. Portugal was seeking a sea route around Africa to India. A sea route would enable them to trade directly with India rather than using the expensive and increasingly unreliable overland route.

Eurasia

During the formation of the modern era, Eurasia became increasingly interconnected, a pattern which the Eurasian Age of the Machine would later extend to the rest of the globe. For the first 1500 years of the current era, the far northern regions of Eurasia remained comparatively isolated. Various oasis kingdoms flourished in Central Asia, and they were key factors in the transmission of culture and religion through the center of the continent. The other main factor in Central Asia was the pastoral nomads who periodically raided agricultural areas.

Technological innovations occurred in various places in Eurasia. The use of cannon, gunpowder and paper began in China. The zero was invented in Southeast Asia. The lands of Arabie systematized medicine. The nomads of the steppe invented the stirrup which made horse riding safer and easier, and facilitated calvary warfare. Europeans invented the screw as a pressing device for oil presses, and developed fine gearing and precision metalworking for clocks; later they combined the screw and precision gearing to make possible precise boring of cannon, and to produce intricate machinery, including accurate timepieces. Often overlooked by grocery-store-fed moderns are the important advances in agriculture. The Chinese developed ways to obtain the maximum production of crops, fuel, fodder, fish, and fiber per area of available land, and to retain the reproductivity of that land over centuries. Europeans developed the three-field system of crop rotation to retain land fertility in northern climes, and hybridized cattle for better meat and milk production.

East Asia

Throughout the formation of the current era, East Asia remained a world unto itself, and was often a magnet for traders from other areas of the continent. The center of East Asian power and cultural influence was China, which was extraordinarily powerful in the two "Golden Ages" of the Han and Tang Dynasties. China lay under the Mongol yoke during the Yuan Dynasty, and sometimes in other dynasties was a middling or failing political power. But China was always an extraordinary focus of cultural influence and prestige in East Asia.

The Chinese Han dynasty fell in 220 A.D., roughly a century before the fall of the Roman Empire. Buddhism had already entered China along the Silk Road, and it became a popular religion in the time of troubles following the fall of Han. As Europe was to do after the fall of Rome, China broke up into small feudal states which were constantly at war with one another.

In 581, the Sui reunited China under one ruler. The great Sui accomplishment was the construction of the Grand Canal linking the Yellow and the Yangtze rivers. This meant that large quantities of rice from the fertile south of China could now be brought north on barges. But building the canal bankrupt the Sui, and it fell to rebellion.

The succeeding Tang Dynasty (618–907) traded over the trans-Central Asian Silk Road to the Moslem Mediterranean. Just as the Han Dynasty is famed in literature for having the world's first truly monumental historical study, the *History of Sze-Ma Chien*, so the Tang dynasty is famed for its poetry. Tu Fu is known as the "poet of the people" for his straightforward language, used in brilliant poems on everyday themes, such as farming and the seasons. Li Po is known as the "drunken poet" for he wrote best when "in his cups"; he is famed for the brilliant imagery and sound patterns of his poems, written in literary language and allusive style, which dealt with love, romance, and abstract themes. Tu Fu and Li Po knew and respected one another, and have influenced Chinese poetry throughout the centuries since they lived.

On the steppes to the northwest of China, the Mongols, led by Ghengis Khan, established a capital at Karakorum in 1206. Then they raided south, completing the conquest of China in 1279. During the Yuan Dynasty, when the Mongol Emperor Kublai Khan was on the throne of China, Marco Polo and his uncles came from Venice to trade. They traveled along the Silk Road, which was enjoying the Pax Mongolica, the "Mongolian Peace," that made trade and travel safe in the Roman Mediterranean world.

Some 700 years ago, the Chinese took the black firing powder they used for fireworks and began to use it to hurl projectiles from guns. They expelled the Mongols in 1368 and established the Ming Dynasty. After a series of naval expeditions under Cheng Ho to India, Arabia, Africa, and Southwest Asia in the early 1400's, the Ming Chinese slammed shut their doors to the outside world. The Portuguese who came in the early 1500's found themselves confined to the small island of Macao, and their interactions with the Chinese carefully controlled by a strong central government.

Despite repeated invasions and setbacks, Korea developed and maintained a unique national culture. The world's first moveable type was developed in Korea, and spread first to China, and then to Europe where it led to the modern age of mass literature and literacy.

The Korean Yi Dynasty founded in 1392 saw increasing anarchy and the rise of the Samurai warrior class, responsible to their feudal lords. Note the parallel with the rise of the European knights which began around the same time. In 1274 and 1281, the Japanese successfully repelled Mongol invasion attempts. The late 1400's saw Japan plunged into chronic warfare in a period whose anarchy paralleled that of the warring states in China of the 400's B.C. Only with the establishment of the Tokugawa shogunate in the 1600's, did the time of anarchy end.

Central Asia

In Central Asia, the Uighur Empire flourished in the region south of Lake Baikal during the Tang Dynasty "heyday" of the Silk Road in the 700's A.D. Mongols later used Uighurs to administer their empire, and the Uighur script was modified to provide the Mongolian script.

The city of Samarkand in the 1400's had massive onion-domed mosques, decorated with blue tile mosaics. Samarkand was the center of Islamic culture, and boasted high literacy attainments; it was also a trade center. What needs to be remembered here is that in the Islamic world, as in the Chinese world, literary attainment either in the written literature of the elite or in the oral literature of the populace was perceived as being one of the highest accomplishments; thus, to be a center of literary brilliance was a desired and admired attribute for a city.

Of all the many groups who swirled and struggled their way through varied vastness of Inner Asia, it is the Mongols who are best remembered in fame and infamy. In the 13th century, the charismatic leader Ghengis Khan united various groups of steppe pastoral nomads into one fighting rampaging group, the Mongols, and led them on a series of conquests which struck terror into most of Eurasia and resulted in an empire that spanned much of the continent. For centuries, the Central Asian trade and communication routes were the strategic heart of the continent, and provided a source of power and wealth to the kingdoms that controlled them. Under the Pax Mongolica, immense quantities of trade and tribute flowed along the Silk Road, and the Mongolian pony express messengers who rode relays of horses day and night across some of the fiercest desert and mountain terrain on earth could go from what is now Warsaw to the Mongolian capital in the steppe north of China, taking only six weeks to make the journey which girded nearly a quarter of the Earth's circumference. Not until the completion of the trans-Siberian railroad in the later 1800's would such trans-Eurasian speed ever be attained again. The final weakening and disintegration of the Mongol Empire in the 1400's made the trans-Central Asia route impassable, and led to the Spanish and Portuguese search for a sea-borne route to East Asia which resulted in the opening of the New World to Europeans, and in the around-Africa sea route to Southern and East Asia. In short, the disintegration of a pastoral nomadic empire in Central Asia eventually led to the European expansion over the globe.

Southeast Asia

Southeast Asia followed a complex course during the formation of the modern world. Cultural influences from India and China played a part in forming the regional pattern of important trading towns, which were headed by semi-divine kings and had international contacts and spheres of influence, contrasting with semi-isolated farming regions and hunter-gatherers in the remote jungle hills.

Buddhism arrived in Southeast Asia during the early centuries of the current era. The monument of Borobodur on Java, built in the 700's, symbolized in stone the Buddhist quest for enlightenment. It also reproduced the sacred world mountain. Climbing to the top of Borobudur symbolized attaining enlightenment and thus being released from the endless wheel of rebirth.

In the 900's, the Khmer, who lived in what is now Cambodia, invaded and destroyed the Cham capital in what is now Southern Vietnam. The Khmer then conquered the Chao Phraya River delta, site of modern Bangkok, Thailand. King Suryavarman II of Khmer built the massive stone Buddhist temple complex of Angkor Wat in the early 1100's, partly in celebration of his attacks on the Cham in the Mekong delta and on the Viet side in the Red River delta. In retaliation, the Cham raided the Khmer empire in 1177 and sacked the capital, but in 1200 the Khmer king Jayavarman VII, took the Khmer throne, attacked Cham, and occupied it for 20 years. This perspective makes it clear that the present Vietnamese-Kampuchean hostilities are the continuation of an ancient pattern.

The Mongols stormed south from China to raid Pagan, the capital of Burma, in 1287.

But the Cham and Viet repelled a Mongol attack made by the Mongol rulers of China in 1300.

The kingdom of Majapahit on Java, an island in Southeast Asia, rose in the 1300's. Majapahit grew wealthy from control over the key sea lanes for the China-India trade.

Malacca rose to prominence on the southeast coast of the Malay Peninsula in the late 1400's. Again, the source of power lay in the control of key sea-lanes for the China-India trade. Because of its importance as the main trading center of Island Southeast Asia, the Portuguese attacked and conquered Malacca in 1511, marking the first significant foothold of Europeans in the region.

On the mainland, the Thai, who had been moving into the region from southwest China, conquered the Khmer capital in 1594. The Khmer abandoned their capital of Angkor and moved south to Phnom Penh. In 1593 Burma was united under one ruler, and the Thai-Burmese warfare would occur sporadically for the next several centuries.

South Asia

Like China, South Asia has had two "golden ages"; the first was the reign of Ashoka (273–232 B.C.), the second golden age was the Gupta Empire (320–455 A.D.). South Asia played an important role as the homeland of Buddhism, as the transmitter of Buddhism to East Asia, and as a source of major cultural influence in Southeast Asia.

The Kushan Kingdom of the 0–200's A.D. in the northwest part of South Asia synchronized Hindu and Hellenic art traditions into Buddhist art. Kushans made the first images of Buddha. Previously the Buddha had been symbolized by a footprint which represented his wanderings, or by a wheel which symbolized his teachings.

In the Ganges region of India, the Gupta Empire arose, noted for its lawgiver Harsha,

Figure 3.13 The heads on this ancient Khmer gateway symbolized the power of the king as a divine ruler. The elephants are bearers of Hindu gods, and the hooded serpents are *naga,* the cosmic serpent who churned the Primordial Sea to create the Earth.

whose code of laws formed the basis for the legal codes of subsequent kingdoms and empires. Hinduism resurged against Buddhism under the Gupta, and there was a flourishing of Sanskrit belles-lettres. In 450, Hun nomads invaded the Gupta Empire and hastened its downfall.

Buddhism became firmly established in Tibet in the 100's and monasteries flourished. The yellow hat sect of Buddhist monasticism arose in the 1500's. It was a reformist movement which sought to promulgate a "purer" Buddhism; one less mixed with traditional non-Buddhist Tibetan religious practices than was the earlier "red hat" monasticism. The yellow hats established the theocratic government, headed by the Dalai Lama (a Mongol title bestowed by the Mongol emperor of China) which lasted until the Chinese Communist invasion of the 1950's; today the Dalai Lama is in exile.

On the southeast coast of India the Chola Kingdom waxed strong in the second and third centuries A.D. The Chola made exquisite bronze sculptures, of which the dancing Sivas are most famous. The Chola also invaded Sri Lanka, as other Tamil-speaking dynasties before them had done, and as did others after them. It is the memory of these invasions which makes the Sinhalese Sri Lankans so bitter against the Tamils, and has engendered the Sinhalese Tamil conflicts which disturb Sri Lanka today. Marco Polo passed through Sri Lanka on his way home from China in 1292. Marco Polo traveled homeward by sea because the Pax Mongolica had faltered and the overland route was no longer safe.

Mongol incursions on South Asia effected significant damage when Timur the Lame invaded and destroyed Delhi in 1398 as an offshoot of his raiding and conquering in Southwest Asia. In 1526 the Mughul Babur, a direct descendant of the Mongol leader Ghengis Khan, conquered and held the Delhi sultanate. From this base the Mughul conquest of India proceeded, unifying the kingdom under one rule. The official language of the Mughul Empire was Persian. The Mughuls kept Europeans at bay until princely rivalries weakened the dynasty. Beginning in the late 1600's, Europeans fought against one another and against the local princes. Only in the 1800's did the British reunite the subcontinent under one rule.

Southwest Asia

The turmoils and troubles of Southwest Asia today have roots reaching far back into the past. For at least 5,000 years, kingdoms and power centers have warred and contested with one another. With the disintegration of the Roman Empire in the 400's A.D., another round of fighting and power struggle began in Southwest Asia. Areas which had once traded for imported goods now began to make them, and in many areas the standard of living declined drastically. A series of droughts created hardship for the traders and pastoralists of the Arabian Peninsula in the early years of the 600's.

In the windswept desert near his home city, the Meccan merchant Muhammad received a call to prophecy, and founded the religion of Islam. Hounded and persecuted by Meccans unwilling to embrace Islam, Muhammad fled with his followers from Mecca to Medina in 622 A.D. It is from this flight, the hejira, that the Muslim calendar begins. July 16, 622 A.D. is the beginning of the year 1 A.H. of the Muslim calendar; A.H. stands for *anno hegirae,* "year of the hejira," the flight from Mecca to Medina. Because the Muslim calendar is a lunar one, it does not correspond to the western solar calendar. For Moslems, November 23, 1979 was the first day of the year 1400 A.H., and the Muslim year 1421 A.H. will begin on April 6, 2000 A.D.

The Prophet and his followers later conquered Mecca and established the Kabbah in Mecca as the sacred shrine of Islam. After

Muhammad's death in 632, Islam split into two factions, Sunni and Shiite, over the succession to religious and temporal leadership.

Islam expanded rapidly; by 714 Moslem armies had swept over Eurasia from Spain to Northwestern India. In 732, Moslem expansion northward into Europe was halted at the Battle of Tours, France. Eastward expansion halted in Central Asia where the Moslem armies defeated the Chinese at the Battle of Talas River in 751. This same battle also halted the Tang Chinese expansion west.

Scholarship flourished throughout Moslem realms in the 800's. Baghdad in Iraq was a flourishing center of learning and literature. In the 990's, the Shiite Moslem Fatimids conquered Egypt and in Cairo established Al-Azhar University, which still holds classes today.

Meanwhile the schism of Byzantine and Roman Christianity was solidifying; this schism effectively divided the Christian world against itself. European crusaders seeking to reconquer the Holy Land for Christianity attacked the Moslem Empire in 1099. Several small European princedoms were established, but soon fell.

Mongols attacked Persia and destroyed Baghdad in the 1200's. They massacred the population of Baghdad and let the complex irrigation system necessary for Baghdad's survival fall into ruin. To this day, the city has not recovered its former glory. The glory and fall of Baghdad are well-known from contemporary written sources. Extrapolating back from this, we can understand some of the human dimension of the many cities that once flourished in Mesopotamia and elsewhere, then fell, and now appear only as names or ruins in the historical and archaeological record.

The Arab geographer and traveler, Ibn Battuta, visited Mecca, Europe, Africa, and Asia in the early 1300's. His written account, the *Travels of Ibn Battuta* is a classic of geographic literature.

Nomadic Ottoman Turks moved out of Central Asia into Anatolia in the late 1200's. They completely conquered the area which is known today as "Turkey," from the name "Turk."

Constantinople, the last bastion of the Byzantine Empire, fell to the Turks in 1452 and was renamed "Istanbul." From the 1480's until World War I, the Ottoman Turk Empire dominated Southwest Asia and much of the Mediterranean. The final end of the Ottoman threat to Northern Europe came with the defeat of the Ottoman armies at the walls of Vienna in 1693. But the Ottoman Empire remained a major world power until the present century, and only dissolved in the aftermath of World War I.

Europe

During the time of the formation of the modern world, Europe as a whole had three major historical periods; first, the time of the Roman Empire, second, the centuries of chaos and disunion following the fall of Rome, and third, an awakening of intellectual curiosity and exploration which led to the great European sea-borne expansion and ultimately to our modern industrial-technological world.

During the first two centuries of the current era Rome reached the peak of power and influence, but the combination of internal weakness and problems of increasing pressures from without set the Empire into decline from the end of the third century onward.

One factor in the fate of Rome was a chilling of climate in the 270's which led to a decrease in rainfall in Italy, Arabia, and Central Asia. Diminished rainfall in Central Asia meant poorer pasture for the powerful pastoral nomadic Huns (pastoral nomadism is discussed in chapter 7). In an effort to get more pastures, the Huns raided their neighbors.

Hun movements in Central Asia pushed neighboring nomadic and farming groups out of their previous habitats. These displaced groups appeared on the Roman frontiers and increasingly stressed the Roman Empire. These external pressures, combined with internal economic and political differences, led to the weakening of the Roman Empire.

In 410, the Visigoths captured Rome, ending the Roman Empire. The eastern portion of the Roman Empire continued on as the Byzantine Empire, headquartered in Constantinople. But the sacred language of the Roman Catholic Church continued to be Latin, and the Church's hierarchical ecclesiastical organization carried on Roman patterns. In Europe, people responded to the loss of Roman security by submitting themselves to local strong leaders for protection, thus giving rise to the feudal system.

The Roman Empire had legally recognized Christian churches in 313, following the vision of Emperor Constantine who in a dream saw a cross and heard the words, "*in hoc signo vinces,*" "under this sign you shall conquer." He accepted Christianity and was victorious. He renamed the Anatolian capital Constantinople, "City of Constantine," and ordered the building of the largest church in Christendom, the present day Hagia Sophia. The Byzantine Empire reached its greatest height in 532 under the emperor Justinian who promulgated a *Code of Laws* which served as the model for many later European codes of law, including the Napoleonic code which is still basic to French law today.

Germans were using the moldboard plow by the 500's A.D. At this time, the Slavs migrated from Central Europe into Eastern Europe and the forest zone of Russia. In the 600's, they settled in the Balkan Peninsula.

In 793 Viking raiders from Scandinavia sacked the Celtic Christian monastery of Lindisfarne off the Irish coast and destroyed a center of brilliant manuscript writing. Other Vikings moved down the river system of Europe to Byzantium, where they served as elite military forces and palace guards for the Byzantine emperors. Vikings also established the state of Kiev, in the south of Russia. The bulk of the population in Kiev was Slavic, and the records of Kiev were written in the Slavic language.

While some Vikings raided the British Isles in the 850's, others raided as far north as Africa. By the 900's, there was a significant Viking settlement in England. These were the Anglo-Saxons whose preserved masterpiece of literature is the epic poem *Beowulf.*

Christianity spread in Europe as an intellectual and religious force. In 966, the Poles converted to Roman Christianity and in 988, the Russians converted to Eastern Christianity, which had its spiritual center in Constantinople, just as Roman Christianity had its spiritual center in Rome. In 1054, the eastern church formally and decisively broke with Rome. Christianity flourished in the art, churches, and monasteries of the French empire of Charlemagne, who was crowned Holy Roman Emperor by the pope on Christmas Day, 800 A.D.

The Normans, or "north men" were descendants of the Vikings who had settled in Northern France and adopted the French language and culture. The Normans conquered England with a decisive victory at the Battle of Hastings Down in 1066. The amalgamation of the Norman French language with the Anglo-Saxon language of England eventually gave rise to modern-day English.

Invading Mongols in the early 1200's destroyed the city of Kiev and conquered most of Russia. Only in the 1500's did the Russians expel the Mongols and extend their control south along the Volga River and east to the Ural Mountains. It is in large measure the heritage of the Mongol conquest that made the Russians hateful of a perceived outside threat, a situation that continues today under the Soviets. The first wooden *kremlin,* "fortress," was built in Moscow in 1156.

In England the Tudor Dynasty rose in the late 1400's. Patterns of mercantile trade sent the British looking for overseas outlets. And

THE CURRENT ERA

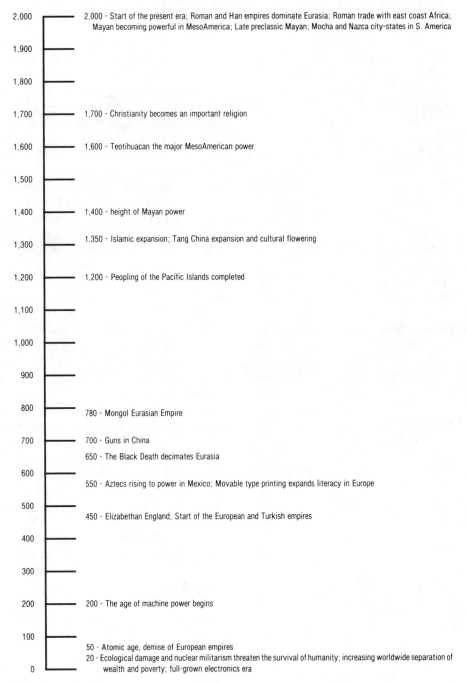

2,000	2,000 - Start of the present era; Roman and Han empires dominate Eurasia; Roman trade with east coast Africa; Mayan becoming powerful in MesoAmerica; Late preclassic Mayan; Mocha and Nazca city-states in S. America
1,900	
1,800	
1,700	1,700 - Christianity becomes an important religion
1,600	1,600 - Teotihuacan the major MesoAmerican power
1,500	
1,400	1,400 - height of Mayan power
1,300	1,350 - Islamic expansion; Tang China expansion and cultural flowering
1,200	1,200 - Peopling of the Pacific Islands completed
1,100	
1,000	
900	
800	780 - Mongol Eurasian Empire
700	700 - Guns in China
	650 - The Black Death decimates Eurasia
600	550 - Aztecs rising to power in Mexico; Movable type printing expands literacy in Europe
500	450 - Elizabethan England; Start of the European and Turkish empires
400	
300	
200	200 - The age of machine power begins
100	
	50 - Atomic age, demise of European empires
0	20 - Ecological damage and nuclear militarism threaten the survival of humanity; increasing worldwide separation of wealth and poverty; full-grown electronics era

Figure 3.14

56

news of the Spanish discovery of a sea route across the Atlantic to a New World caused an excitement about exploration for knowledge and gain.

The Age of European Expansion

Europeans expanded rapidly over the face of the globe during the period from 1500–1800. In this expansion, the Europeans brought along their Indo-European languages, their capitalists and mercantile economy, and many cultural values, including the Christian religion, an emphasis on the importance of works as a justification for one's life, a pre-occupation with time, and the rapidly developing scientific worldview and its associated technology.

The prelude to this period of European geographic expansion was the formation of the Renaissance in the 1400's. This period saw the rediscovery of classical Greek and Roman culture and language, and also fostered an intellectual curiosity and sense of exploration, be it in the realms of nature and geography or in the realms of the mind. European printing with moveable type began in Germany in 1455 and spread rapidly. Books, charts, mathematical tables, maps, popular ballads and doggerel issued from the presses.

European sea-borne exploration went on at a rapid pace during the three decades from 1492–1522, with consequences still felt today. In 1492, Christopher Columbus sailed to the west and discovered the Americas. The Spanish and Portuguese rapidly followed up this initial voyage with conquests and colonization. Meanwhile in 1498, the Portuguese reached India by sea and in 1514 reached China. This effectively began the direct overseas trade from Europe to China and spelled the demise of the Central Asian powers dependent upon overland trade from the Mediterranean to China. Ferdinand Magellan's expedition completed the first circumnavigation of the world in 1522, opening the trans-Pacific route to European shipping and trade.

European-introduced diseases, such as measles, smallpox and tuberculosis, decimated the population of the Americas, and facilitated its conquest. Gold from the Americas altered the balance of power in Europe and tempted people of many nations to explore. Added to the economic motives were the political motives arising from the religious eruption of the Protestant Reformation which began in 1521.

The Reformation unleashed tremendous spiritual, economic, and social forces which ultimately propelled the European invention of the modern world. Henry the VIII of England dissolved the monasteries and other Roman Catholic institutions in England and appropriated their wealth to the crown, thus freeing a large sum of capital for secular use, including building a navy. Similar patterns of using newly-obtained wealth for secular use took place in other countries.

England, in what is now called the "Elizabethan Age," under Elizabeth I in the late 16th century, prospered and began overseas trade and exploration. William Shakespeare wrote down the lusty Elizabethan language in powerful dramas still performed today.

By 1600, Spain and Portugal were the two dominant European powers. Protestantism was firmly entrenched in Northern Europe. In India the Mughul Dynasty, descendants of the Mongols, ruled the land. In China, rebellions and disorders were common as the Ming Dynasty steadily declined.

One factor encouraging immigration from Europe to the New World and elsewhere was the Little Ice Age, which began in 1530 and lasted until 1850. During the Little Ice Age, the European climate became much cooler than it had been; glaciers expanded on many of the mountains, literally burying whole villages under ice; agriculture became impossible in some of the extreme areas to which it had been pushed, such as the English uplands, and was much less productive in other areas.

Hardships brought on by the Little Ice Age pushed the Russians outward from their heartland. The Russians had freed themselves from paying tribute to the Mongols in 1480. As the Russian peasants were increasingly enserfed, in effect, made into slaves, many began to escape to seek opportunities elsewhere. Peasant movements followed the explorers across the Urals in 1586. Crossing the Urals opened up the vast expanses of Siberia and Central Asia for Russian explorers, just as the crossing of the Atlantic had opened up the vast expanses of the Americas for the western European seaboard nations. In 1649, Russian explorer-traders reached the Pacific, and settlers soon followed. Russian trading settlements ultimately extended into the New World, down the coast of Alaska and into California.

Major crop exchanges between the Old and New Worlds began in the late 1500's. Europeans brought the potato, tomato, corn (maize) and tobacco from the New World to the Old, while introducing the Old World crops of tea and coffee to the New, along with plantation agriculture, especially of sugar-cane.

Turmoil seethed in China and Europe of the 1600's. In Europe the religious wars, of Protestant against Catholic, and Protestant against Protestant, devastated one land after another. The European wars were also fought out on the high seas and in their overseas possessions. China fell to the invading Manchu, descendants of pastoral nomads, who overthrew the Ming and founded the alien Ching Dynasty.

The intellectual climate of Europe altered during the 1600's, as first-hand observation and experimental science became an important means of acquiring knowledge. Newton's *Principia* provided a mathematical description of gravity and the motion of the moon around the Earth and the Earth and other planets around the Sun. This removed cosmology from the reality of religion and tradition, and placed it in the realm of mathematical analysis and description, where it remains today.

The Manchu conquest of China brought peace and prosperity to the land. The introduction of maize and potatoes which could be grown on upland areas not suited to rice and wheat agriculture led to a rapid increase in the population of China, because the new crops made more food available than there had been before. Emperor Kang Hsi of the Ching Dynasty commanded the compilation of a massive dictionary which would include all the words in the written Chinese language. Chinese scholars produced the *Kang Hsi Dictionary* of more than 50,000 major entries, which is one of the greatest attainments of the human intellect. This *Dictionary* preceded by more than half a century the world's first true encyclopedia, the *Encyclopedie* compiled by Diderot in France.

European expansion and exploration continued throughout the 1700's and led to the emergence of a pattern which remains important today: the conflicts among European powers were played out worldwide, whether directly or indirectly through third parties. The British and French fought one another on the North American continent, in India, and on the high seas, while the Dutch defeated Portugal in the Indonesian region. China, Japan, and Korea remained ioslated and repelled European attempts at penetration, though some Catholic priests served as intellectuals at the Chinese court.

In 1788, the British began to colonize Australia; the last large area still inhabited by hunter-gatherers. The British saw the American Declaration of Independence in 1776 as the rebel manifesto of an important but not vital colony. The French Revolution of 1789 unseated a thousand-year old monarchy and eventually brought to power Napoleon Bonaparte who sought to conquer all Europe.

British Admiral Horatio Nelson defeated the French and Spanish combined fleets at the Battle of Trafalgar in 1806; this gave the British a supremacy of the seas which they retained until World War I. At the Battle of Waterloo, in 1814, Napoleon's land army was defeated and Napoleon was sent into the exile where he died. Thus, the phrase, "his/her Waterloo" has entered English as an expression meaning "something which utterly defeats someone's intentions."

The battles of Trafalgar and Waterloo were modern annihilative warfare and mark the beginning of modern Europe.

The Age of the Machine

The period from 1814 to 1914 was the "Golden Age" of Europe. Europe had widespread economic, social, political and intellectual power all over the globe. Although the Spanish American colonies freed themselves in the 1800's, as did Canada, Europe became increasingly powerful in Africa and Asia.

The European intellectual climate during this "Golden Age" was one of optimism and faith in "progress" that the future would be better than the past had been. Advances in urban sanitation and water supplies led to decreased death rates and an increase in European population. The world became interconnected in a manner undreamed of at the turn of the 19th century. Machine power was substituted for human power on a massive scale, and relatively abundant material goods became available to the masses.

The industrialization of Europe exacted a high toll of human misery as jobless rural people migrated to factory towns where they worked for a pittance and lived degraded in slums. This human misery inspired reform movements. In reaction to this misery of industrialization, Karl Marx wrote the *Communist Manifesto* which stressed the interconnectedness between social power and the control of modes of production. Adapted and interpreted as the guide for various revolutionary political movements, the work of Marx remains influential today. The Soviet Union, for example, claims to follow Marxist philosophy, though objective anthropological economic analysis would suggest that it does not do so in actuality.

The application of high-power steam engines for transportation and machinery became significant with the opening of the first passenger railroad in 1825, in Britain. Railroads opened up hitherto remote areas to mass movements of people and goods, with their associated ideas and culture. Nowhere is this more apparent than in the United States where transcontinental railroads made the final connection in 1869, bringing immigrants and settlers to formerly sparsely settled areas of the continent. Steamships sailed on schedule across the oceans, not dependent upon the vagaries of the wind.

The 1868 Meiji restoration in Japan brought Japan into the modern world. Japan flexed military muscles by defeating the Russian battle fleet in East Asia and the Battle of Tsushima Strait in 1905, an event which marked the entry of non-European power into global competition.

The summer of 1914 in Europe was unusually gentle, a long succession of soft sweet days which flowed one into the other. Suddenly, on August 8, guns blazed across the continent as World War I erupted. An era had ended. World War I marked the start of the most recent era, the Age of Flight.

The Age of Flight

"Flight" has a multiplicity of meanings. Most obvious is that of flight through the air. Referring to the present time, it is the flight of the airplane, first flown in 1903, first used as a weapon of war in 1914, and which now provide transportation links across the globe. The trip from San Francisco to Japan no longer lasts six weeks hard sailing by fast clipper ship, but a matter of less than twenty hours in the air. The more recent era is an age of flight in other respects as well. There have been extreme flights of technology and materialism, ranging from nuclear bombs to pocket computers, from chemical "junk food" to canned and frozen food on a mass scale. At the same time, it has been an age of flight from tradition to modernity; and latterly, it has been a time of flight from the modern to a recreated or imagined tradition as a reaction to the pressures and discomfitures of scientific, technologized, bureaucratized life.

World War I caused the destruction of the old European social order and began a new one. The overthrow of the Russian monarchy and the subsequent establishment of the Lenin-led communists in power brought an intensity and terror of totalitarian power new to the world, one increasingly adopted elsewhere. Poison gas and aerial bombing added to the horrors of war. The influenza epidemic of 1918 killed more people than World War I had done; a reminder that disease could still wreak major havoc.

China experienced violent fluctuations during the course of the 20th century. The overthrow of the Manchu Dynasty in the 1930's caused immense sufferings, as did the later civil war which the Communists finally won, and took over the country in 1949. The Red Guards of the 1960's disrupted the Chinese economic and social fabric and destroyed many traditional monuments, antiquities, and libraries. The 1980's were a time of revitalization and modernization, of movement toward once more becoming a major world power.

A characteristic of the most recent era is that events in one part of the world have an influence on ordinary people in other parts of the world to an unprecedented degree.

The Great Depression of 1929 began in the United States and soon affected the world economy, bottoming out in 1933. Dutch factories and rubber plantations as far off as India and Borneo shut down. Farmers on plowed-up prairie land, marginal agricultural land in the interior of the United States and Canada, suddenly found drought and windstorms destroying them in the "dust bowl" region. Yet, ironically, much of the remainder of the world had better weather than had been experienced in the last 900 years, and the population worldwide began an enormous increase.

World War II lasted from 1939–1945. During the War, the insecticide DDT received its first wide usage; antibiotics cut the casualty rate from wounds; computers cranked out tables for accurate gunnery; German rockets carried bombs to London; the first jet airplane flew; and the atomic bomb dropped twice on Japan ended the War and inaugurated the nuclear age.

In the aftermath of World War II, the European empires dissolved, except for the Soviet land-based empire which carved up the world with the United States; Soviet colonies such as Cuba and Vietnam serve as overseas power centers for the empire. The Soviets continued expanding their land-based empire with the take-over of Afghanistan in 1979, and consider the 1989 withdrawal only temporary. The Soviets view the United States as also being an empire with overseas bases, including Guam and the Philippines.

Since 1960, the world climate has worsened. Fickle weather in the years since 1972 has led to mass crop failures and famines in various areas, including the Sahel (edge of the Sahara Desert in Africa) and Brazil.

The 1960's were the time of massive decolonization and the trauma of the Vietnam War; the 1970's brought declining expectations. Significantly, 1977 saw the eradication of smallpox from the Earth, and the end of the scourge that had killed and maimed for thousands of years.

In the 1980's, fewer than half the humans on Earth were occupied in agriculture. For this reason there is much talk of the "post agricultural age." But whether this will last or not remains to be seen. In many areas human population is pushing resources to the limit, and beyond, with destructive results. One striking example is the Chinese destruction of much of the flora and fauna of Tibet in less than two decades; another is the massive deforestation of the Himalayas as people seek fuel for their cooking fires. For many humans in the world, one or more of three shortages is critical to survival: shortages of food, of drinking water, or of cooking fuel.

Into the Future

How far from the ancient mammoth hunters is the present era! In the last third of the 20th century, electronic communications and space satellites linked the world, spied on it, and provided fascinating pictures of global weather. Offsetting the technological wizardry were the socially disrupting factors of the increasing worldwide separation of wealth for the few and poverty for the many, and the threat to human survival posed by ecological damage, epidemic disease, and nuclear militarism. The "Achilles Heel" of the electronic age is the absolute dependence upon electricity; any interruption in the supply of electricity disrupts life, and in developed countries so much food is shipped long-distances instead of being grown locally that an interruption in the fossil fuel supply needed to fuel shipping could lead to mass starvation, especially in the urban areas where most of the population live.

Looked at in the long-term perspective of human habitation on Earth, the present technological hypertrophy may be just a passing phenomenon. Two major threats to human survival lie in hybridized agriculture and in pollution. Modern agriculture relies heavily on hybridized crops. Concomitant with this has been the loss of the earlier non-hybridized forms of crops, so that if blight (plant disease) ravages crops, there is little or no genetic pool of older crops available to be raided or bred into new hybrids. Modern technology pollutes the entire environment. Acid rain is killing forests in Europe, America, and Japan. The long-lasting pollution of spent nuclear fuel and highly toxic chemicals, which remain lethal to humans and the environment for centuries, is surely a Pandora's box of horrors for future generations. The use of fossil fuel in industry, for generating electricity and to supply transportation, poses another problem for human survival. It is now apparent that the Green House effect is upon us and that the long-term predictions for our present ecosystem are not optimistic. On a personal level, many people feel themselves to be the pawns, not of a deity who can be supplicated, but of amorphous implacable forces.

Yet there is hope. Humankind over the past 100,000 years and more have successfully faced large climatic forces and great change. The end may have come for particular individuals or groups of individuals, but humanity as a whole survived. Survival is an active affair: one cannot relax in comfort; one must do that which is necessary, face the challenges, and live each day to the full.

Each of us is here now because of the past. We should learn from the past, and take comfort in it, so that we can live a better today and alertly face the future.

SUGGESTED READINGS

Calder, Nigel, *Timescale: An Atlas of the Fourth Dimension,* The Viking Press, New York, 1983. Presents an overview of Earth history from the distant beginnings to the present, from trilobites to dinosaurs and pyramids.

Coe, Michael, Dean Snow and Elizabeth Benson, *Atlas of Ancient America,* Facts on File, New York, 1986.
This book is a lively, lavishly illustrated account of Indians of the Americas from the time of their first entry until today. Extensive maps, illustrations, and timelines make this a valuable reference as well as good reading.

Past Worlds: The Times Atlas of Archaeology, Hammond, Maplewood, 1988.
A lavishly illustrated large-format work which brings the past vividly to life, this readable atlas provides hours of happy reading. Through the many pictures and maps one can feel a real connection with the human past.

Being Human—Enculturation and Life Cycle

4

Culture is all-encompassing. Humans are born into a culture, live by cultural rules, and die wrapped in a cultural shroud. Culture is not instinctive, it is learned. This process of learning a culture is called *enculturation.*

Humans are social beings. During a human life on earth, one is related to physical surroundings, humans, animals, and spirits that dwell on earth, and to the entities that exist or dwell above or below the earth.

Throughout the life cycle, each human is part of a particular culture. The stages of the life cycle consist of conception, birth, childhood, sexual maturity, marriage, reproduction, raising of the next generation, old age, and death. Many cultures mark key life passages with formal rites (rites of passage). These may include birth, first steps, maturity, marriage, first child, first child married, and death.

The Beginning

Life on this earth begins with conception, usually resulting in birth. Some cultures attribute conception to causes other than sexual intercourse, although they may realize that sex is somehow related to conception. Among the Trobriand Islanders conception is believed to occur when an ancestral spirit enters the woman's womb while she is wading in a lagoon (Malinowski, 1927). The belief that the child is a reincarnation of an ancestral spirit who somehow slipped into the womb occurs in many cultures. For example, the Arunta believe that a spirit-child enters the woman's womb.

A woman who wishes to conceive will act upon her cultural beliefs regarding conception. Because barrenness is an acceptable reason for divorce in many cultures, women often try desperately to overcome infertility. For Catholics barrenness has been the only sanctioned reason for divorce. In an effort to conceive women may wear charms and amulets, take special medicines, and perform various tasks (such as pilgrimages) to supplicate the gods. A Navajo woman who has had difficulty conceiving will have sex with her partner during her menstrual period, an act which is normally considered taboo. Brunei Malay women make a special pilgrimage to a folk saint's grave, asking to be granted a child.

Women who wish to avoid having a child also act upon their cultural concept of conception. Groups with limited ecological and economic resources often need to limit population. A family may be unable to support another child, or may not want to risk loss of the mother's life. Women in many cultures use one or more of four methods to limit family size: abstinence, contraception, abortion, and infanticide.

Abstinence is refraining from sexual intercourse. Many cultures have post-partum taboos, which proscribe sexual intercourse for a specified period following the birth of a child, often lasting from one to three years.

Contraception is the prevention of conception. Methods include ingesting medicines, using condoms during sex, practicing coitus-interruptus, placing objects in the vaginal canal, using charms and amulets, and sterilization. Invoking or relying on supernatural aid as a contraceptive measure appears all over the world. After her first experience with sexual intercourse, an American teenage woman is likely to say "Oh God, please don't let me be pregnant!" Birth control pills are an effective modern contraceptive widely used as a means of population control.

Sometimes an unwanted child is conceived. Then abortion or infanticide may occur. Both methods are controversial in Euro-American culture today, but both are practiced worldwide.

Abortion is induced expulsion of a fetus. Spontaneous abortion, or miscarriage, occurs when a woman's body "throws off" a fetus, often because it is malformed. Abortion may be induced by ingesting a strong emetic, sticking a sharp object into the vaginal canal, beating the abdomen violently, or surgically removing the fetus. Abortion is a widely used method of birth control, although cultures differ widely with respect to sanctioning or forbidding it legally or morally, as the controversies over abortion in the United States and Canada show.

When an unwanted infant is born it may be killed, which is known as *infanticide*. Many cultures practice infanticide. The Greeks of ancient Sparta exposed physically deformed children to the elements. A !Kung infant born too soon after a previous child, was buried in the sand before it had time to take its first breath. It should be noted that in many cultures, a child is not considered fully human until it reaches a certain level of development (such as making its first sound, or taking its first step). Therefore, infanticide is not considered to be murder in these cultures.

Traditional China had a high rate of female infanticide. Males were wanted to carry on the family line, since kinship was patrilineal. Children of both sexes had to be supported by the family until they were old enough to work. But as soon as a daughter was old enough to contribute valuable labor she was married and became a part of her husband's family. Thus, a family had all the expense of raising a daughter but received nothing in return for this investment (Wolf 1974). To provide desperately needed population control, modern China forces couples to have only one child, which has made female infanticide so prevalent that the government holds official "girls are nice" campaigns.

Lest one assume that infanticide is found only in "other" cultures, it should be noted that the practice exists in the United States today. Violent child abuse may be a form of infanticide, and many newborns are abandoned by mothers who cannot afford to raise them, or are silently neglected until they die.

Most women who conceive accept the pregnancy. For many it is a much-wanted and eagerly accepted event in life. Pregnancy can be a time of many wonders for a woman, for now she bears within herself a child who is at once a part of herself and yet is also a nascent human being, a new life being created.

Traditional cultures emphasize the importance of motherhood. Thus, when conception has been verified and accepted the pregnant woman is enveloped within a cloud of ritualistic behavior and taboos. The belief that all the mother's activities and experiences influence the development of the child is prevalent in many cultures. The Chinese speak of this as "education in the womb." Upsetting experiences, certain activities, and certain foods are thought to cause fetal deformities and/or a difficult labor for the woman. Many traditional Native American cultures believe that eating chicken feet, or the feet of any other animal, will cause the baby to be born feet first. In Guatemala, a Pedrano pregnant woman who ventures out during a thunderstorm can expect the child to be born with club feet and to be claimed by the rain gods as their helper (Paul,

1974). Many Native Americans held the belief that eating too many berries would cause the child to have red-colored birthmarks. Among the Brunei Malays the mother is told not to go out alone at night, lest certain kinds of evil spirits attack her.

Sexual restrictions associated with pregnancies vary. The Hopi of northern Arizona believe that the father's semen strengthens the child. But the Apache believed that a pregnant woman must cease all sexual activity to avoid damaging the baby (Niethammer 1977).

Some cultures have pregnancy taboos which greatly restrict what a woman may do or eat. Brunei Malays say that it is particularly important for a woman pregnant with her first child to observe all the restrictions. In later pregnancies, after she already "knows how to give birth," the restrictions may be eased. Women from traditional societies who have received formal education may face conflicts over pregnancy restrictions. One Malaysian university graduate who lost her first child at birth tearfully exclaimed that she didn't think all those taboos mattered anymore, but she supposed she'd have to observe them next time. The latent meaning behind her statement was that perhaps her failure to observe the traditional restrictions had caused her baby to be born dead.

Pregnancy and childbirth hold many hazards for both the mother and the unborn child; hence, many cultures allow the cravings of the mother-to-be to be satisfied. In North America a pregnant woman's food cravings are considered normal and should be fulfilled, even if what she wants to eat is a little earth from the yard, or a dill pickle, peanut butter and chocolate sandwich. And the Iroquois tell a story about a husband who made a hundred mile trek to a trading post and sold his horse, just to satisfy his pregnant wife's desire for a special kind of corn (Neithammer 1977).

Birth

Birth, especially a first birth, is a time of trauma for a woman. In the days before modern hygiene and medicine, the mortality rate of women in childbirth was high. For this reason, women in many cultures are given a great deal of emotional support and/or medical assistance while they are in labor. Brunei Malays surround a woman giving birth with the attention of many women, in addition to the assistance of a midwife and a traditional medical practitioner. They maintain that a woman in childbirth should not be left alone or with only a few people nearby, lest she become lonely or afraid. Other cultures also allow the birthing woman to be assisted by female relatives and women who have special knowledge of birth customs. The other women talk to and comfort the mother to help ease her trauma, while at the same time creating and reaffirming a strong sense of female solidarity. She is not the first woman to go through childbirth, nor shall she be the last.

Sometimes, something goes wrong, and a specialist is called in to invoke supernatural aid. The decision regarding whom shall be saved, the mother or the child, is a difficult one, and it is arrived at differently in each culture. It is, however, usually the mother's life which is deemed more important. Among the Brunei Malays, if the choice lies between the life of the mother and that of the child, that of the mother is chosen, because she can have another child soon, but the baby cannot take a full place in society for many years.

Some cultures permit a woman to express the pain she feels during childbirth, and others do not. In Euro-American culture it is permissible for a woman in labor to yell and scream—indeed, it is even expected. But such behavior is not permissible for a Crow woman. One explanation that has been proposed is that if a Crow woman gave birth while the group was on the move and being pursued by enemies (such as the Cheyenne), her cries would reveal the position of the group, thus precipitating an enemy attack. To prevent this, women were taught that however great the pain, they must remain quiet.

The father's role at birth also differs among cultures. The traditional Euro-American role for the father was to be uninvolved in the birthing procedure, and to see the baby and mother only after it was over and they had been tidied up for presentation. As a colloquial maritime saying expressed it, "the father is needed for the keel laying but not for the launching." This attitude is changing somewhat; fathers can assist in the birthing rooms of many hospitals, if they so desire.

Among some of the traditional Indian groups of the Amazon Basin, the men practice *couvade*. While his wife is giving birth, the husband lays in his hammock and goes through a simulacrum of the birth process. *Couvade* is a French word meaning "brood" or "hatch," and the practice takes various forms in different societies. One anthropological explanation of this phenomenon attributes it to male envy of the woman's ability to give birth ("womb envy"). Members of cultures who engage in this practice, however, usually give different reasons. For instance, it is often believed that by pretending to give birth himself, the father diverts the attention of evil spirits from the mother and child, thus protecting them from harm (Kupferer 1965). A variant of couvade occurs among some Euro-American males who are stricken with "sympathetic" morning sickness or labor pains.

In many cultures the birth of her first child marks a female's transition from childhood to womanhood. Indeed, bearing children is often seen as one of the central roles of a woman. In bringing a child into the world, the woman contributes to the continuation of the group and reinforces kinship ties, while elevating her own status. The traditional Chinese considered that a woman who had not yet borne a son to carry on her husband's descent line was a wife who had not fulfilled her proper function (Wolf 1974).

Euro-Americans mark the specialness of a first birth (and often of subsequent births) through the "baby shower," a party which is given for a woman by her female friends. Part of the ritual is the giving of gifts to the pregnant woman, usually items which will be used by the new baby. The shower is given near the time of birth, usually within the last month of pregnancy, and serves several functions. It has the practical aspect of providing many necessities for the baby soon to be born; it serves as a marker of female solidarity and cohesiveness; it provides comfort and encouragement in the face of an impending event which entails some danger and which will mark a drastic alteration of life-style; and it serves as a formal marker of the life passage from young womanhood to "motherhood."

By contrast, the Brunei Malays, while surrounding a pregnant woman with care and attention, consider it bad luck to prepare anything for the baby about to be born. Only after the baby is safely born are "baby needs" assembled. To do so earlier is to incur risk by making evil spirits aware of what will happen, because evil spirits are especially fond of infants, and it also risks incurring the wrath of Allah by presuming to know the outcome of an event, which only He can decide.

One of the most famous descriptions of birth ever written is that found in the Bible. "And the days were accomplished that she should be delivered. And she brought forth a son and wrapped him in swaddling clothes and laid him in a manger." This description makes vividly clear that once a child is born it enters the world of human culture (English uses the neuter pronoun for infants spoken of in the generality, itself a cultural statement). Modern Euro-American children are no longer wrapped in swaddling clothes, which cover the infant from head to toe, leaving only the face exposed. But in many areas of the world, swaddling clothes are still used. They are thought to protect the infant from harm by preventing it from wiggling and falling, and by protecting it from wind and drafts as well as from cold. The child may be put into a crib in American culture, into a baby sling in Brunei Malay culture, into the mother's hammock among the Amazon Indians, or laid beside the mother on the ground, as among the Bushmen of the Kalahari, or carried in a cradleboard as among the Crow. From the first moments of life then, the new-born child is exposed to and influenced by its particular culture.

Post-Partum

The time immediately following birth is a crucial one for both mother and child. Each culture prescribes post-partum treatment and care for the mother and infant. Often mother and child are kept in seclusion, and the mother may need to follow a special diet. Among the Nez Perce of northern Idaho a woman enters a special underground lodge two to three months prior to giving birth, and stays there until two weeks after delivery (Spinden 1908).

Post-partum seclusion is an effort to allow the mother and child to recuperate from the birthing ordeal. Brunei Malays say that the new mother should rest for 40 days, with a warm fire beside her abdomen. This is to help the uterus shrink to its normal size, to prevent the mother from catching a chill which could presage fever, and to enable her to regain her strength.

Many cultures consider birthing to be defiling or unclean; post-partum seclusion is therefore sometimes seen as a way to protect people from the mother's dangerous and polluting powers. In addition, the mother may also go through a specific purification ceremony before re-entering social life. In the Greek Orthodox religion, a woman must wait 40 days and then undergo special ceremonies before she

Figure 4.1. Map of Borneo

can attend services in the church again. Among the Hopi, a woman remains in seclusion for 20 days with her female relatives. On the 20th day the mother and baby are ceremonially washed in yucca suds and the infant is given a name by its grandmothers and aunts. The child is then presented to the father so that the mother and child may rejoin the people (Smith 1931). In Brunei Malay society, if the first-born lives for 40 days and the mother herself is safe, a special feast and ceremony are held to mark the 40th day after the birth. This is a rite of passage for both parents, signifying that they have safely produced a live child. The couple dresses in finery such as they wore for their wedding, and they sit on a special platform to be seen by the guests. Afterwards, a feast is served and prayers of thanksgiving are held.

Sometimes an infant dies soon after birth. In many cultures, the grieving mother must recover in seclusion, and go through the purification ceremonies alone. Infant mortality in the first year is high in some areas of the world and low in others.

An Alorese child of eastern Indonesia is not permitted to set foot on the ground during its first year of life. Then a special ceremony is held for the child's first step upon the earth, symbolizing a final transition from the state of one who comes into being to one who walks upon the earth (DuBois 1960).

Male Jewish infants are circumcized on the seventh day after birth, to mark their reception into the Jewish religion and culture. An Omaha Indian mother protects her child from early death by giving it a pair of moccasins with a hole in them so the child can tell the Great Spirit, "I can't travel with you now, my moccasins are worn out" (Niethammer 1977).

Childhood

All humans must make a transition from the complete dependency of early infancy to the comparative independence of early childhood. This transition may be gradual or abrupt. Among Euro-Americans it is comparatively gradual, as it is among the Brunei Malays. The Alorese child of eastern Indonesia, however, experiences the transition as a sudden trauma. One day, the mother simply stops keeping the child with her all of the time. Instead, she leaves it behind to fend for itself with the other village children. Its tantrums are ignored or even egged on, and it no longer is soothed and comforted (DuBois 1960).

Three developments accompanying the transition from infancy to childhood appear to be universal. First, the child learns to walk, which gives it a certain degree of independence. Second, the child becomes, or is, toilet-trained. For example, among the Japanese intensive toilet training is a feature of life. By contrast, among the Brunei Malays it is assumed that the child will toilet train itself when ready (although hints and encouragement are given). The third event, and one that forever marks the child as a human being, is the acquisition of language.

In many cultures the acquisition of language marks the child's transition into a fully human being. The English language reflects this concept in the usage of pronouns. When referring to a young child who has language, the pronouns "she" or "he" must be used, whereas when one is referring to a child too young to speak, the pronoun "it" is commonly used. Brunei Malay funeral customs display this same bias. A child who dies before acquiring language is accorded a simplified version of the funeral ceremony. But a child who dies after learning to speak is given a funeral every bit as elaborate as that of an adult.

Children who have acquired language gradually become a part of the play and activity groups of other children. Modern Euro-American culture often marks the full transition into childhood through entrance into nursery school. The entrance of Prince William of England into a nursery school signified that he was now unequivocally a young boy, and that the proper time had arrived to begin his formal schooling.

Children are *enculturated,* that is, they learn to be members of their culture, in many ways. Children observe and seek to imitate adult behavior, often by playing "make-believe" games or by carrying out chores appropriate to their age, sex, and status.

Another aspect of enculturation is formal instruction. In the U.S. today, this is conducted in schools where attendance is obligatory, whereas in many traditional groups attendance is not obligatory and the process of instruction is casual. Story-telling is a very important mode of instruction in many nonliterate societies.

Among the Brunei Malays children of both sexes were taught to recite the *Koran,* but only boys learned to read Malay written in the

Arabic script and to write. Such division of knowledge by sex is common cross-culturally. Among the Bushmen of the Kalahari, girls accompanied their mothers on gathering expeditions, and were given the specialized technical knowledge that every woman needed to successfully provide for her family. Boys listened to the men as they recounted events of the hunt, thus beginning their education in subsistence activities.

Maturity

Eventually, signs of physical maturity begin to appear in the child. Around the time this occurs, many cultures mark the passage from childhood to adulthood with some special rite of passage ceremony. This transition from the status of child to adult is accomplished through rites of initiation. Through initiation, a body of rites and oral teachings, the initiate gains access to the traditional adult knowledge, behavior patterns, techniques and institutions of the culture.

The onset of menarche often denotes a young girl's readiness for puberty initiation. At the sign of the first flow of menstrual blood, the young woman undergoes ritual changes that signify her transition from child to adult status. Three elements that are frequently associated with such rites are isolation of pubescent girls, learning of traditional knowledge in regard to their role as women, and a joyful celebration that they now belong to the company of women and are able to produce children to increase the group.

Among some Native American women, the practice of isolation in "moon huts" was common. From menarche to menopause, women gathered in these huts during the time of menstruation. It should be noted that this was not personal isolation. It was often a social time, a time of bonding and reaffirming connections among women. It is also interesting to note that in many cultures, men consider menstruating women to be dangerous, and young women must learn to control both their creative and destructive powers. This is often evidenced, as it is in Euro-American culture, in a taboo against engaging in sexual intercourse during menstruation.

During the puberty initiation a young women often receives instruction on the "art" of being a proper woman. This instruction indoctrinates the girl into the proper behavior of a woman and the traditional female lore. Among the northeastern Australian people, pubescent girls were initiated by the *cooborees,* the women's secret societies. Members of the cooboree chanted songs to bring on sexual maturity. They taught the young women secret rituals to prevent hemmorhaging and cramping, to stop the blood flow, and to facilitate childbirth (Rohrlich-Leavitt 1975). In modern American society a young woman receives her knowledge about menarche from several sources; sex education classes in school, peer gossip, magazines, and from her mother, sister, or some other female relative. There is no overt rite of passage ceremony celebrated to mark her new status as a woman. She learns that menstruation is something shameful which must be concealed from everybody, particularly from males, and that she is expected to "carry on" with full normal activities as though nothing were happening. This does not mean, however, that menarche is unimportant in Euro-American culture. Young women recognize it as a time of transition; they discuss it among themselves, worry about it if it occurs later than they think it should, and often congratulate each other when they reach this milestone in their lives.

For boys, there is no such clear physical manifestation of maturity, and perhaps the fact that male initiation ceremonies tend to be more complex than those for females is related to this. Among the Australian aboriginies, males

Figure 4.2 Children are an important part of Navajo life. This mother is holding and comforting her child while also weaving. Another woman is weaving on the second loom; the two women provide company for each other as they chat while working. (Photograph by Harry Teller)

undergo a series of ceremonies which symbolically separate them from the world of children through a ritual enactment of death. They are then educated in the lore of men, including valuable hunting and magico-religious knowledge. They are also marked physically in various ways, and then are symbolically reborn as adult men. Brunei Malay boys' circumcision marks their entrance into adulthood and full responsibilities as Moslem men. The Bar Mitzvah ceremony transforms a Jewish boy into a man. Among other things, this signifies that he is now eligible to constitute one of the

Figure 4.3 Formal instruction is an important part of enculturation in the United States. The child in this photograph is receiving formal instruction in the Early Childhood Education Center of Pierce Community College, Tacoma, Washington, in 1988. (Photograph by Brian Benedetti)

although the rites and customs surrounding entrance into high school often seem to serve as a surrogate to the participants. But because the larger society does not recognize such a transition, there is a period when individuals who are physically at or near maturity are still classified as children, and a problem of self-identity occurs. In Euro-American culture, graduation from high school (or being old enough to do so) is generally considered to mark passage into adulthood.

An individual who has become an adult continues to be enculturated. Much enculturation takes place through participation in such groups as women's or men's societies, voluntary organizations, military societies, or special groups of contemporaries. Secret societies and many other groups have initiation rites. Various adult groups are small subcultures with their own customs and rules. These adult groups play an important role in many people's lives.

In many West African cultures the women gather in their special house to have fun, set trading rules, chastize women who have broken their laws, prepare for their daughters' initiation ceremonies and to reaffirm a sense of female solidarity. The London coffee houses of Samuel Johnson's time were male group preserves. Here, men gathered by occupation or class to discuss issues of their time, to exchange news and information, and to gossip.

In cultures with a strong military organization, young adult males are conscripted or obligated to serve. Traditional Chinese literature contains numerous poems recounting how the strong young men of a village were forcibly conscripted, leaving only the women, the old men, and the children behind, and of the disastrous consequences this had for the village. Among the Iroquois of eastern North America all men were expected to be warriors. This was also the expectation among the Crow,

ten men necessary to make a *minyan,* the minimum group necessary to hold a religious service. In the absence of any physical manifestation of maturity, these ceremonies can assume vast importance in the "making of a man." Among some African groups, for example, a 60 year old male may still be called a boy if he has never been through initiation.

In Euro-American culture no such formal demarcation occurs, either for girls or for boys,

Figure 4.4 This young member of the Crow tribe is learning the importance of her ethnic identity by participating in activities associated with her cultural heritage. She is standing in front of one of the tipis erected for the Crow fair at Crow Agency, Montana, in 1988. (Photograph by Dale McGinnis)

but any man who could not fulfill it had the option of becoming a *berdache* (a male who takes on the female role). And an Iban man of Borneo had to take a head on a head-hunting raid before he was considered a real man and therefore eligible to marry.

Marriage

All human groups order the relations between women and men. What constitutes "marriage" differs in various cultures, but marriage is basically a way of pairing a woman and a man to form the basis of a new family. This basic kinship unit is intricately connected to all other aspects of culture and is discussed in depth in Chapter 6.

Adulthood

Learning and growth continue throughout adult life. For example, the rearing of children is a two-decade education process both for the children themselves, and for their parents. Adults are, by and large, no longer acquiring the basics of their culture, but they are acquiring refinements. The introspective life of an adult may be very rich or very poor, but there is little way of documenting this. Yet this interior life is an important part of every individual's existence, and may have a key influence upon how one deals with life.

Adulthood, then, is a time of deepening and enriching that which was learned in childhood. Imagine the difficulties faced by a person raised in one culture who, as an adult, is thrust into another culture. Little of her knowledge or past experience is useful to her now; she must literally start over from the beginning, learning a new language and a new way of life. Her adulthood, instead of being a time of refining what she has already learned, becomes more a return to childhood. This is one of the elements of what anthropologists refer to as *culture shock,* and is something with which refugees all over the world must deal. Some manage to adjust fully to the new culture, others adjust partially, and still others cannot handle the strain. Such trauma at any stage of life can have a life-long effect. Children tend to be more resilient in the face of such trauma; as people who are not yet fully enculturated, they adapt more easily to a new culture. But adults, in whom cultural concepts and mores have been fully internalized, find adjustment to such radical change far more difficult, and often impossible.

One characteristic of modern industrialized society is incessant change. Adults, and children to a certain extent, must constantly adapt to new circumstances. Again, not everyone is equally capable of making such adjustments, and the "stress of modern life" is often partially attributed to such difficulties.

Old Age

"Old" is a relative term. Among the earliest modern humans, 40 was ancient, but for members of modern industrial societies 40 does not even mark the beginning of middle age. The beginning of old age is signified in various ways in different cultures, and attitudes toward aging and the aged are also diverse.

Cessation of menses, or menopause, often signifies the beginning of old age for women. As with the onset of puberty, the "death of youth" is not so clearly marked for men; they simply experience a gradual loss of vitality. Among the Inuit of northern Canada, the elderly who could no longer carry out their economic role were allowed to die, because the harsh reality was that life was lived on the margin of survival, and there was no surplus to support unproductive persons. The traditional Chinese venerated their elders for their wisdom and knowledge, yet among the poor the elderly could eat and survive only as long as they could work.

Among Euro-Americans, the elderly are treated in an ambiguous manner. On the one hand there are remnants of the earlier tradition of respecting the elderly for their knowledge and wisdom. But on the other hand is the fact that Euro-American culture is extremely youth-oriented, tending to value only those people who are actively productive. The elderly are thus cast out because they are no longer young, and because they are no longer as intensely competitive and income-producing as are the younger people.

Modern Euro-Americans segregate the elderly into "old age communities" set apart from the rest of the social world and largely ignored by it. In many large cities criminals prey especially upon the elderly and force them to become virtual prisoners in their own homes or in their old age community dwellings. Yet, paradoxically, there is a reluctance to let the elderly die in the fullness of their days; rather, expensive medical measures are used to prolong their biological existence, even though their social existence has ceased.

Old age has its own compensations. As women become older they gain more freedom in many societies. For example, among the Brunei Malays older women can move about more freely than younger ones, and can talk to men in circumstances where it would be improper for a younger woman to do so. This is due in part to the belief that older women are not sexual beings; hence there can be no sexual component to their dealings with men.

Rosaldo (1974:28), in her discussion of women and power says "The rituals of authority are not available to woman; only when

Figure 4.5 The late Mrs. Anna Old Crow, a member of the Crow tribe and a matron of the Big Lodge Clan, as she appeared in 1972. (Photograph by Dale McGinnis)

she is old and free of the responsibility of children, when she is disassociated from child rearing and also from sexuality, can a woman build the respect that comes with authority."

To a lesser extent, such freedom comes also to aging men in traditional societies. An older man can sit and chat with a group of women, where it would not be proper for a younger man to do so. And older men often have the privilege of sitting and ruminating upon the world.

Older women and men may become experts in traditional medicine or literature. In fact, they will have been acquiring this knowledge during their adulthood, but begin to use it only when freed from the constant demands of rearing a family. With their children grown and married, they now have more time to visit and to engage in various activities.

Traditionally, older people were respected for their knowledge, and in the traditional social and political hierarchy they played important roles. But now, with the modern world impinging in the form of westernized education, modern technology and bureaucracy, the Brunei Malay elders complain that only those who "wear neckties" (younger men in the bureaucracy) are paid any attention. Many younger women attend high-school, then marry and raise families full-time. They may begin with their school-acquired ideas, but are then socialized into the more traditional ways. In other words, after marriage they acquire much of the traditional culture they would otherwise have acquired before marriage. To a lesser extent this is also true of men outside the higher bureaucratic ranks. On the other hand, a significant number of educated women continue to work after marrying, often to help the family acquire desired material goods or to build a house. It seems likely that life for old people in Brunei will become increasingly difficult in the future, as modern houses and apartments have no place for them, and as the desire for material goods by the younger family members makes them reluctant to divert resources for the care of the aged.

Death

Eventually, old age leads to death. Among many groups one cause of respect for elders is their longevity, because by living so long they have demonstrated a "power" of life. And the elderly may be thought special because they are nearer to the ancestors, being so close to being ancestors themselves.

The final rite of passage is death and incorporation into the world of the dead. Attitudes toward death differ not only between cultures, but also within a culture, depending on how and to whom death has come.

Brunei Malays regard a death in childbirth or in holy war against infidels as good deaths; the person who dies goes straight to heaven. The Aztecs of Mexico also held that the death of a woman in childbirth was like that of a warrior in battle and that both went to heaven. Among the Brunei Malays the death of a vigorous healthy individual in her or his prime, especially if the death is not due to an accident or one of the common fatal diseases, is suspected to be due to poisoning or the sending of evil spirits. The sudden decline and death of a vigorous old person is attributed to like causes. But the death of a child is often seen as the result of some evil spirit getting hold of that child, because evil spirits like to kill children. If there has been an unusual pattern of deaths, or an excessive number of them occurring regularly in a community, it is assumed that someone who commands an evil spirit lives in the community and must be ferreted out. But the gradual decline of an old person and the ensuing death are considered normal, and the cause of death is stated as "old age."

Just as the infant at birth was enmeshed in its culture, so the individual at death is parted from it. Disposal of the body ranges from burial, as among Brunei Malays and most Euro-Americans, to cremation as among the Hindus, to exposure on a mountaintop so that the soul can find release on the wind, as among many groups dwelling in the Himalayas. The dead person leaves a gap, a rent in the fabric of society. Funeral ceremonies serve to mend this gap.

The modern Euro-American funeral is a single ceremony, but the Brunei Malays hold prayers on the day of death (which is also the day of burial), as well as on the third, seventh, and fortieth days after death. By the fortieth day all affairs of the dead person should have been attended to, the inheritance divided, and after the large memorial feast on the fortieth day, people are supposed to cease mourning for the departed and to continue with the living of life. Thenceforward, the deceased will be publically mourned only on the annual day of the dead.

Afterlife

All humans face the ineffable mystery of death. And most cultures have ideas and beliefs concerning what happens after death. The Brunei Malays follow the Islamic idea that on Judgement Day all souls will be judged and go to heaven or hell for eternity. Hindus and Buddhists believe that unless a person has attained release from the endless round of being reborn, she or he must return to live another life on earth. One of the beliefs of the Mongols was that the soul would forever ride the wind that swept across the vast steppe of Eurasia. And the Hopi believe that the souls of the dead live on as benevolent spirits who bring rain to those still living.

Many people believe that the dead are capable of returning to visit the living; hence the admonition in Euro-American culture "Don't speak ill of the dead."

Cultural attitudes toward death and the dead vary. Mexicans have a fascination with it, as seen in the bullfight. And on "El Dia del Muerte" ("The Day of the Dead") they even become intimate with death and joke about it. Families gather together eating, talking, and laughing at the graveyards. Special candies shaped like skulls and coffins are part of the food. At the graves, the family reassures the dead that they have not been forgotten, brings the dead up to date on the latest family gossip, and asks them not to hurt or bother the living.

In the United States, major public deaths (such as the assassination of President Kennedy or the death of the seven astronauts of the Challenger space shuttle) inspire national mourning, symbolized by flags at half-mast and by televised funeral or memorial rites.

They are often later commemorated in other ways, for instance, by the erection of public monuments. Modern American culture has two official days set aside for remembering the dead: Veteran's Day and Memorial Day. On Memorial Day particularly, families take flowers to the gravesite and spruce up the grave, or they may share their memories of the departed in other ways.

Beyond the Life Cycle

The mourning customs of any culture allow the individual to see the continuity of life and to realize that she or he will also be remembered after death. Such observances also give the living cause to ponder the ephemerality of life, and are a time to order one's interior life so as to deal with the realization that one will not always be here.

"To everything there is a season . . .
A time to be born, and a time to die."
(Ecclesiastes)
"What begins shall end, whatever being is born must also die,
and the river flows into the sea."
(Brunei Malay)

SUGGESTED READINGS

Linderman, Frank B. *Pretty-Shield: Medicine Woman of the Crow*. Lincoln: University of Nebraska Press, 1972.
This book offers the reader an exciting story of a woman's life as a Plains Indian. The story includes such cultural events as courtship, marriage, and childbirth.

Mead, Margaret. *Coming of Age in Samoa*. New York: Dell, 1961.
A classic anthropological study on adolescence.

Read, Margaret. *Children of Their Fathers: Growing Up Among the Ngoni of Malawi*. New York: Holt, Rinehart, and Winston, 1968.
A study of the Ngoni of Central Africa. This ethnography focuses on the enculturation practices of the Ngoni.

Turnbull, Colin M. *The Human Cycle*. New York: Simon and Schuster, 1983.
A cross-cultural work that spans four continents in an effort to examine the human life cycle, and how culture acts upon the individual in the various stages of life.

Van Gennep, Arnold. *The Rites of Passage*. Chicago: University of Chicago Press, 1960.
This work is a classic in the field of life cycle and transition rites.

Language and Communication 5

Communication

Humans communicate from the first cry at birth to the last sigh at death. Communication takes many forms, of which the most distinctly human is spoken language. Languages change over space and time, providing a living communication framework for cultural interactions and individual identity. The study of language is the study of being human.

A Model for Basic Communications

Anthropology searches for understanding through many avenues. One approach is the construction of models which include a wide range of data. A single basic communications model (Figure 5.1) fits all the forms of human communication.

For speech, the *sender* is the speaker and the *receiver* is the hearer or listener. The *message,* the spoken utterance, is transmitted through the *medium* of air (because sound travels as waves in the air). *Feedback* is the reaction of the listener, perhaps a facial indication of interest or boredom. The sender will then modify further communication on the basis of the feedback received. A teacher who sees nodding heads and hears snores in the classroom is receiving feedback that the lecture is too boring. The teacher may tell a few jokes or try other ways to liven up the lecture.

Interference (or *noise*) is anything which hampers transmission or reception of the message. A blaring television or a jet passing low overhead creates interference.

The concepts of sender, receiver, and message, as well as feedback and interference, apply to any communication, verbal or nonverbal. A man or woman wearing fragrance on a date is sending a message of attraction, hoping for a feedback of affection. The other person having a severe head cold presents massive interference right at the receiver. If a skunk wanders across the area where the couple are, a clear case of interference in the medium of transmission may occur.

Modes of Communication

Whether midnight movie, murmured affection, or Thanksgiving Feast, each mode of human communication has three main aspects. First, it is culturally learned and patterned. We speak, gesture, and smell in the ways we were taught. Second, the basic communications model applies to it. Any communication has the components of sender, receiver, message, feedback and interference. Finally, all human communication involves some aspect of human physiology. The following discussion covers the six basic modes of human communication.

Oral-Aural

Oral-aural communication includes language and all other types of communication through sound. Opera and rock concerts, jackhammers and whispers, bird-song and thunderstorm, all constitute part of the sound environment and all convey some sort of message.

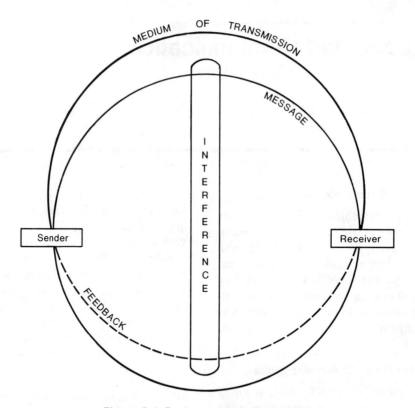

Figure 5.1. Basic communication model

Listen to the noise of rain and the silence of snow, hear the quiet of early dawn and the noise of traffic.

Speech uses the wind-tract, which serves primarily for breathing, and the mouth-stomach part of the digestive tract. A severe head cold can interfere with the wind-tract, as can a peanut butter sandwich interfere with the digestive tract. Interference at either point hinders efforts at speech.

Another hindrance to spoken language is problems with hearing, or the aural portion of speech. Individuals in the United States who have severe hearing problems rely on the visual-kinetic language, American Sign Language (Ameslan). Ameslan is as fully developed a language as any spoken language. Because of interference in the receiver, the aural area, deaf people have developed visual alternatives to oral-aural communication.

Visual

By reading this book you are learning through the medium of *visual* communication, messages received through the eyes. Facial expressions, dance movements, styles of dress and decoration are all forms of visual communication. The message we receive through visual communication is, like oral-aural communication, determined by our culture. People with deficient eyesight cannot rely on vision but depend upon aural cues. For reading, blind people use a tactile form of communication, a series of raised-dot letters called Braille.

Tactile

American culture underemphasizes *tactile* communication, communication through touch. Think of the limitations imposed on hugging, kissing, and holding hands in public.

Two American men holding hands in public may be judged homosexual; among Arabs two men holding hands will be recognized as close friends, and nothing more. Shoes insulate the feet from feeling the terrain over which they walk, and cement sidewalks provide a monotonous tactile environment for the feet.

A student of martial arts and yoga attempts be aware of the very air through which she or he moves. Normally we are aware of moving through the air only when there is a heavy wind. Traditional Polynesian and Micronesian navigators used tactile cues of subsurface water currents, combined with the kinesic feeling of boat movements, as important locational clues.

Kinesic

Kinesic communication, communication through body movements, forms the heart of dance and of traditional cultural postures. Each culture teaches different kinesics for walking, sitting, and moving. Americans, who are used to chairs, are often unable to squat or to sit for prolonged periods on a level surface like the floor. By contrast the Japanese traditionally knelt with their feet tucked under them. The Brunei Malay sitting position is cross-legged for men and women keep their feet tucked underneath and slightly to one side. A person accustomed to sitting in the Japanese or Brunei Malay position finds prolonged sitting in a chair uncomfortable. Similarly, a mountain-bred person finds prolonged walking on level ground a painful experience.

The term "body language" refers to kinesic communication. But body language, too, varies in meaning from culture to culture. If someone stands too close to another person in North America, that person will tend to move away to keep a "safe distance" between them. In Latin America, to back away from someone who is standing close is an indication of coldness and insincerity. No matter what the cultural way of kinesic communication, it is important to communication. The absence of visually-received kinesic cues makes telephone conversations more difficult to follow and interpret than face-to-face interactions.

Gustatory

American culture has a tradition of "good eating" as a means of communicating comfort and contentment. *Gustatory* communication is communication through taste and eating. In America, one way of expressing friendship is an invitation to dinner.

In many cultures, the giving of food and hosting of feasts forms an important means of communication. Prestige at a Brunei Malay wedding stems in large measure from the number of people fed and the lavishness of the food provided. In America, too, wedding receptions are often judged by the quality of the catering.

Gustatory communication often involves symbolism. A classic instance is the American ritual over-eating during the Christmas to New Year's period. Following the ritual overindulgence comes the ritual antithesis, the penance of "New Year's resolutions," symbolizing a break from the old and a start of the new and "better."

Olfactory

Olfactory communication, communication through smell, like other modes of communication, is culturally patterned. Each culture determines what are "socially acceptable" smells. Italians and Lebanese enjoy the smell of culinary garlic. Many Americans dislike it. On the other hand, it is perfectly acceptable for Americans to smell like a mint field, hence all the mint-flavored mouthwashes and "breath sweeteners" sold in stores.

Animal Communication

Animals use the same modes of communication that humans use. But different modes have greater importance and the manner of use differs among animals. For example, humans "sound each other out," while dogs "sniff each other out." Most land mammals have a far better developed sense of smell than humans, and use scent as a primary means of communication. Though well aware of the scent of the skunk, humans remain utterly oblivious to the rich olfactory world experienced by cats and dogs. We use primarily visual and verbal markers, not olfactory ones. Such also seems true of most apes and monkeys.

Cats combine sound and kinesic cues, as in the spitting hair-raised arched back yowling of a cat fight. Many birds have elaborate kinesic courtship rituals. Birdsong attracts mates, demarcates territoriality, and warns of danger.

Humans communicating with animals use mixed-mode communication, a combination of modes. A horse rider knows the warning meaning of a horse's laid-back ears or mincing and shying movements. The rider transmits both verbal cues ("giddyap") and tactile-kinesic cues (using the heels to nudge the horse's flanks). Animals communicating with humans also use mixed-mode communication. A cat meowing and brushing against a person's leg is hinting for food or petting. A dog wagging its tail and bringing a stick or ball wants its human to play.

After prolonged skillful coaching, a gorilla and a few chimpanzees have learned to communicate to a limited extent using a simplified version of Ameslan or using plastic chip symbols. With these skills, apes are able to teach other apes to communicate in the new language. They appear to be able to form creative sentences and to use some abstract concepts. But this is still far from being the rich, flexible and complex language communication that permeates human culture. It is to the study of human language in all its complexity that we now turn.

Linguistics

One of the most important developments of the past two centuries has been the emergence of the science of *linguistics,* the scientific description and analysis of contemporary and past languages, and of language change through time. Linguists have ventured to the far corners of the earth to record and study living languages, often at the cost of great personal hardship and danger, the same kinds of hardship often met by cultural anthropologists studying living cultures. Anthropologists confronted with unknown or poorly studied languages and dialects need to analyze the speech sounds encountered, identify the sounds crucial to meaning, understand how words combine to form utterances, and then systematically approach the study of what those utterances mean.

Five Aspects of Linguistics

Phonology

The precise description of how sounds are produced is *phonetics.* The larger study of speech sounds is *phonology.* The root *phone,* which is also found in "telephone" is Greek, meaning "a sound."

A brief consideration of the English sounds *b, p,* and *m* shows some of the complexities involved in phonology. The difference between the sounds *b* and *p* lies in the fact that the *b* is produced by vibrating the vocal chords, while *p* is produced without vibrating the vocal chords. Thus, *b* is a *voiced* sound, because the voice box, the *larynx,* produces sound by vibration of the vocal chords during the production of the sound *b;* no such sound is produced with the sound *p,* and *p* is therefore *unvoiced.* If you place your hand on your throat and pronounce first *baa,* then *pa,* you will feel your vocal chords vibrating in the first case but not in the second.

The difference between b and m lies in the fact that when pronouncing b, the air carrying the sound is expelled through the mouth, while with m the air is expelled through the nose. B is thus an *oral* (mouth) sound, while m is a *nasal* (nose) sound.

These are a few of the important characteristics considered by linguists who study phonetics, or the way sounds are produced. Many other characteristics exist as well, including whether the air flows freely during pronunciation or is stopped, and where the sound is produced—lips, throat, roof of mouth.

The complete description of a language's phonology is more complex, however, than merely describing how a sound is produced. The anthropologist must first learn to hear sounds that differ from those of English, and then to pronounce them. To help distinguish different sounds, and to be able to record them, linguists learn the International Phonetic Alphabet (IPA) or some other phonetic writing system. In a *phonetic alphabet,* each symbol corresponds to one and only one of the several hundred speech sounds used in various languages. But, description, analysis, and notation of sounds form only the first step in the larger linguistic analysis.

Phonemics

Phonemics studies sounds crucial to the determination of meaning. A *phoneme* is the smallest unit of sound which distinguishes meaning in a word. Note that *a phoneme is a sound, not a letter.*

Consider the English words *men* and *pen,* which are alike except for the initial sound. In this case both m and p are phonemes, because they are the smallest units of sound which distinguish the meaning of "men" and "pen." Likewise the words *pen* and *pet* differ only in their final sounds, n and t; but that single sound difference distinguishes meaning. These are examples of consonant phonemes. Vowels can

be phonemes too, as in the words *pen* and *pan;* it is the vowel sounds e and a which change the meaning of the word.

Phonemes may have variant pronunciations which can be recognized or not recognized in a particular culture. In Southern and Black English, *pen* and *pin* are pronounced identically. To those speakers, e is a variant of i, and when other speakers pronounce the two words differently, the difference is not heard by Southern or Black English speakers. In English, the t sound in *tip* and *pit* is considered to be the same sound. But if you place your hand in front of your lips as you pronounce both words, you find that in the first case, a rush of air accompanies the t sound. In the second case, there is no air. The first is an *aspirated* sound (from the Latin *aspirare,* "to breathe upon"); the second which has no puff of air is *unaspirated.* To a speaker of Chinese, these two sounds are different and use of one or the other will change the meaning of a word. Some languages, such as Spanish, do not use the aspirated variant of the letter at all, and this makes it difficult for English speakers to speak those languages without an accent. These variants of basic phonemes are called *allophones,* from Greek *allo,* "other, else" and *phone.* The basic phoneme is the usual pronunciation of a sound, and the allophone is a variant pronunciation.

If someone speaking a foreign language mispronounces a phoneme and uses an allophone, or variant, of the phoneme, that person will "sound funny" but usually will be understood. On the other hand, if that individual uses an incorrect phoneme there will be misunderstanding or total lack of comprehension.

Morphology

Morphology is concerned with the ways sounds can be combined to form meaningful units, which we usually call words. *Morphemics,* which concerns us here, studies small units of meaning directly linked to sound. A *morpheme* is the smallest unit of sound which has its own inherent meaning. Note that *a morpheme is not a word.*

Book, books, and *booked* are all English words which have meaning. But the smallest unit of sound that is the basis for all these words is *book. Book* is called a *root morpheme* because it carries the basic meaning of all these words. Other morphemes are *s,* indicating plurality, and *ed,* indicating past tense of a verb. These are not root morphemes because they have no basic meaning unless they are attached to a root morpheme. Try to determine the root morpheme and the others for the words *do, undo, doing, doings.* How do the other morphemes change the meaning of the root morpheme? What do all of the words have in common in terms of meaning?

Just as phonemes have variant pronunciations, or allophones, so too do morphemes have variant pronunciations. These are called *allomorphs.* The normal English plural morpheme is *s,* as in book*s.* But in some words, the plural is pronounced *z,* as in zoo*s.* In this case, the *z* pronunciation is an allomorph of the usual morpheme *s.*

Like any other student of a foreign language, the anthropologist must understand all the normally encountered morphemes and their allomorphs. Memorizing vocabulary for a foreign language class, such as French, is basically the memorizing of a list of root morphemes and their meanings. But the anthropologist dealing with an unrecorded language is in the position of a small child: it is necessary to figure out what the roots are and what they mean before memorizing them. The next step is to find out how these morphemes are combined into words, and how words are combined into phrases and sentences.

Syntax

Syntax is the study of morpheme combinations and word combinations into phrases and sentences. Anthropologists in field situations usually use item-and-arrangement syntax, or analyzing word order and the placement of grammatical indicators.

Every language uses a limited number of sounds. Likewise every language uses a limited number of patterns of syntax. In many languages, the order of morphemes is important. For example, *The dog bit John* has a meaning different from *John bit the dog.* In other languages, there are grammatical indicators to distinguish subjects and objects of action.

Each language has a structure which underlies its syntactical peculiarities. Consider the English sentences, "I read the book," and "The book was read by me." The first is an active sentence, the second passive. English speakers recognize that the active and passive sentences are transformations of one another. Both indicate who did what, even though they are put together in different ways; the simple and elaborate forms have the same basic underlying structure. *Item and arrangement* essentially looks at "What goes with what and how are they connected?" Figure 5.2 shows one method of diagramming syntax, starting with the spoken sentence, and grouping ever larger units until at the highest level, the entire sentence is itself a single "item."

Semantics

Beyond the formal structural constructs of syntax, morphology, phonemics, and phonology lies the vast realm of *semantics,* the study of meaning. The classical pattern of Western semantic studies derives from the ancient Greek techniques of questioning and discursive analysis.

The anthropologist in the field usually deals with elementary semantic questions: what does this word or phrase mean? With

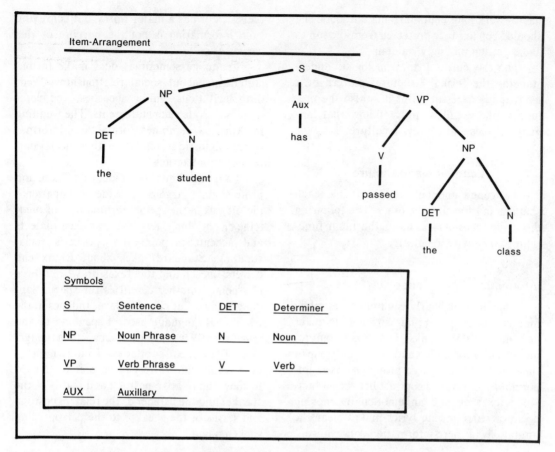

Figure 5.2. Diagramming syntax

what does it contrast or compare? What is the context of usage, or in what context is usage avoided? What are the synonyms and antonyms of this item, and what shades of meaning differentiate them? Are there any special poetical or allusive usages? Has the meaning changed over time, or are there dialectical special usages?

Take the American English word, *poke*. Used as a verb, it means "to jab," as in, "to poke the fire." To "poke someone in the ribs" means to remind them with a jolt, bring them back from inattention. By extension, "to poke fun at" means "to make fun of," with the connotation of doing so at the expense of the other person. As a noun, in some dialects, poke means what in other dialects may be called a "bag" or "sack." A "poke of flour" is a "sack of flour." But "a pig in a poke" is something unidentified and probably useless. One would always buy flour in a poke, or sack, but never livestock. A "poke bonnet" was a woman's bonnet with a great long curved-down front brim to protect the woman's face from the sun, so that she was hidden, as though wearing a poke. In other places the same bonnet was called a "scoop bonnet," reflecting its shape. Underlying the wearing of a poke bonnet was the cultural value that even though a woman had to work long hours farming outdoors, she should keep her face protected from the sun to avoid getting an "ugly" suntan.

For the cultural anthropologist, understanding the formal structural pattern of a language is necessary. But it is also the prelude to the detailed study of how that language shapes and conveys a culture.

Language and Culture

Language and culture intertwine, each shaping and forming the other. The following discussion considers some of the main functions of language in culture.

Information Conveyance

Language obviously communicates information. But people are humans, not almanacs or computer data banks. The direct communication of information and data is only one of the functions of language, although it is an important function. The contrast between a fact-laden textbook and an emotionally moving poem or stirring song lyrics makes clear the limitations of mere information conveyance.

Social Facilitator

Language often serves as "social grease," providing an informal interaction whose purpose and intent is reinforcement of a casual social link. The following is not an exchange of information:

Hi!
Hi! How are you?
Fine, and you?
Fine, thanks. See ya.
Bye now.

This conversation "greases" a casual acquaintanceship. Perhaps one of the speakers really feels sick or has a major worry, but conveying such information is not the purpose of this conversation.

Language sometimes does make formal statements about social relationships. Wedding invitations, public speeches, and ceremonies provide such statements. The wedding in America combines formal and informational linguistic statements with a special pattern of ritual actions.

Language knits social identity. Trade and professional jargons provide occupational identity, as in the special terminology of medicine or plumbing. Regional and class dialects and accents pinpoint the speaker's social standing. Standard jokes about Bronx cab drivers' speech and the Texas drawl reinforce this point. In other countries the special language may differ more. In Java, Indonesia, the traditional language used in speaking to and about royalty was almost a separate language. One of the great subtleties of modern Japanese is the wide variety of verb endings used to show the relative position and status of the speaker and the listener or the relative position and status of the speaker to the person being spoken about.

Emotional Reservoir

Language also provides a vehicle for the expression of deep emotions. Traditional literature contains eloquently expressed emotions, feelings, descriptions, and analyses of a culture. Literature often embodies cultural ideals or cultural statements. But the sound and feeling of a work may be almost more important than the narrative contents. In Brunei, for example, everyone knows the plots of the traditional epic tales. The enjoyment lies in hearing the language and appreciating its richness. Such also was true of the *Iliad* and *Odyssey,* and remains true of Shakespeare's work and the work of the great poets.

Figure 5.3 An Australian Aborigine boy is learning the traditional symbols of his people while watching his father draw the history of their clan ancestors.

Identity Focus

National identity and individual and group self-worth often are inextricably involved with language use. For nations whose people have many native tongues, the establishment of a national language standard may be crucial for the unity of the country. The recurrent "language question" in Canada reflects on a linguistic level the social and economic differences between French-speaking and English-speaking Canadians. The fight of many American Indian groups to retain or to regain their own language shows the importance of language in self-identity.

Cosmic Connection

On a deeper level, language serves to relate humans to the universe. To a Hindu the proper pronunciation of the sacred syllable *om* can link one to the ultimate. For a Muslim, reading the Koran means producing the proper sound of the Arabic in the correct chant form. It is the very sound pattern of the recitation which is pleasing to Allah. In contrast, Christians and Jews emphasize the need to understand scriptural content, though both groups use chanting to some extent. Shamanic traditions focus on verbal communications to and from the spirits.

The absence of verbal communication also plays a role in religion. "Silent worship" Quakers believe that worship should be silent so that worshippers can hear the voice of God. Zen Buddhism teaches that profound understanding arises only when one transcends the confines of language.

Language Families

Linguists have grouped together languages which are similar to one another and seem to have common origins. English has been classified as a part of the Indo-European family, a group of languages which are closely related. The Indo-European family includes languages in several sub-families; among these are Germanic (English, German, Danish), Latin, Romance (French, Spanish, Italian), Slavic (Russian, Bulgarian, Polish), Greek, and Indo-Iranian (Persian, Hindi, Punjabi, Sanskrit). Malay belongs to the Austronesian language family, which also includes Tagalog (national language of the Philippines), Hawaiian, Samoan, and Chamorro (indigenous language of Guam). Arabic and Hebrew, along with Ancient Egyptian, belong to the Semitic language family.

Language Change

Languages, like the humans who speak them, can live or die. Like individuals and cultures, languages change through time. The history of Latin exemplifies the connection between language history and culture events.

The "Epic of the Latin Language" spans two and a half millennia, features a cast of millions, and centers on a melodramatic plot. In 700 B.C. Latin was a small local dialect spoken in the neighborhood of seven warring villages which only later would unite to become Rome. By 200 B.C., the villages had united, set up their central meeting place in the middle of a swamp, and begun to conquer their neighbors. Concurrently with conquest, the Latin language spread, stamping out Etruscan to the north and Greek to the south. By the start of the present era, the Roman Empire included most of the area around the Mediterranean Sea and had reached north into Europe, spreading Latin all the way from England to the borders of Mesopotamia. Latin was the language of progress, engineering, government, science, and international commerce.

Wars and riots, mystic cults and sports mania, all beset the empire. Megalomaniac emperors' torrid love affairs alternated with reforming emperors' violent purges. Staging a coup or starting a civil war became the paths to the throne. By the fourth century, a combination of corruption, economic decline, and violent invasions had weakened the empire. The city of Rome soon fell to northern invaders.

Meanwhile the small Christian fringe cult grew steadily, spread by missionaries who traveled the Roman roads and sea lanes. Obeying a prophetic dream, Emperor Constantine made Christianity the official religion of the Roman Empire.

Different parts of the Empire fell to various invaders who brought their own languages. But the Christian Church continued to grow. The Church spread Latin as the ecclesiastical language, and as the language of learning.

The whirlwind of Islamic conquests in the 700s substituted Arabic for Latin as the language of the southern and eastern Mediterranean shores. But the expansion of Christianity through Europe spread Latin as a language of scholarship and international communication. As science grew and developed during the Middle Ages and subsequent periods, Latin terminology grew and developed with it.

As European science moved into Asia, Africa, and the Americas, so too did the associated Latin terminology. Over the past three centuries the scholarly use of Latin has diminished slowly, though it remains important in science and is the official language of the Roman Catholic Church. Latin still remains a prime source of scientific terminology. But the computer jargon of the post-World War II era derived from English rather than from Latin. Thus, in the latter part of the twentieth century the last great flourish of Latin wanes.

Beginning as an obscure dialect spoken in a hilly riverside swamp, Latin grew and endured through all the turbulence which formed the modern world, and traveled to the moon ("lunar" is Latin). The Epic of Latin has been a resounding language success.

The Destiny of English

The English language also has a history linked with cultural events. Early English bards recounted historical narratives in verse form, because verse is easy to remember. But the allusions and references in verse narrative history often presuppose a certain amount of knowledge on the part of the listener. The verse history of the English language presented in Figure 5.4 provides an example of the type of oral history which for most of humankind's time on earth has been the only available account of the past.

Modern English continues to change in response to cultural events. This change is particularly evident in technical vocabulary. Over the past 20 years, computer jargon has proliferated and infiltrated English. "Input, throughput, output, downtime, system crash"—these are becoming commonplace English words. The term "feedback" originated in radio engineering and has become important in computer development. Such words as "byte" and "floppy disk" show a touch of whimsy. But terms also vanish and die. Most English speakers do not know the meaning of "whipple-tree," "surcingle," or "hackamore," all terms pertaining to horse harnessing and driving. These terms were in common use a century ago. The coming of mass automotive transportation and its associated terminology doomed horse transport and its terminology.

Note the contrast of automotive terminology, with its terms derived from Latin (radiator, carburetor, transmission), to computer terminology with terms derived from English. This change in the derivation of terminology reflects a cultural shift that is occurring now. No longer is Latin the "language of learning," and the source (together with Greek) for all new scientific engineering terms. Modern English chemical and biological nomenclature follow patterns formalized in the eighteenth and nineteenth centuries and are in Latin and Greek. But computer terminology originated in the post-World War II period and uses English words, or words whose formation is based on English. Note that European nationalism in the early nineteenth century doomed Latin as the universal scholarly language of Europe. It may well be that the current global nationalism will in similar fashion doom English as a widespread language of communication or, perhaps, technological and business interconnections will strengthen the position of English. Only time can tell.

Writing

For over a hundred thousand years, hunting and gathering humans lived, dreamed, sang, and spoke their way over the face of the earth. Yet, of all those songs and words, nothing remains. Spoken words vanish on the breeze.

"Go where the path rises up amid the snow
  Go to find what you shall know."
[from an old hunter-gatherer]

Glaciers flourished, receded, and came no more
  to England's long and varied shore.
Forest and flat fed the game
  in search of which hunter-gatherers came;
The tongue they spoke we'll never know
  it vanished as the melting snow.

Farmers worked to tame the land,
  in awe and wonder turned their hand
To hoist up great megaliths tall
  Stonehenge, Avebury, and all
Predict the course of sun and moon.
  The centuries flowed on and soon
From Britain in France Celtic speakers came
  To give the island their old home's name.

The Roman trumpets' blazing sound
  Meant soldier feet tramping ground.
Boadacia the valiant queen
  fought the last stand of the Celtic dream;
Her forces from the world of old
  fell before the legions cold.
Hadrian's wall marked the north,
  "stay out, wild Celts, come not forth."
For in the south the Latin tongue
  ruled supreme Londinium.
Town and village free from strife
  lived a golden Roman life
Which later ages would recall
  as high noon before Rome's fall.

Troubled times and movements mark
  succeeding centuries cold and stark.
Villas abandoned, hill-forts built
  seething chaos to the hilt.
Viking invaders, a burning brand,
  killed and stole, scarring the land.
Celtic speech in Scotland and Wales
  elsewhere dragon Germanic tales.
Beowulf the hero famed
  of those who soon the island named
Angeland, an island home,
  for those who once the wide seas roamed.
Alfred the king whose sunlit day
  of song and learning passed away.
Monasteries wrote and taught
  while petty kingdoms warred and fought.

Autumn was fair that distant year
  King Harold fought for all he held dear

And fell to the blow of invading foe
  who onward conquering would go.
Ten sixty-six at Hasting's Down
  William the Conquerer gained renown.
Scion of Vikings who came to France
  changed their language, song and dance,
But kept the Northman-Norman name
  hurled by Frenchmen to defame.
Norman French nobles, king and law
  in stone-built bastions ruled over all,
Norman French at lordly table
  Anglo-Saxon in field and stable.
Became the tangled, English giver
  two streams formed a mighty river.

Chaucer wrote the English speech
  of places close in London's reach.
But in the wild Cornish coast
  lingered on a Celtic host;
And few beyond the seas around
  ever heard the English sound.
Wars of the Roses rent the land
  finally stopped by Henry's hand
That tore the church away from Rome
  and set great fleets the seas to roam.

Under Elizabethan lights
  England rose to climb the heights.
Shakespeare strode the London stage
  his English plays all the rage.
The King James *Bible* crested a tide
  that rapidly sank to regicide.
The Puritan wave found a height
  in Milton's strong poetic flight.
English spread across the seas
  ship-borne on the ocean breeze.
In America did many settle,
  spread the language and prove their mettle.
Conflict and commerce coursed the earth
  from farmer's field to harbor birth.

Nelson, Victoria, sail to power,
  English spread, a great wild flower,
As first and second speech,
  attaining global reach.
India, China, computer chatter
  festooning extra-terrestrial matter.

A light in the forest, a beacon at sea,
  so many things English can be,
Ever-changing, renewed with an infant's cry,
  plumbing the depths and soaring the sky.

The tale is done
  new time begun.

Figure 5.4

One of the greatest human cultural creations was writing. *Writing* is a systematic graphic recording of language such that a future reader can grasp the meaning of the original spoken utterance. Shakespeare has lain in his tomb for centuries, yet readers today still mourn Romeo and Juliet or guffaw at Falstaff.

But writing has limits. Languages die and are forgotten. Only the immense scholarly toil and genius of Champollion made possible the decipherment of Ancient Egyptian hieroglyphs, providing the key to a literature which lasted from 3000 B.C. to 100 A.D. Builders of the monumental pyramids, the Egyptians wrote only the consonants of their language. They omitted the vowels, so we can never really know how their spoken language sounded. The often recited words of Lincoln's Gettysburg Address, or the dramas of Shakespeare, are not the very sounds of those person's voices and speech, but rather our reconstruction of sounds from written notation. Spoken language is as fleeting as is the moment of its utterance. The word spoken now vanishes forever, remaining only as a memory in the listener, for until less than a century ago there was no way to preserve sound itself. Hence the importance of writing.

Writing as Cultural Event

The act of writing constitutes a cultural event. Who wrote what and why? What were the circumstances calling forth the effort of writing and word preservation? Many mercantile accounts remain preserved in writing, but few lullabies or musings.

Sacred writings may be considered to imbue the material on which they are written with sacredness or special power. To a Moslem the *Koran* is a sacred book and is treated with special respect, always stored in a high location, handled only by individuals in a state of ritual purity. To the Buddhist passages from the Buddhist scriptures written on paper and folded up may serve as protection from harm when worn inside a person's clothing. Traditional Chinese at New Year's put special inscriptions, newly written in gold or black ink on red paper, outside the front door of their house to ward off evil spirits and other harm.

Many different substances serve for writing material. The ancient Sumerians of Mesopotamia wrote cuneiform (wedge-shaped) script with reed styluses on clay tablets. Pen and velum or parchment served medieval Europe, while the Chinese wrote with brush on paper for over two thousand years. The computer age uses electromagnetic impulses recorded on floppy or rigid disks. The traditional writing methods were slow and even clumsy, but they endured. Scholars today read 5,000 year old Sumerian clay tablets, and inscriptions on 4,000 year old Chinese bronze ritual vessels.

Chinese

The sophisticated and beautiful Chinese writing system was modified into its present form during the last centuries B.C. The First Emperor of Chin (221–206 B.C.) lives in infamy because he ordered the burning of all the old classics. He wanted the past forgotten and only the new order known. But he effectively united China into a single country ruled by one emperor. At the time of its unification under Chin, the country of China consisted of several main regions, each with its own dialect and script. The First Emperor of Chin ordered that one standard writing system, the Small Seal Script, be used everywhere (Fig. 5.5). Since that time the Chinese have used one single writing system understood by all literate Chinese, regardless of the dialect they speak. The Small Seal Script was a lasting achievement because it unified the written Chinese language.

Figure 5.5. Small seal script (courtesy of T. Y. Pang)

During the Han Dynasty (206 B.C.–220 A.D.) the Chinese empire reached overland to trade with Rome, and overseas into Southeast Asia. Han scholars and bureaucrats wrote on silk and bamboo scrolls with writing brushes. They developed the Official Script during the early Han dynasty. The square and stiff Official Script (Fig. 5.6) is a rather slavish modification of the Small Seal Script. Note that the characters are basically the same in both scripts, but that in the Official Script the shape of the characters has altered somewhat. Each character is a complete word.

During the stormy Three Kingdoms Period (220–265 A.D.) following the fall of Han, scholars developed the Regular Script. The Regular Script (Fig. 5.7) has more rounded forms to go with the flow of the writing brush. The Regular Script is alive; it has a whole new spirit.

The Tang Dynasty (618–907) was the Golden Age of Chinese poetry. Calligraphers carried the art of writing to new heights. Paper and woodblock printing made books more widely available than they had been before. By the Tang times, the Cursive Script (also known as Running Script or Grass Script) had developed out of the Official Script. Cursive Script (Fig. 5.8) uses strokes of the characters which are blended into one another, and some characters are run together in one sweeping unit of brush stroke. The Running Script can be written very fast to serve practical clerical needs. In the hands of a skilled calligrapher the Cursive Script becomes a graceful and lively dance, filled with a spirit of vitality.

One tale recounts how a famous Tang dynasty calligrapher's art improved dramatically after he watched a beautiful dance. Many of the famous Tang poems which have inspired Chinese for over a thousand years were first written in the dancing Cursive Script.

Figure 5.6. Official script (courtesy of T. Y. Pang)

Figure 5.7. Regular script (courtesy of T. Y. Pang)

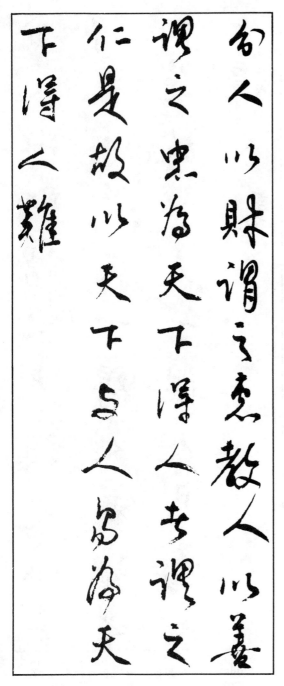

Figure 5.8. Cursive (running, grass) script (courtesy of T. Y. Pang)

By the time of the Tang Dynasty Chinese calligraphy had become the multi-faceted art which it remains today. On the practical side, the unified Chinese system of writing serves to form a common written link among people speaking very different dialects. And that script has remained essentially the same for the past 2,000 years, since the Official Script. A student who learns Chinese today can read some poems written more than a thousand years ago. Calligraphy is also art with its own inherent worth as an art.

The enduring nature of writing appears in the passage used for the examples of calligraphy given above. It is a quote from the philosopher Mencius (c. 372–284 B.C.). His philosophy was first written down in one of the regional scripts of the time. With the coming of the Han Dynasty Mencius' works were copied out in Official Script and have continued as important philosophical works ever since.

In one of his disquisitions, Mencius described the earliest history of China, when several excellent rulers governed the people. Each of these rulers took great care to pass the throne on to a successor who would selflessly govern the people wisely. Mencius, in the passage written in Chinese calligraphy in figures 5.5–5.8, emphasized how difficult it is to choose a new ruler for the country.

> Sharing your wealth with others is kindness,
> Teaching and inspiring the people is a deed of fidelity,
> Finding an individual who will see to the welfare of the people is kindness.
> Although it is easy to pass the throne on to just anyone
> It is very hard to find the right person to govern the people
>
> (trans. T. Y. Pang, pers. comm.)

The continuing tradition of the Chinese writing system, and the literary tradition it transmits, is important to understanding Chinese culture today.

Southwest Asia

In marked contrast to China, Southwest Asia has been an ever-changing mosaic of cultures, languages, and literature. The Southwest Asian writing systems changed periodically as speakers of different languages became dominant in the region. By the early centuries A.D., various alphabets were used over the region, and the older scripts, including Egyptian hieroglyphs, were forgotten. With the spread of Islam from the mid-seventh century A.D. onward, the Arabic script came to predominate. The Romans developed the Latin alphabet, which was spread through the Roman Empire. After the fall of Rome, the Latin alphabet continued as the script of the Church, and was eventually used to write Western European languages. This book, for instance, is written in the Latin alphabet.

Central America

Central Americans developed a writing system during the latter centuries B.C. They wrote out sophisticated calendars, recorded dynastic histories, and inscribed important monuments. Unfortunately, the Spanish conquerors saw it as their duty, in the name of destroying pagan religion, to destroy all the available books and inscriptions. Only recently, after enormous intellectual labor, has it become possible to read some of the materials with relative certainty.

Tradition and Modernity

The differences between traditional and electronic writing materials contain a cultural comment. Computer and word processor writing are fast and compact. But they depend on the availability of a sophisticated technology operated by electricity. Should either technology or power supply fail, the writing becomes utterly inaccessible. A similar pattern characterizes much of modern technology. It provides an abundance and luxury only dreamed of in the past, but at the same time it is a rapacious and fragilely interdependent system. Modern technology destroys proven traditional patterns, thus removing viable alternatives. As a result, the failure of modern technology can cause disaster on an unprecedented scale. When all the floppy disks have vanished the ancient Latin stone inscriptions will remain.

Language and Being Human

Language lies at the heart of being human. Many cultures mark this fact in the way they treat those who cannot speak. Often, children are considered human only when they have learned to speak.

Among the Brunei Malays all children who cannot yet speak are addressed and referred to as *lai*. Only when a child has learned to speak is he or she called by the given name. The funeral service for a child who cannot yet speak differs from that of a speaking child. Older children and adults who cannot speak are considered handicapped marginal members of society. And the old who can no longer speak are considered to be already apart from human society and nearing the realm of the dead. In broad outline this pattern holds true for most cultures.

Learning how to properly communicate and to interpret communications presents a difficult task to an anthropologist or business person entering a new culture. Often the newcomer inadvertently sends unintended messages. For example, the standard New York City upraised thumb to summon a taxi does not apply in Malaysia, where such a gesture is very obscene. By the same token, the Malaysian taxi summoning gesture of holding the right arm out straight at shoulder height and waving the down-hanging hand back and forth from the wrist, would not summon a cab in New York, and might be interpreted as a vulgar gesture. Euro-Americans point with the index finger, Navajos with the chin. Brunei Malays and Crow Indians point with the lips. Because an anthropologist in the field must learn to use another language, and must learn to acquire at least the rudiments of another culture's non-language means of communications, the anthropologist must, in reality, learn another way of being human. The experience is a difficult one, and a deep one, which is shared by all students who learn a new language and go to a different country for education. Yet despite the difficulties involved, many adults do learn another language and another culture. This shows the flexibility and adaptability of humans. Herein lies great possibility for building a better future.

SUGGESTED READINGS

Rogers, E. M. with L. Svenning. *Modernization Among Peasants: The Impact of Communication.* New York: Holt Rinehart and Winston, 1969.
This book investigates five Columbian communities in an effort to determine the effects of changing communication systems.

Slater, Philip. *Earthwalk.* New York: Bantam, 1975.
This work examines modern technological society and the problems associated with distorted communications.

Hall, Edward T. *The Hidden Dimension.* Garden City, New York: Doubleday, 1969.
This book deals with proxemics in a cross-cultural framework. The author presents the idea that knowledge of a culture's use of space is critical in the understanding of the behavior of individuals in a particular culture.

Ladefoged, Peter. *A Course in Phonetics,* second edition, Harcourt Brace Jovanovich, San Diego, 1982.
Ladefoged gives a technical, but readable, introduction to the fascinating world of speech sounds, and stresses learning to pronounce the sounds.

A Critique of the Notion that Language Imprisons the Mind

6

by Edward J. Vajda

The relation of language and mind has interested philosophers for many centuries. The Greeks assumed that the structure of language had some connection with the process of thought. This idea took root in Europe long before people realized how diverse languages could be.

Only recently did linguists begin the serious study of languages that were very different from their own. Two anthropologist-linguists, Franz Boas and Edward Sapir, were pioneers in describing many native languages of North and South America during the first half of the twentieth century. We are indebted to them because some of these languages have since vanished, as the peoples who spoke them died out or became assimilated and lost their native languages. Other linguists in the earlier part of this century, however, who were less eager to deal with bizarre data from "exotic" language, were not always so grateful. The newly described languages were often so strikingly different from the well studied languages of Europe and Southwest Asia that some scholars even accused Boas and Sapir of fabricating their data. Native American languages are indeed different, so much so in fact that Navajo could be used by the US military as a code during World War II to send secret messages.

Sapir's pupil, Benjamin Lee Whorf (1897–1941), continued the study of American Indian languages. Being interested in the relationship of language and thought, Whorf developed the idea that the structure of language determines the structure of habitual thought in a society. He reasoned that because it is easier to formulate certain concepts and not others in a given language, the speakers of that language think along one track and not along another. Whorf came to believe in a sort of linguistic determinism which, in its strongest form, states that language imprisons the mind, and that the grammatical patterns in a language can produce far reaching consequences for the culture of a society. Later, this idea became to be known as the Sapir-Whorf hypothesis, but this appellation is somewhat of a misnomer. Although both Sapir and Whorf emphasized the diversity of languages, Sapir himself never explicitly supported the notion of linguistic determinism.

Let us first see how Whorf came to the conclusion that language imprisons the mind and then critique his view.

Whorf studied the Hopi Indian language of the American southwest. He observed that Hopi has no grammatical tense. In other words, a Hopi verb might be interpreted as referring to past, present or future time. In contrast, European languages have complicated tense systems. Compare, for instance, the large number of tense forms in English, "I was, I had been, I used to be, I am, I will be, I will have been." Whorf felt that the linguistic emphasis on time in European languages favored the development of recordkeeping, nurtured the concept of history, and inclined Europeans

Figure 6.1 Isolated heights have special spiritual significance for the Navajo. These two girls perceive the world and its meanings through the lens of the Navajo language. (Photograph by Harry Teller)

toward a general awareness of temporal categories. In short, the structure of the European languages predestined Europeans to pay attention to time.

A preoccupation with temporal cycles is evident in many European words for time, which usually involve the idea of cycles: Russian *vremya* stems from the concept of "whirl, spin." German *Zeit* comes from the same source that provides the English word "tide," another repetitive motion. One can surmise that the repetition of the seasons was of central importance in the culture of the ancient Indo-Europeans.

Whorf pointed out that this association of time with the idea of repeatable and countable units is totally absent in the grammar of Hopi. Spatial terms cannot be used as metaphors for time in Hopi. One cannot say "a long time," since only objects can be long. One can count twigs or stones, which can be gathered together in a visible pile, but not days or months, which cannot be gathered together in spatial terms. Unlike European time, Hopi duration is inconceivable in spatial terms. Instead of saying, "He waited for five days," in Hopi one must say approximately, "He waited for a duration which ended on the fifth day." Nor can

Figure 6.2 The Hopi language provides a name for each of the items in this interior of a Hopi pueblo, and expresses the culturally accepted ways of using those items.

the idea of intensity of action be expressed in terms of speed. Instead of saying, "The man runs fast," a Hopi must say, "The man very runs." Instead of saying, "The corn grows fast," a Hopi must say, "The corn very grows." Whorf connected these grammatical facts with the fact that the Hopi were a peaceful agricultural society in a land of scanty rainfall isolated by geographic features. Time and speed (which is a correlation of time over distance) were unimportant in a world that rarely changed. What was important were the concepts of duration and intensity. Whorf also observed that the modern Hopi had difficulty dealing with European concepts involving units of time, such as programs, schedules, budgets and deadlines, and he connected this behavior with the grammatical structure of the Hopi language.

On the other hand, Whorf argued that the structure of European languages constrained thought in other ways. For example, perhaps because they were preoccupied with time, the Europeans were late in coming up with the theory of relativity, for which the traditional categories of time, form and space no longer maintain separate relevance. Whorf's hypothesis suggests that if Aristotle or Newton had spoken Hopi or Navajo, their thoughts might have taken quite a different direction. If language truly imprisons the mind, then even the discoveries of geniuses should be viewed as somehow predetermined by the structure of the languages these geniuses spoke.

The material that Whorf uncovered when developing the idea that language imprisons the mind is indeed fascinating, but there are problems with his hypothesis.

First, speakers are not conscious of the grammatical rules that go into creating a statement. They perceive only the meaning of the statement. The grammatical rules that build each utterance are ancillary. Speakers need not be any more aware of them than the

runner need be aware of the name or particular function of each leg muscle. A speaker of English who has not studied linguistics might not even be aware that English contains progressive verbs or a pluperfect tense. The English sentence, "He runs fast," and the Hopi equivalent of, "He very runs," evoke an identical conceptual image in spite of their disparate grammatical underpinnings. It is not clear how grammatical subtleties of which speakers are often not even aware could influence conscious thought in any profound way.

Second, if language constrains the mind in the strictest sense, then foreign language learning and translation would be impossible. It would only be possible to express or grasp concepts prevalent in the grammatical structure of each particular language. But translations as well as foreign language learning are very obviously possible, although by no means perfect. The Bible, for example, with its sophisticated references to past, present and future time has been translated into Hopi, Navajo and hundreds of other languages. Many of these languages contain grammatical categories that differ radically from those of the original Greek, Hebrew and Aramaic, as well as from English.

Whorf's comparison of Hopi grammar with Hopi culture is fascinating and even seems convincing. On the one hand, languages lacking grammatical tense may be spoken by peoples such as the Hopi for whom the concept of time as understood in European terms is of no central importance. Such instances would seem to support the hypothesis. However, to prove that grammar universally constrains the mind, one would have to survey other languages without tense and note whether the peoples speaking them likewise lack the concept of time, as Whorf claimed the Hopi did. When one undertakes such a survey, Whorf's hypothesis begins to fall apart because no systematic correlation exists. Peoples with a complex system of temporal concepts and an enduring preoccupation with recording history often speak languages with no grammatical tense. One such language is Mandarin Chinese. Chinese grammar lacks tense, but Chinese culture cannot be said to lack the concept of time or history in the same sense as traditional Hopi culture. And, in fact, a recent study, by Malotki (1983), has shown that the Hopi do have sophisticated temporal concepts, but the manner of their expression is very different from that of European languages. The correlation between grammatical structure and culture turns out to be random, more a matter of coincidence than the product of linguistic determinism.

The randomness of such grammar-culture correlations becomes even more obvious when one looks at grammatical forms lacking in English but present in other languages.

Russian has separate verb forms, called aspects, to convey completed and incompleted action. An English verb is often ambiguous with respect to completion of action. The sentence, "I wrote my homework last night," might refer to a completed action ("I got my homework written."). Or it might mean that I simply worked on the homework but didn't complete it. In Russian there is no ambiguity, since completed action is marked by the perfective form *napisal* "finished writing" as opposed to the imperfective *pisal* "engaged in writing." Although English does not contain a grammatical category of completed vs. incompleted action, no one would dream of accusing Americans of being oblivious to the concept of deadlines.

Another illustrative example comes from Bulgarian, which has separate verb forms to mark witnessed action vs. hearsay. This grammatical distinction is also present in Turkish, Navajo and many other languages. It is lacking in English, however. An English verb is ambiguous. The sentence, "John stole the money," may convey an event that the speaker himself has witnessed or an event that is known from another source. Although English lacks the grammatical forms in question, English speaking societies are obviously well aware of the distinctions involved and find other means of expressing them: for instance, a newspaper headline might read, "suspect allegedly fires gun at allegedly unsuspecting bystander." Once again, the presence or absence of a grammatical form in a language has little predictive power regarding the structure of habitual thought in the society where that language is spoken.

One final example of grammar-culture correlations is gender. Many European languages contain grammatical gender. In French and Spanish, for instance, nouns may be masculine or feminine, which affects the form of articles and adjectives added to them. Typically, the distinction extends beyond biological gender to encompass also the world of inanimate objects and of abstract concepts. In such a language, the sun might be masculine, and the moon feminine. Other languages, for instance Chinese, Hungarian, Malay and Georgian lack grammatical gender and even have a single word to express the concepts of "he, she," and "it." The absence of grammatical gender certainly cannot be construed to reflect the speaker's attitude toward biological gender.

If the structure of language does not determine the structure of thought, then the question remains as to just what the relationship between language and mind actually is. Not only does the notion of linguistic determinism as expressed in Whorf's writing seem grossly exaggerated, the very opposite correlation turns out to be more prevalent. Concepts present in the speaker's environment that come to be stored in the mind have a much greater effect on the structure of language than the structure of language has on culture and thought. This becomes most apparent when one compares the vocabulary of diverse languages. Concepts that are extremely important to a society tend to give rise to a large and very precise inventory of words, each of which conveys a particular aspect of the phenomenon in question. Examples of this phenomenon are numerous across languages. The Old English epic, *Beowulf,* contains no less than 37 terms for "hero" and 17 terms for "sea." The language of the Alaskan Eskimos contains 40 words for "snow" and 16 words for "seal." One need not go so far afield to find pertinent examples. Modern English displays analogous multiple terms for what in another culture might seem to be a single concept. Witness, for instance, the innumerable American brand names for cars, cereal, beer and other products.

Conversely, a language may have a single term to cover a number of related but different phenomena. Hopi has only one word, *masa'ytaka,* to denote "bird, airplane," or "insect." This does not mean a Hopi cannot see or tell the difference between the three. Rather, it might imply that at one time the distinction between various flying things was not important in Hopi culture. The vocabulary stock of a language often contains much revealing information about the cultural history of a people. In pre-Christian northern Europe, for example, the bear was considered a sacred animal and people avoided the original name for the animal, which probably sounded something like the Latin *ursus* "bear." Thus modern English retained only the euphemistic appellation, "bear," meaning, "the brown one." Similarly, Russians today call the bear, *medved,* originally a euphemism meaning, "the honey knower." This was not the case in southern Europe, where the bear was not held to be sacred, and so the original Latin name of the bear, *ursus,* was preserved. Thus, culture and environment can easily influence language. There is no evidence that language influences thought and perception to an equally significant extent.

Rather than being a rigid prison, each human language seems equally well equipped to react to the effects of a changing cultural environment. If a new concept is introduced to a culture, a word can easily be coined to describe it, either by direct borrowing, such as "zebra" or "glasnost," or by loan translation, such as the English calque "forgive," which is based on a translation into English morphemes of both parts of the French word "pardon."

The lack of a word in a particular language in no way prevents speakers from recognizing a new concept and verbalizing about it in some creative manner. The Mandarin Chinese term for "telephone pole" is *dian xian gan,* "lightning thread pole." English has only one word "snow," but this does not prevent skiers from understanding and talking about powdery snow, packed snow, wet snow, spring snow, or ice-crusted snow. This is why phrases rather than single words often express significant concepts, as exemplified by the English phrases: nervous breakdown, the arms race, post nasal drip and numerous other collocations. In languages without tense, such as Hopi, Chinese, or Malay time can be indicated by adverbs or circumlocutions. Hawaiian has two words for water, *wai* "fresh water" and *kai* "sea water." English has only one word, but we can just as easily express the distinction by saying "fresh water" and "salt water." Classical Greek had five words for "love," English has only one, but we still know and can express the difference between "brotherly love," "romantic love," "love for God," and so forth.

It is important to note that significant cultural differences tend to be reflected in the vocabulary of a language and not in the grammar. Perhaps the grammatical categories of a language likewise developed under the influence of culture and thereby reflect certain bygone values or environmental influences. There is certainly no proof that grammatical patterns inherited from the past constrain thought in the present. In fact, there is ample indication that the opposite is true. It is quite possible to grasp concepts which lack any established linguistic expression. Russian has no precise word for privacy, but Russians have no trouble being private when necessary. Swahili has such unusual words as *mumagamagama,* meaning "a person who habitually loses other people's possessions," and *muwavi,* "a good looking woman who can't cook." English does not have these words, but this obviously does not preclude expressing these concepts in English, as the glosses prove. Russians use a single verb, *opoxmelit'sa,* to refer to what people do when they take a sip of vodka the next morning to battle a hangover. English has no concise equivalent, and so we use the phrase "to eat some of the hair of the dog that bit you." But the concept is the same, dog or no dog.

One final example of how languages react to a changing cultural environment is the way they cope with new technology. The sentence, "I filled my gas tank and changed a headlight," is not expressed in many languages simply because the concept "motor vehicle" is unknown to the speakers. But this does not prevent speakers of these languages from acquiring the concept and easily coining a new word or phrase for it. The Apache language of today has names for every part of an automobile. For instance, *pit,* literally meaning "stomach," has come also to mean "gas tank"; *jnda,* meaning "eye," now also means "headlight." If language truly imprisoned the mind, then the acquisition of new vocabulary as well as creative new uses and combinations of old vocabulary would not be the ubiquitous phenomena that they are.

Although the vocabulary of a language clearly depends upon culture and environment, the complexity of a language's grammar does not seem to depend upon any particular level of cultural sophistication. All grammars are equally complex in the sense that all are capable of verbalizing about new concepts and new ideas. All languages contain this capacity for potentially unlimited creativity. It has been estimated that a thousand nouns and a thousand verbs could produce a million utterances.

If one added a thousand adjectives, the total number of possible utterances would be over a billion. And every language has thousands of words. True, there are a limited number of words in every language, and some languages have more words than other languages do. (English is said to have the largest number of words.) But each language can produce a potentially unlimited number of combinations using this finite quantity of words.

Languages differ then, not in their creative potential, but rather in terms of the level upon which particular distinctions are realized in a particular language. What is grammatical in one language must be expressed by a standard or improvised combination of words in another language. Russian might have a concise way of expressing the concept of completed action, but English can express the same concept with equal ease by using a phrase. Thus, the creative potential of the human mind overrides whether or not a particular distinction is inherent in the grammar or depends upon the vocabulary of a given language.

This linguistic creativity should not be underestimated. It is central to understanding the uniqueness of the human mind. As far as we know at the present time, only human languages are creative in a true sense. Apes, birds and bees all have "languages," to be sure. But animal systems of communication convey only a limited number of messages and seem to be conditioned responses to external stimuli. Animals simply do not recombine the basic units of their "languages" with the same creativity evident in the use of human grammar. In contrast, each of the several thousand diverse human languages, regardless of the particulars of its grammatical structure, is an equally ingenious means of extending reality beyond the here and now. The wondrous phenomenon of language, which is universally present in all human societies, symbolizes better than anything else the unity and basic equality of all peoples.

Sapir, Boas and Whorf were undoubtedly justified in emphasizing the amazing diversity of languages. In fact, modern linguists more often than not incorrectly gloss over the true extent of this diversity. The diversity of languages, however, has fewer psychological implications than one might assume. It is easier to break out of the habits of language than Whorf believed. People have imaginations and can find a way to say anything. Languages cannot for long constrain the inquiring mind of an Albert Einstein or a Marie Curie. Many of the discoveries of modern physics and chemistry cannot be said to derive from the structure of European languages or from the structure of any other language. There is no grammatical pattern in any European language that could have predicted or predetermined Maxwell's equations for electromagnetic radiation, Mendeleev's periodic table of chemical elements or Bohr's model of the atom. No significant intellectual difference arising from grammatical differences in the structures of various languages has ever been shown to exist.

In conclusion, it is important to soften the categorical tone of Whorf's hypothesis but not disregard it altogether. Language obviously contains the potential to confuse as well as to clarify. And different individuals use language more creatively than others. But there is no compelling reason to look upon language as a prison of the mind. Language and mind interact, to be sure, but the predominant direction of cause and effect is from mind to language rather than from language to mind as Whorf hypothesized. Anthropologists should take note and approach languages as priceless scrapbooks filled with keen images of the past and insightful glimpses into the present of the societies who speak them. Through conscientious study of the vocabulary of various languages, anthropologists can excavate lost

Figure 6.3 Does language imprison on the mind, or is it a structure of many possibilities? (This picture shows the framework of a house in Borneo; builders climb up the notched log ladder to the right.) (Photograph by L. A. Kimball)

details from ancient cultures and use this information to better understand the cultures of today. In this sense, the painstaking descriptions of new languages and vanishing cultures undertaken by Sapir, Boas and Whorf represent a true and lasting contribution. The work of these linguists, in both its successes and its shortcomings, underscores the need for linguists to be anthropologists and for anthropologists to be linguists.

SUGGESTED READINGS

Malotki, Ekkehart, *Hopi Time: A Linguistic Analysis of the Temporal Concepts in the Hopi Language,* Mouton, Berlin, 1983.
A technical, but fascinating, account of the world of Hopi time, this book provides a unique insight into Hopi culture.

Sampson, Geoffrey, *Schools of Linguistics,* "The Sapir-Whorf Hypothesis," pp. 81–102, Stanford University Press, Stanford, 1980.

Whorf, Benjamin L. *Language, Thought and Reality.* Cambridge, Massachusetts: MIT Press, 1956.
Whorf attempts to illustrate the ties between the linguistic categories and cultural categories by relating meaning to form.

Strategies for Economic Survival

7

All humans have biological, psychological, and cultural wants and needs. The most basic needs are sustenance, shelter, and society, the three "S's" necessary for human survival. *Sustenance* is whatever is needed for the continuance and viability of life. It includes food, materials for technology, domestic animals, and fire. *Shelter* is protection from the elements. We all need human companionship, which is found in *society*. In achieving the basic needs, human behavior interacts with the environment by using tools and technology. *Tools* are any instruments used by human beings to perform a task. They may be specially made, or they may be found and used as they are. *Technology* is the sum total of the adaptive strategies which humans use in the course of their lives. Technology includes all of the knowledge necessary to make and use tools in a particular environment in order to survive. When people in the United States go camping, they often take a tent for shelter. Knowing how to put up the tent and stake it involves technology. A tool may be necessary to drive the stakes, and this tool can be a special tent stake mallet, a hammer, the flat edge of a hatchet or a large rock.

From this broad perspective of the necessities of human survival in the physical world, anthropologists consider economy. *Economy* may be defined as the acquisition, production, distribution, and consumption of goods and services which meet the needs of the individual and society. The descriptive and interpretive study of a given culture can show the strategies it uses for economic survival. Economy can be studied from two perspectives, the formalist and the substantivist.

The *formalist* approach to economy applies Western economic concepts such as money and profit to non-Western groups. It acts on the assumption that all economic systems in all times and places operate on the same principles as Western economic systems. This assumption does not take into consideration the fact that economic systems reflect the values of a particular culture. For example, gift giving has little to do with money or profit, but in many cultures it is an integral part of social interaction and helps to distribute goods as a part of the economy.

The *substantivist* approach maintains that non-Western economic systems operate on principles different from those in Western systems. The substantivists focus on the social, ritual and ideological aspects of economy as well as on the material aspects studied by formalists.

Two Economic Systems

Different economic systems have different technologies as their basis. In a broad sense, two types of economies exist in the world today, the non-industrial and the industrial. Non-industrial economies include hunting-gathering-fishing, horticulture-agriculture, and pastoralism. Industrial economies are prevalent in the world today, and include wage labor and peasant farming.

Figure 7.1 Erecting the poles for a tipi requires skill. (Crow Fair, Crow Agency, Montana, 1988, Photograph by Margaret McGinnis)

Hunting-gathering-fishing, horticulture-agriculture, and pastoralism have some similarities. First, people in non-industrial economies have a preoccupation with daily and seasonal food supply, partially because they have difficulties storing and transporting food. Second, they are often dependent on one or two major resources. In industrial economies, people depend on the sale of their products through market exchange as a primary source of livelihood (Dalton 1967). Labor, land and produce are commodities that are accorded monetary values and can be bought and sold.

Four Aspects of Economy

Anthropologists find it useful to look at four different aspects of economy. The first aspect is the technology required for an economy and how labor is divided. The second aspect is the structure of productive units and the ways that membership in productive units is determined. The third aspect is the system of exchange—what is exchanged and how it is exchanged. The fourth aspect that can be examined is the control of culturally valued items, or wealth (Nash 1967). Both non-industrial and industrial forms of economy will be looked at from these four aspects.

Man the Hunter, Woman the Gatherer

Seen in the long perspective of human life on earth over the past 100,000 years, hunting and gathering has been the predominant lifestyle. Yet agriculture, which began around 15,000 years ago, has accompanied such a high density of population that the majority of

Figure 7.2 The tipi provided a functional dwelling for the nomadic Plains Indians. In traditional times a buffalo-hide cover was placed over the poles. A Crow tipi could easily house a family of ten to twelve members. These modern tipis, covered with cloth, were erected at the Crow Fair, Crow Agency, Montana, in 1988. (Photograph by Margaret McGinnis)

humans who walked the earth have lived in an agricultural society.

At the time when hunting-gathering flourished as the livelihood of all humans, groups inhabited and survived in the richest and poorest of environments. Hunter-gatherers who lived in the caves near what is modern-day Peking some 100,000 years ago survived in harsh sub-arctic conditions. Others lived in temperate climates with an abundance of game and plant food. The hunter-gatherers remaining in the world today inhabit harsh locales, deserts and jungles and tundra. Their way of life is similar to that of early hunter-gatherers, but cannot be assumed to be identical.

Hunter-gatherers today are vanishing, their land and livelihood seized and manipulated by agriculturalists. The few remaining groups live in areas where survival is difficult. Approximately 175 hunting-gathering societies in Oceania, Asia, Africa, and America have been studied by anthropologists (Gough 1975), but most of these societies have since disappeared.

The essence of the hunting-gathering life is mobility. Hunters must follow the wandering game, or intersect its path, and gatherers must move on after they have used much of the plant food in an area. Some plant growth must be left to regenerate and provide the next year's supply. Mobility, however, does not imply aimless wandering. A large part of the technology of hunting-gathering people is the knowledge of when and where food is available. Hunting-gathering groups time their movements seasonally to take advantage of different resources. Groups who use fishing as an economic strategy must know in what season to fish, and where the best fishing stations are.

Mobility restricts the amount and weight of possessions an individual can own. They must be few enough and light enough to be carried easily. If they can not be carried, they must be cached somewhere for future use. Likewise, when a large animal is killed, it is easier to move the camp of humans to the kill site than to move the beast to the camp.

The material culture of hunting-gathering groups includes bows and arrows, spears, bone needles, skin or bark clothing, and temporary shelters such as the igloos of the Eskimo or the tipis of the Plains Indians. Fishing groups such as the Northwest Coast Indians use different technology. They might require fish hooks, nets, lines, or boats.

Labor in hunting-gathering groups is commonly divided by sex and age. This is by no means true of all hunting-gathering groups, however, as you will see when the fishing lifeway of the Northwest Coast Indians is discussed below. In general, though, men hunted and women gathered and raised their young. Hunting required cooperation among males, planning, knowledge of many species and large areas, and technical skill (Washburn and Lancaster 1968). Gathering required knowledge of the varieties and locations of plant foods, skill in judging seasonal patterns, and techniques of collection and preparation (Slocum 1975). When game is scarce or the hunt unsuccessful, the women's gathering supports the group. In the case of the !Kung San of the Kalahari Desert, it has been estimated that the

Figure 7.3 A slash-and-burn field is filled with debris which helps to lesson soil erosion. This Bornean woman will use a dibble-stick to make holes in the ground and plant seeds. Adventitious vegetable crops will be planted near some of the larger logs. (Photograph by L. A. Kimball)

women provide 85% of the dietary needs of the group. There are only two technological activities in which women appear not to participate: hunting large sea mammals, such as whales, and smelting ores (Murdock and Provost 1973). Because it is the woman's responsibility to raise and care for children, one of the first important tools was the baby carrying sling, which allows women to carry children as they gather.

The basic productive unit in hunting-gathering groups is the family. Families, however, tend to travel in a cooperative economic unit called the band. *Bands* are groups of families, consisting of about 20 to 50 people, who travel together and cooperate in getting food. Families in hunting-gathering groups are usually nuclear, composed of a woman, a man and their children. Bands of families have no formal government. Leadership is based on the individual's ability to lead and to provide for the general welfare of the band. This type of political system is known as *egalitarian*.

Figure 7.4 This Borneo woman used the dibble-stick in her right hand to make a hole in the ground; with her left hand she is planting rice seeds in the hole. (Photograph by L. A. Kimball)

Among hunting-gathering groups, land and resources are communally owned. Private property consists of whatever resources are collected by individuals and whatever tools are made by individuals. Within a nuclear family, all of these might be shared. Within the band, exchange takes the form of reciprocity. *Reciprocity* involves the exchange of resources with the mutual expectation that the value of the goods or services will be returned eventually to the distributor. Reciprocity is based on role obligations and is embedded in the network of social relations. In groups of hunter-gatherers, reciprocity functions very well as a manner of exchange in small bands where everyone is known. If a woman has recently given birth to a child and is unable to gather one day, other women will share the products of their day's work with her. At some other time, she will reciprocate. If a hunter kills a large animal, he will give the greater portion of it away in the expectation that another hunter will share a future animal.

Because of a system of communal ownership of resources and an exchange system of reciprocity, wealth is not usually an important concept in hunting-gathering groups. If a new item is introduced, such as a steel axe, it may be shared among members of a group, or passed around so that each has an opportunity to "own" it for a while.

Among many of the Plains tribes of North America resources were exchanged within the tribe by means of give-aways and "*giftexchange*. The Wichita of the Southern Plains held gift dances periodically. The participants in the gift dance would visit every lodge of the encampment, and at each lodge recited the gifts they desired. The families within the lodge would attempt to grant the dancers' wish by supplying them with gifts (Curtis 1930).

The Crow of the Northern Plains circulated material wealth within the tribe by means of the give-away and gift exchange. The give-away was an important part of most tribal festivities. During social dances elder males would give away presents to members of the tribe. During initiation into the various societies, such as the Tobacco Society, and the numerous military societies, the initiate gave gifts to clansmen, relative, and participants. Wealth was also circulated by the giving of gifts to brother-in-law and sister-in-law. The paternal clansmen of a married girl made sure that their brother-in-law was provided with the things that a man valued, such as weapons and horses. Sister-in-laws also gave one another gifts of value.

When a member of the tribe died almost all of the dead person's possessions were given to members of the tribe (McGinnis and Sharrock 1972). Because of the give-away customs, there was, and still is today, no static ownership of goods among the Crow, and the result is general goodwill with no extreme cases of either poverty or prosperity (Medicine Crow 1939).

The Northwest Coast—An Exception

Most hunting-gathering cultures have the characteristics of mobility, egalitarianism, and reciprocal exchange. An exception to all of these were the Indians of the Northwest Coast of North America.

The hunter-gatherer-fishers of the Pacific Northwest lived in a lush environment. Salmon runs, shellfish and vegetable resources, and game in the nearby mountains provided year-round supplies of food in one locale. Except for annual moves to fish camps, people on the Northwest Coast lived a settled life. Thus, they developed many of the cultural features more often associated with sedentary farmers.

Northwest Coast Indians developed an elaborate technology for fishing, hunting and gathering. Cedar was the main material, and from it they made houses, canoes, clothing and fishing equipment. Bone provided the material for fish hooks, needles, awls, and many decorative items. Copper and certain shells were used as wealth.

The division of labor was not based solely on the factors of age and sex. The status and rank of an individual largely determined what tasks were to be performed and in what context. Certain clans owned certain fishing stations and other resource areas, and controlled access to those areas.

The basic social and productive unit on the Northwest Coast was the clan. Classes of nobility, commoners, and slaves existed, but the individual's status was determined by clan membership.

The method of exchange included reciprocity, but had the added feature of *redistribution*. Redistribution occurs as a prominent economic mode of distribution in cultures where ranking and stratification are present. It will be discussed and defined further as a feature of agricultural societies. On the Northwest Coast, coppers, slaves, cedar blankets, and other artifacts were accumulated and given value within the society. During a potlatch ceremony the accumulated goods were given to another clan and redistributed throughout that clan. This not only spread the wealth around, but cemented kinship and other social bonds. If, for example, you are given the place of honor at the potlatch and accorded many valuable gifts, you are then beholden to reciprocate when you are able to be the giver. This ability to potlatch, however, was reserved as a right of the nobility, and commoner clans depended on the generosity of the wealthy nobility.

Horticultural-Agricultural

The main characteristic of horticultural-agricultural lifestyle is that people produce their own food rather than gather it. It is clear that a series of steps could have led from the gathering of food to the producing of it. The agricultural transformation, though it extended over millenia, was a revolution in the sense that it utterly altered the lifestyle and world-view of humans. We are almost all influenced and molded by an agricultural perspective. And so profound was the alteration that in any emotional or empathetic sense we cannot comprehend what the hunting-gathering life was like, though we can understand it intellectually.

Four "F's", food, fodder, fiber and fuel, are essential in agricultural life. Humans need adequate *food* in order to survive. *Fodder* is food for herbivorous animals; pack and draft animals need adequate fodder or they will not be able to work. In our modern world of synthetics, we often forget the important role of *fibers*, fibers for thread to weave cloth and blankets, string, rope, and twine of all kinds, including binding twine for use in construction and making tools. *Fuel* is essential for cooking food, providing warmth, and lighting the night. Traditional agriculturalists must balance their needs for the four F's against the land and labor resources available to produce them. More land in fodder means less for food, fiber, and fuel. Using more fuel to light the night could mean fewer fibers and less food and fodder available. If the same oil is used for both cooking and lighting, more oil used in cooking means darker nights.

Horticulture is usually applied to farming which requires no plow or draft animals. Horticultural farmers are sometimes called "gardeners," and their staple crops tend to be root crops. *Agriculture* refers to farming which requires mechanical energy, such as plow, draft animal or tractor. Agricultural farmers usually have a grain as their staple crop.

Horticultural farmers use such tools as machetes and axes to clear land, hoes to break up the earth, and dibble sticks to make holes to put seeds in. Dibble sticks are used to uproot tubers. Agricultural farmers use plows, often harnessed to draft animals, to make furrows in which seeds are scattered. In addition to the basic tools required for planting, farmers must be able to store and preserve their food. Pots, baskets, grain grinders and other fairly portable equipment are necessary for this task, but

farmers also tend to have more permanent facilities. Grain silos and pits for root storage require labor and energy to build. Building of permanent facilities and infrequent moving of fields tend to make farmers sedentary.

Division of labor in horticultural-agricultural societies continues to reflect the differences of sex and age, but further divides labor in stratified ways. Some part-time specialists may exist, such as religious practitioners, who have great prestige and are supported by the products of other's work. Many farming cultures divide labor between the sexes with men doing clearing, plowing and other heavy work, and the women planting, reaping and preserving food. In some societies, labor becomes further specialized as basketmakers, pottery experts, blacksmiths, and other artisans do not produce their own food, but are maintained by the surplus food that growers produce. This specialization often leads to stratification, as certain groups lay claim to higher rank depending on birth and occupation.

Figure 7.5 Rice harvest time in Borneo is a time of hot hard work, but also a time of happiness. When the harvest is safely in there will be rice to eat for the coming year. (Photograph by L. A. Kimball)

Figure 7.6 The Iban of Borneo believe that the rice has a "spirit" which will be frightened if they harvest roughly. This Iban harvesting knife is partially concealed in the hand and gently cuts the rice ear-by-ear. (Photograph by L. A. Kimball)

Unilineal kinship patterns, or tracing descent through only male or female ancestors, is common in horticultural-agricultural societies. Land may belong to one of these kin groups or to a family or even to a particular individual. In stratified agricultural societies, individual land ownership tends to be the common pattern.

Agriculture and horticulture brought the development of conflict for land or possessions, or developed preexisting patterns of conflict further. Along with this conflict came the need for bartering. An individual had to trade goods or services in order to receive those which could not be produced locally. *Barter* is the direct exchange of two goods for one another, or of a service for certain goods. Barter is direct or immediate reciprocity; the exchange takes place without any delay.

In stratified societies, another form of exchange that takes place within the community is *redistribution*. Redistribution involves the acquisition of goods and services by a central collecting source which then redistributes the resources according to economic, political, and kinship relationships.

Redistribution occurs as a prominent economic mode of distribution in cultures where ranking and stratification are present. A simple type of redistribution occurs at Brunei Malay wedding feasts. The family amasses large quantities of foodstuffs, then at the feast redistributes that food into the mouths of the numerous guests. A more complicated system of redistribution is found in New Guinea. The Melanesian Big Men use redistribution to further their power among the people. A Big Man amasses goods and services which he redistributes as gifts to his followers, in exchange for which they offer political support. There is usually an element of political power and control associated with redistribution.

In farming societies, land, crops, and permanent facilities are regarded as wealth. Individuals and families try to amass greater wealth, which provides access to specialized services. This individual acquisition of wealth may be at the expense of others, and ranking according to amount of wealth may occur. The idea of private ownership carries with it the need to protect the wealth of an individual and community, and often leads to levels of warfare, especially as population increases.

Pastoral Nomadism

Pastoral nomads raise animals rather than plants. Yet they share patterns in common with farmers. The welfare of the pastoral group depends on the welfare of the animals raised. Like the hunter-gatherers, the pastoral nomads must be mobile. The possessiveness toward their herds, however, parallels the possessiveness of farmers toward their crops. Much of the pastoral nomadism of Eurasia developed from a mixed farming and herding economy during a time of dry climate at the end of the second millenium B.C. (Khazanov 1984).

Pastoral nomadic world view often centers around the animals and the environment affecting the animals. Thus, for some African groups, such as the Nuer, the highest compliment that can be paid is to liken someone to a bull or a cow. The Nuer also perceive the world as different qualities of cow pasture, which occur in different places throughout the year (Evans-Pritchard 1968).

Among the Karamojong, subsistence cattle herders in Uganda, cattle are acquired and treated with great care. A young male Karimojong is given a specially-named male calf during his initiation. Whenever the boy talks about himself it is in reference to his calf (Dyson-Hudson 1969).

Pastoralists are located in various areas, such as the arid zones of the Sahara, Central Asia, Siberia, Arizona, and Columbia. The most common domesticated animals are sheep, camels, llamas, and goats. Pastoralists are small nomadic or semi-nomadic groups that move in search of grazing and water.

Figure 7.7 Sheepherding can be long, lonely work. This Navajo shepherd is taking a rest from his work, but will spring into instant action if the sheep begin to stray. (Photograph by Harry Teller)

The two patterns of pastoralism are *nomadism* and *transhumance*. In a nomadic pattern the entire population moves with the herds, as the Mongols did. In transhumance, a portion of the population moves with the herds, and the remainder stays behind at a fixed locale. In the European alpine transhumance pattern, the men remained at the farms to work the fields in summer, while the women took the herds of cattle to the high summer pastures. Among the Nuer, transhumance meant that the men wandered with the herds, while the women and children remained behind to farm the land around their settled village.

Pastoral nomads, whether nomadic or transhumant, have to be mobile. This limits the amount of possessions they can carry. However, a common pattern is to use some of the animals to transport the goods, so that more things can be carried by pastoralists than by hunter-gatherers.

In pastoral nomadism, the animals which are the economic resources are privately owned, but the land is usually considered communal property. Both men and women may own and tend their livestock. The degree to which ownership of these animal resources is open to both sexes and various kinship statuses indicates a great deal about the social structure, emphasizing the worth and ranking of the individuals within society. Among the Tibetan pastoral nomads, ownership of livestock lies essentially with the tenthold or family (Ekvall 1968). Private ownership or claim to use of individual animals may be acquired through inheritance, raiding, hunting, or special individual skills, such as veterinary expertise.

Sometimes the concept of ownership is even extended toward the supernatural as seen in the "God Yak" of Tibet. These yaks are ceremonially presented to the gods and then set free where they may not be used or even handled by anyone. If the yaks follow the tribe in their seasonal move, it is a good omen. The pastoral community acts as guardians of these livestock of the gods. Ekvall (1968:30) states that these "free" god yaks seem to be an acknowledgement that domestication of the livestock on which pastoralism depends is an infringement of the natural rights of the gods.

Statuses and expectations are means for distributing tasks and resources. Livestock care involves the provision of pasture, protection and veterinary care. Commonly among nomadic pastoralists the herding and care of domestic animals is men's work, whereas milking and preparing dairy food such as cheese and yogurt is women's work. Among the Tibetan pastoral nomads, the caring for the animal at birth, the raising of its young, and particularly milking are done only by women (Ekvall 1968).

Pastoralists are predominantly divided into father-centered extended family groups. Descent is usually reckoned only through the male line. However, not all pastoralists follow this pattern. The Navajo live in mother-centered family groups with descent reckoned through the mother's line.

Many pastoralists combine some other form of subsistence with herding. Pastoralists must engage in reciprocal exchange systems with agriculturalists when they are not fully self-sufficient. This often leads to conflict between the two groups with increasing amounts of aggression and warfare. Pastoralists must protect their right to grazing land for their "field on hoof" (Ekvall 1968) and agriculturalists must defend their fields of crops from being destroyed or denuded by the herding animals.

Pastoralists, however, engage in aggression and warfare among themselves, too. They raid one another to obtain animals and economic resources, and they must band together to protect themselves from raids. Pastoral nomadism is a chancy life. Today's rich herds may be devastated tomorrow by sickness, natural disaster, or raiding. But raiding another group can change a person's fortunes for the better.

Modern governments do not want people roaming with the freedom of nomadic pastoralists, and are making efforts to settle them and convert them into farmers, urban dwellers, or ranchers. This is the fate of the Mongols in the Soviet Union and China, as well as of other groups.

Industrial Economies

With farming came an increase in hierarchy, and forms of government and social organization which included individuals who were full-time specialists in non-farming activities. Along with this came the development of towns and later cities. Food was funneled from the country where people produced it, to the city where specialists consumed it. This meant both extraction by trade and by coercion in the form of taxes and labor conscription. Urban areas were concentration centers for wealth. The apex of the hierarchy lived in the cities with their greater abundance of material goods both in life and the grave.

The *peasant* is a farmer whose link with those outside the village is through an economic tie which brings the peasant goods which cannot be produced in the village, and also brings new ideas, customs, and technology. Peasants are found in all parts of the world including Russia, Europe, Africa, Latin America, and much of Asia. The peasant usually relies on one or two cash crops, and these vary. It is how and to whom they can dispose of what they produce that determines their standing as peasants.

With farming, a fundamental shift occurred in the attitude toward land. Land now equalled both wealth and survival. Ownership of land was necessary in order to be able to use it. Usually, the peasant does not own land, but has certain rights of use to it in return for a portion of the yield being given to the owner. One of the functions of the owner is to provide protection from outside enemies.

Peasants as a class provide economic resources for the other higher classes. Peasants have represented the majority of the world's population (Foster 1967). They are and have been a huge reserve of cheap and available labor. The women work with the men in the fields, but are attributed an unequal status by the menfolk.

Three types of economic exchange, reciprocal, redistribution, and market, are used in peasant societies. *Market exchange* is open bartering or buying and selling which is based on the laws of supply and demand. The two parties involved in market exchange usually have no intimate social bonds. This means that kinship ties and cultural role expectations do not enter into the exchange as major factors.

Market exchange can be barter exchange, but is more usually based on some accepted medium of exchange. In ancient China, cowrie shells could be given in exchange for many items. But cowrie shells were a limited medium of exchange and many things could not be bought with them.

In the modern industrial world, money is a universal medium of exchange. This means that every conceivable good or service can be purchased with money. *Money* is a mutually agreed-upon measure of value by which goods and services can be exchanged. Specially printed paper serves as money in much of the modern world. But the expressions, "not worth a plug nickel," and "not worth a Confederate dollar," make the point that the value of any

Figure 7.8 Fishnets need constant mending. In Brunei, some old women specialize in this work. (Photograph by L. A. Kimball)

type of money is culturally assigned. In countries with high rates of inflation, gold or other items considered intrinsically valuable serve as media of exchange.

Within the village, peasants may use reciprocity and redistribution to gain items. Peasants usually sell their crops for money to markets outside the local village. At the other extreme of industrial economy lies the urban center, filled with specialists who sell their labor for money.

In the industrial economy, subsistence becomes more linked to uncontrollable events in distant places. Most people work for money rather than being subsistence producers. Many shelters depend on artificial materials and on the presence of electric power. Many buildings have no windows to let in sunshine. The long-distance transportation of foodstuffs means that the local farms and market gardens that once supplied cities and towns have been put out of business, so that any disruption in the transportation could cause catastrophe. The development of almost completely mechanized farming machinery has devastated the peasant lifeway, leading peasants in many parts of the world to move to cities to find wage labor. This process can be seen clearly in Mexico City, which grows by an estimated 2,000 people, mostly peasants, every day.

Meanwhile, improvement in sanitation and public health has brought about a decrease in the death rate in many areas of the world. As a result there is a growing population in much of the world, which strains the resources of individual countries, past their limits in some cases.

Industrialization has also changed social patterns. In farming areas, the extended family is a vital social unit. When portions of these families migrate to cities in search of work, the kinship ties begin to change. Often it is the personal *social network,* the group of kin, co-workers, friends and acquaintances who interact with the individual, which becomes the most important social unit in the city. Social networks, unlike kin relations, can shift and change over short periods of time. Where peasants maintain contact with rural groups, the social networks in cities tend to be strong and functional. Among Americans, though, who may have no links to a rural base, social networks are often ephemeral things and provide little of the stability of a kinship group.

Economy and Culture

In analyzing economy, anthropologists distinguish between the structure and the individual. Cultural customs and beliefs, as well as environment, relationships with other groups, and all other aspects of the cultural and economic system are the structural framework. Within this framework, the individual lives and maneuvers. In looking at the human element of economy, anthropologists consider the motives and behaviors of the individual, and the actual behavior involved in all economic activities.

Each culture is an integral whole. Economy is thoroughly interrelated with other parts of the culture, including politics, kinship, physical environment, and religion. Thus the study of the interactions and interrelationships between economy and other aspects of the culture helps broaden our understanding of that culture (Nash 1967). Such study, done more broadly from a cross-cultural perspective, helps our understanding of cultures throughout the world now and in the past.

SUGGESTED READINGS

Dalton, George, ed. *Tribal and Peasant Economics*. Garden City, New York: Natural History Press, 1967.
This book contains many of the most important papers in the field of economic anthropology.

Malinowski, Bronislaw. *Argonauts of the Western Pacific*. New York: E. P. Dutton, 1961.
A book considered by many to be the classic on the Kula exchange.

Mauss, Marcel. *The Gift.* New York: Free Press, 1954.
An attempt to arrive at the principles that govern the behavior associated with giving and ceremonial exchange. A basic work in economic anthropology.

Rubel, Rosemary, Abraham, and Paula G. *Feasting with Mine Enemy: Rank and Exchange Among Northwest Coast Societies*. New York: Columbia University Press, 1971.
This work concentrates on six Northwest Coast societies in an attempt to analyze the relationship between social structure and the potlatch.

Sahlins, Marshall. *Stone Age Economics*. Chicago: Aldine-Atherton, 1972.
This book is a thorough and provocative study of economic exchange and its social importance at the household level.

Marriage

8

Marriage is a rite of passage that marks the relationship and merging of two individuals, usually a male and a female, into a basic cooperative social unit. Two individuals united through marriage form the basic kinship unit. Marriage is connected with all other aspects of culture, particularly with the kinship and economic systems. Every culture recognizes at least two types of marriage partners: permitted and prohibited.

Types of Marriage

Prohibited Marriages

A prohibited marriage is a forbidden marriage. Every culture forbids certain marriages and has sanctions against them. These sanctions range from killing the offenders to expelling them for life from the culture.

In every culture, *incest* is prohibited. Usually incest means marriage to or sexual relations with a relative deemed too close for marriage. However, sexual prohibitions are subject to cultural interpretation. For example, among the Crow, if one sits too close to a prohibited sexual partner, it is considered to be incest, and among the Balinese male and female twins are considered to have committed incest in the womb and must be ritually purified at birth. In America, marriage with one's child, parent, sibling, aunt, uncle, grandparent, or any lineal ascendant or descendant is considered incest. In most states, marriage with one's second cousin (the child of one's

parent's first cousin) is permitted, but not marriage with one's first cousin. Some states, however, such as Alabama and Massachusetts, do permit first cousin marriage. Other cultures may define incest quite differently, but all have incest taboos.

People may be prohibited as marriage partners for other reasons than kinship. Social status, membership in a cultural group, religious differences, and many other factors may cause a marriage to be defined as prohibited. For example, in India one must marry only within one's own caste, which is an hereditary social group. In traditional times in southern China, the children of boatmen were not allowed to marry the children of landsmen. In the orthodox understanding, Moslem women are not allowed to marry non-Moslem men. A similar situation once existed in the Roman Catholic Church, though now mixed marriage is permitted if the non-Catholic partner agrees to allow the children to be brought up as Catholics.

Permitted Marriages

A permitted marriage is one which is allowed. Permitted marriages include marriages which are preferred. Some cultural groups specify in detail who is the preferred marriage partner, while others leave the matter open. In "small town North America" there was, and remains, a marriage preference for the "hometown boy or girl," because one knows the individual and the family, and therefore is marrying a known friend and not a stranger.

Figure 8.1 Travel to a wedding can be arduous in Borneo. The canopied boat in the center is bearing a groom to his wedding; members of the groom's extended family are traveling in the other two boats. (Photograph by L. A. Kimball)

This reflects the fact that in American culture, geographic closeness and longterm interaction serve as a partial substitute for kinship relations.

Similarity of background and socioeconomic class are factors in urban marriage preference. For example, upper class people who have inherited their wealth, and those who are in well-paying professions, encourage their children to "mix" with certain social groups where they may find a partner with similar background and status. In this case, social status is partially equated with financial position. This contrasts with feudal Europe, where social status was hereditary, although wealth was concentrated in the hands of the higher status people. In feudal Europe, pre-ferred marriages among princes and nobility, the highest statuses, involved the formation of favorable alliances combined with profitable economic maneuvers. Wealth was directly linked to land ownership, so princely and noble marriages were often arranged to keep large estates within the groom's family, or to augment the groom's estate.

Arabs prefer to marry first cousins, (the father's brother's child), because such a marriage keeps property within the man's kinship group. Brunei Malays also prefer marriage to the first cousin, but of a different type. The parent of the groom must be the elder sibling of the parent of the bride in precise mirroring of the fact that in the marriage relationship, the husband is senior to the wife. He is dominant and she is subordinate.

Figure 8.2 The arrival of a groom at his wedding in Brunei is a moment of excitement and high anticipation. The decorated candlestick and the umbrella symbolize the groom's status as "king for a day," just as the bride is "queen for a day." (Photograph by L. A. Kimball)

Endogamy and Exogamy

Many cultures specify the group from which one must or may select a marriage partner. One frequently occurring specification is that marriage must be within a particular group or outside of a particular group.

In _exogamy (out-marriage)_ one must marry outside of one's own social group. For example, among traditional Chinese, people having the same surname are considered to be somehow related to one another, and are too close for marriage. One must marry a person with a different surname. This could be called "name exogamy." In many cultures, one must marry someone outside the village. They practice "village exogamy."

In _endogamy (in-marriage)_, one must marry within a defined group. In America, Catholics are supposed to marry Catholics, and Orthodox Jews are supposed to marry Orthodox Jews.

Exogamy and endogamy may work together. For example, in some Plains Indian tribes, such as the Crow, one must marry out of one's own clan, but must marry within the tribe. In India, members of a particular caste must marry outside of the village, but must marry within their own caste.

Bear in mind that marriage is more than just two people coming together. Marriage is rather the uniting of two kinship units in bonds of cooperation.

Affinal Marriages

Affinal marriage is marriage to one's in-laws. There are two forms of affinal marriage, the levirate and the sororate. In the _levirate,_ a woman who has been widowed marries her dead husband's brother (her brother-in-law). In the *sororate*, a man who has been widowed marries his dead wife's sister (his sister-in-law).

The levirate and sororate are found among many Native American societies, the Arabs, and is recorded in the Old Testament as having been a marriage practice of the ancient Hebrew. These two forms of affinal marriage serve to continue the alliance between two families who have been bonded by marriage. Affinal marriage also strengthens the lineage and ensures that a widow or widower is not left without a spouse.

Often, in groups that practice affinal marriage, there is a behavior known as "anticipatory levirate" and "anticipatory sororate," sometimes also referred to as a "joking relationship." The anticipatory levirate or sororate is a flirting behavior between the brother-in-law and the sister-in-law; this flirting is in anticipation of their possibly one day being man and wife. The anticipatory sororate and levirate are found among the Blackfeet, Omaha, and Crow; and the anticipatory levirate and sororate are still a common practice today among the Crow.

Patterns of Spouses

Different societies permit different numbers of spouses. In North America today, *monogamy*, marriage to only one spouse, is the law. At any time, however, if a husband or wife dies or is divorced, the remaining spouse can remarry. This means that over the course of a lifetime, a man or woman may be married to several spouses one after the other. This series of marriages is called *serial monogamy*.

Polygamy is the term for marriage to more than one spouse at a time. The most common form of polygamy is *polygyny* (from *poly*, "many" and *gyny*, "women"), in which many women are married to one man at the same time. Islam, for example, permits a man to have as many as four wives simultaneously. In some societies of West Africa, the first wife sometimes insists that her husband take more wives. She may even pay the bride price to their families because she wants more women to help with the work. In some North American Indian societies, such as the Blackfeet, Crow, and the Hidatsa, polygyny takes the sororal (sisters) form whereby a man may marry the younger sister of his first wife. This particular type of polygyny seems to function smoothly because the younger sister is already accustomed to taking orders from her older sibling and the two sisters are less likely to quarrel than are unrelated co-wives. The rarer form of polygamy is *polyandry* (*poly* and *andry*, "men"), in which one woman has more than one husband at the same time. The Nayar warrior caste of Kerala in Southwest India had polyandry, as did some of the traders in the Himalaya region (Mencher 1965, Levine 1988). The Nayar husbands were frequently away on war expeditions, and the Himalayan trader husbands were frequently off on long trading journeys. In both cases, polyandry provided a means to ensure that the wife was not left alone for months or years on end. Polyandry often takes the form of fraternal (brothers) form in which a woman will marry her husband's younger brother or brothers. Fraternal polyandry often occurs in order to prevent family landholdings from being subdivided or fragmented.

Marriage as Alliance

The basic principle of marriage is that it constitutes an alliance between two kinship groups. The couple concerned is merely the most conspicuous link. In other words, a man or a woman marries not only the spouse but also the kinship group of the spouse.

Very few societies leave it to the individual to choose whom to marry. In this respect, North America today is something of an exception. Even here, there are often exceptions, and the family may influence the choice of partner.

Figure 8.3 In many cultures, marriage is the joining of two kinship groups as well as two individuals. The numerous guests at a Malay wedding are the human reality of the kinship groups joined through marriage. (Photograph by L. A. Kimball)

An *arranged marriage* is one in which the parents of the couple have made the match, or have used a third party or *go-between* to make the match. In some arranged marriages, the couple has chaperoned meetings before the wedding. In other cases, the first time they meet is on their wedding day. Rural marriages in India are arranged matches. The idea of romantic love was an ideal that began in the courts of medieval Europe. Still, almost all medieval European marriages at every level of society were arranged marriages.

Acquiring a Mate

How are mates acquired? There are seven main ways to acquire a mate which are found in the world's cultures. Each will be considered in turn.

Spouse Price

There are two types of spouse price: progeny or bride price, and dowry.

Progeny price or *bride price* is a payment made by the groom's family to the family of the bride. This practice is very common in Africa, where the prestige of a woman is related to the amount of the bride price. Among the Bavenda of South Africa, the price is very high, in fact it is so high that most men must pay it in installments. In this case, the price is paid in cows to the woman's family. The husband makes a down payment and the wife remains in her father's house. The man has visiting rights and sexual relations are permitted. If the payments are not kept up-to-date the father may foreclose on the marriage contract, keep the payments of cows already made, and his daughter and any children involved.

121

The woman is now worth more because she has proven that she can bear children, and a clever father can accumulate a great deal of wealth by this method. On the other hand, if a couple remains childless for two years after a man has paid the full price, he may insist that his wife return to her father's house. The husband may demand to marry the woman's sister or to have his cows returned. If her father no longer has the cows, he must borrow them from his lineage.

Progeny or bride price is *not* a purchase price as understood in our economy. It is an economic payment rooted in, and inseparably part of, a social relationship and interaction, a form of material symbolism of kinship and social linkage. The progeny or bride price represents recognition of the importance and value of the woman to the society.

The Nuer are cattle herders who live on the Upper Nile River in Africa. The standard bride price for the Nuer is 40 cows: 20 for the bride's father and his brothers, 10 for the father's family, and 10 for the mother's brother. When one of the sons of the family is seeking a bride, his whole family must contribute to the bride price. Over a generation or so, there is a cycling of cows, vital for subsistence and prestige.

The Nuer are often at war with themselves and with other tribes. Lineages consisting of grandfathers, fathers, sons, grandsons, and great-grandsons are important to the Nuer. If a Nuer family or lineage has only one male left in the lineage and he is killed, the dead man's family will pay the progeny price for a woman and marry this woman to the dead man's ghost. Thereafter, any children born to this woman will belong to the dead man's lineage. Thus, a fictive marriage serves to ensure that the lineage will continue. *Fictive marriage* is one in which one or both partners are no longer alive.

Another type of spouse price is that found in much of traditional Europe, the dowry. In the *dowry,* the bride brings goods and gifts with her at marriage, and indeed, she will not be accepted as a bride unless she has a dowry to bring to the marriage. In this case, the kinship group of the bride is giving material goods to the kinship group of the groom. The underlying theory is that the groom will supply subsistence for the couple and their children for the lifetime of the marriage, but the bride should provide much or all of the foundation for setting up a household as her approximately equal share of the lifetime transaction.

In Greece, not only must the woman have all the pots, pans, dishes, linens and other cloths she will need, she must also have a house for the couple to live in. Similar to the dowry is the custom in the United States of the "hope chest" in which a young woman collects and saves linens, bedding, and other items for marriage.

Suitor Service

In *suitor service* the intended husband must live with and work for the future father-in-law. The Bible tells of Jacob, who worked for seven years for his wife Leah's father and seven more for his wife Rachel's father.

Among the Kadayans, a rice farming group living in Brunei, Borneo, the future groom worked for a year and lived at the house of his future wife. Only after completing the suitor service would he be accepted as a husband and the wedding be held. The suitor service added the man's labor to the family, to produce the extra rice and other food needed for the wedding. At the same time, the woman's family could assess the man as a potential husband. The family would reject him if they found him weak in providing adequate sustenance or if his personality was in some way displeasing. The prospective groom, likewise, could judge the nature of his bride and would reject her if she was lazy or would not make a

Figure 8.4 This modern cartoonist's view of the past says more about our culture than about the past. (Cartoon by David Flemming)

good wife. Also, by having worked to obtain the right to marry, the man was expected to be more devoted to his wife, and she to him.

Gift Exchange

In *gift exchange,* the family of the bride and the family of the groom exchange gifts with one another. If the two gifts exchanged are equal, neither side has an advantage. Among the Cheyenne, there was an equal exchange of gifts between the family of the bride and the family of the groom, except that the bride had an extra horse which was given to her by her brother. It was the brother who approved the marriage, and the horse was provided so that the woman had a way to come back to her home if things did not work out. A sister was supposed to accept her brother's decision regarding the choice of spouse. If she did not, the brother would then lose face.

Capture

Capture is a way for men to acquire spouses, and is most common in time of war. Cartoons show capture as the "caveman" approach, but there is reason to think that humans have had organized and sophisticated patterns of marriage for at least the last 100,000 years. Furthermore, there is no evidence that "cavemen," or Neanderthals, practiced war and this is the most common situation in which capture seems to occur.

Spouse Inheritance

Among some groups, an individual automatically inherits the spouse of certain deceased relatives. Levirate and sororate marriages (discussed earlier) are a type of *spouse inheritance*. Among the Bura of Nigeria, a man inherits his grandfather's wives, ensuring that they are provided for in old age (Hoebel 1972).

Elopement

Elopement occurs when a couple run away secretly to marry. Elopement often serves as a kind of safety valve. A North American couple who want to marry, despite firm refusal of the bride's family to give permission, often elope. The fictional stereotype of such elopement depicts a woman climbing down the ladder from her window while the man stands below holding ladder and suitcase. The remainder of the stereotype shows the couple being married by a Justice of the Peace in another state.

Brunei Malays who could not afford the price for a full week of elaborate wedding festivities often went off in secret to a religious official to marry. The elopers returned with the marriage certificate, showing that they were legally married in the eyes of Islam. Villagers accepted this as a legitimate marriage. But they felt that it was not quite proper since there had been none of the festivities which serve to symbolize the union of the two kinship groups.

Adoption

In Indonesia and Japan, a family with no sons may adopt one, who will marry one of the daughters. The children of that marriage are then considered the grandchildren of the woman's parents, as though the groom had been their own son by birth. In this way, a woman can acquire a husband through *adoption*.

Romantic Selection

Romantic selection is the common mode of spouse acquisition in modern American culture. Men and women cast about for a member of the opposite sex who attracts them. They then exchange gifts, services, and signs of affection. Meeting the family of the intended spouse signifies an interest in "becoming serious." Sometimes a symbolic gift, such as a special pin, symbolizes that the couple is "engaged to be engaged." Ideally, the man then formally requests permission to marry from the father of the bride. He then formally proposes to the woman, and if she accepts, they are considered engaged. Engagement often is symbolized by the gift of a ring from the man to the woman. This is the general middle and upper class pattern in the United States.

Regional and class variants exist. For example, the couple may have sex and then announce to their families the intention to marry. "Shotgun weddings" occur when the woman has become pregnant and the man is pressured into marrying her. In certain times and locales he was literally led at the point of a shotgun to the wedding. In the United States today, couples may live together for years, with or without children, before they marry.

Variations on a Marriage Theme

Not all marriages are between a living man and a living woman. As noted above, the Nuer practice fictive marriage, in which a woman marries a ghost in order to keep a descent group of males alive. Fictive marriages may occur for other reasons. Traditional Chinese believe that the unhappy ghosts of adult children who died unmarried can disturb the living. In Hong Kong, special matchmakers arrange for marriages between such ghosts. The two families hold a wedding ceremony and feast to marry the ghosts. The ghosts are now satisfied because they have been married and no longer trouble the living (Lau, pers. comm.).

A still different type of marriage is the *pseudo marriage,* a ritual which simulates marriage but is not between two people. The Kwakiutl of the Northwest Coast practice a type of pseudo marriage. The title of a Kwakitul chief passes from the current chief to his daughter's son. If a chief has no daughters, he will lack the son-in-law he needs to transmit chieftancy to his daughter's son. If a chief has only sons, he will perform a pseudo marriage in which one son is "married" to the chief's left leg. The chief's left leg is the man's first wife. He then takes a second wife who bears children. Because these children are the off-spring of the chief's son-in-law, they can inherit the title of chief.

In some cultures, the people who marry may be of the same sex. Among the Nuer, a woman who cannot have children can become a "female husband." As a female husband, she takes a wife and may choose male sexual partners for her wife. The children of the couple are members of the female husband's lineage. Among several Native American groups, men could take on the role of a woman and women could take on the role of a man.

Ending a Marriage

Death of a spouse ends a marriage. Whether or not the surviving spouse can then remarry depends upon the age and sex of the survivor and upon the cultural view of remarriage. In traditional India, a woman dies socially at the death of her husband. She becomes, as it were, a "walking dead," forbidden to wear finery, shunned and avoided. A widower, on the other hand, is expected to remarry soon.

Divorce occurs when both spouses are still living, but the marriage relationship itself dies. In some cultures, such as modern North America, divorce occurs frequently. In others, especially Roman Catholic cultures where divorce is forbidden, it occurs rarely. In many cultures, only the man can initiate a divorce. Among the Brunei Malays, only the man can obtain a divorce. A distressed wife's only recourse is to irritate her husband so he will divorce her in a fit of anger or to ask her male relatives to try to persuade the man to divorce her.

In contrast, in Ireland before 1200 A.D., a man had few rights of divorce. Women, on the other hand, could divorce a husband who "struck one serious blow."

Post-Marital Residence

A vital issue for newlyweds is post-marital residence, where they will live now that they are married. Most cultures dictate where the couple will live. The cultural choice is usually one of the following.

Neolocal

In neolocal residence (neo, "new" and local, "place"), the couple establishes an independent household apart from both families. This is the prevalent pattern in the United States, and may be related to the mobility required of families living in a highly industrialized society. Neolocal residence allows privacy and independence, but it places heavy economic demands on the couple and deprives them of a supporting kin group.

In patrilocal residence (patri, "father"), the couple lives with the husband's father. Patrilocal residence is the most common form of post-marital residence in the world today. This is the residence pattern for most of rural India, traditional China, and Southwest Asia.

In matrilocal residence (matri, "mother"), the couple lives with the bride's mother. Matrilocal residence is frequently found among horticultural societies such as the Hopi of Arizona and the Trukese of Micronesia. This was the pattern among the Nayar of South India and the Iroquois in North America.

In virilocal residence (viri, "man"), the couple lives near the groom's father's house, as among the Crow.

In uxorilocal residence (uxori, "wife"), the couple live near the wife's mother. Newlyweds move to a house located near that of the wife's mother, as in the Atjehnese of northern Sumatra.

In *avunculocal residence* (*avuncu,* "uncle"), the couple lives with or near the groom's mother's brother. Avunculocal residence is most often associated with matrilineal descent, which will be discussed in the next chapter. Avunculocal residence is practiced by the Trobriand Islanders of Melanesia and the Tlingit of southern Alaska (Malinowski 1922, 1929, 1935).

In *bilocal residence* (*bi,* "two"), the couple may live with either the parents of the groom or with those of the bride. The !Kung Bushmen have bilocal residence as do many of the peoples of the South Pacific. It gives the couple access to a wide variety of resources after marriage.

Residence patterns are not absolutes. Political, economic, or social circumstances may affect the choice of post-marital residence. Residence patterns may change over time. For example, among the Brunei Malays the residence is initially matrilocal, but later on may shift to be neolocal or patrilocal, depending on economic circumstances and the realities of social relationships.

Life Cycle of a Marriage

Just as we look at the life cycle of a human, so too can we see the life cycle of a marriage.

The birth of a marriage is at the wedding ceremony, whatever form it may take. For a short time following the ceremony, the marriage is in its infant stage, and special privileges accrue to the couple. For example, the Brunei Malays say that for the first 40 days after a wedding, a couple are besotted with one another and want only to be with each other, day or night. After the 40 days have passed, the marriage is no longer in the very beginning stages and the couple is expected to settle down to the routine of married life and work, enjoying connubial bliss only at night. In the U.S.,

Figure 8.5 Each of these decorations for a Brunei Malay wedding has symbolic meaning. The decorated eggs represent fertility, the flowers happiness, the candles promise of the future; and the raised platform where the newlyweds will sit signifies the importance of married life. (Photograph by L. A. Kimball)

whole resorts are devoted to honeymoons. To the French, being a newlywed is one of the most youthful and exuberant times of a person's life. Newlyweds in France are treated with tender care.

The first years of a marriage are its youth. This is the time when children begin to arrive. Young marriages may founder because the woman is unable to bear children, or is unable to bear male children. Both problems occurred with Henry VIII of England's marriages. When a woman dies in childbirth, death ends the marriage. Many young marriages in

126

North America today founder because of the extraordinarily heavy demands placed on the relationship in times of changing economic patterns and social roles.

As the years pass, the marriage matures. These are the years when children grow up and approach marriageable age. In most cultures, by the time children reach marriageable age, the parents are an established married couple with a significant place in the community. As the couple succeeds in marrying off their children they secure the future of kinship alliances and provide for the survival of the social group. The time of being an established married couple is usually the prime of the two people's lives.

In time, both the couple and the marriage grow old. With all the children married off, and the vigor of prime years slowly diminishing, the patterns and expectations of marriage change. Elderhood is the summing up of a lifetime, looking to the future through grandchildren, and realizing that one is soon to become an ancestor in the world of the dead. For many this is a time of deep thought and understanding, and may well be a time of enormous satisfaction.

Finally comes the death of the marriage. The death of a marriage may occur through death of one of the spouses, or through divorce. But if a couple have grown old together, the dissolution of their marriage is likely to occur through their death in old age. Thus, the life cycle of the marriage ends.

SUGGESTED READINGS

Bohannan, P. and J. Middleton, eds. *Marriage, Family, and Residence*. New York: Natural History Press, 1968.
An assemblage of articles dealing with marriage and the family, with an emphasis on cross-cultural comparison.

Fox, Robin. *Kinship and Marriage in an Anthropological Perspective*. New York: Penguin, 1968.
This book begins with the thesis that there exists a universal biological bond between mother and child and that the husband/father is an intruder into this basic group.

Freidl, Ernestine. *Women and Men: An Anthropologist's View*. New York: Holt, Rinehart and Winston, 1975.
The author offers a number of hypotheses concerning the expressions of sex roles.

Stephens, William N. *The Family in Cross-Cultural Perspective*. New York: Holt, Rinehart and Winston, 1963.
This work contains information on a wide range of topics: plural marriages, arranged marriages, bride price, and adultery presented from a cross-cultural perspective.

Kinship

9

Kinship forms the basis of human life. "Kinship" refers to both biological kinship and to sociocultural kinship.

Biological Kinship

Biological kinship traces the linkages to the "begetter," the male impregnator; the "bearer," the female who gives birth; and the "begotten," the offspring thus produced. Human kinship has an obvious biological basis. The biological aspect of kinship continues after birth. Human infants need prolonged care, and human children remain dependent for years. The demands of nurturing and caring for children serve to band human parents together in the shared endeavor to raise their children. This produces the conjugal-natal family of mother, father, and children. Another term for conjugal-natal family is "nuclear family," stressing that it serves as a base for kinship.

Human biologists (physical anthropologists) study biological kinship. Cultural anthropologists study the cultural definitions and social networks that constitute sociocultural kinship.

Sociocultural Kinship

Kinship, as a cultural system, interrelates with almost all other cultural systems. The kinship structure is a model which both describes and prescribes how a given individual will relate to other individuals.

Biological and sociocultural kinship overlap to some extent, but are two quite different entities.

Most North Americans of European ancestry call their mother's sister "aunt" and their father's brother "uncle." A person's behavior toward people called "aunt" or "uncle" differs considerably from behavior toward those called "mother," or "father." But the Crow of Southeast Montana call their mother's sister "mother," and call their father's brother "father." A Crow's behavior toward mother's sister or father's brother is very similar to the behavior toward his or her own mother and father. The biological relationship of an individual to mother and mother's sister, and father and father's brother is the same for both the Crow and North Americans. But the kinship terminology and the behavior associated with the terms differ greatly in the two cultures.

Two main features characterize human sociocultural kinship. First is actual behavior between individuals, between an individual and a particular kinship group, and between kinship groups themselves. Second is the language of kinship. Every language has a set of terms denoting individuals and referring to them, as well as special terms for describing and analyzing kinship.

Anthropologists use a variety of approaches in order to adequately describe and study the wide panorama of human kinship systems. These approaches include the study of how behavior interacts with kinship categories, practical diagramming of kinship relationships, categorization and comparison of kinship systems, and the analysis of basic processes of kinship systems. For clarity of communication, anthropologists use specific terminology to describe kinship and kinship relationships. This vocabulary is a key which unlocks fascinating areas of study.

Reference and Address

Members of human groups speak to one another and talk about one another. A person directly addressing another individual uses a *term of address*. But a person talking about someone else, whom they are not addressing, uses a *term of reference*. North American Standard English uses the same kinship terms and proper names for both reference and address terms. For example, a daughter might say, "Father, look at this," or "Father gave it to me." In the first case, she is using an address term, and in the second she is using a reference term. Many languages, however, have completely different kinship terms for reference and address. Some languages even have different forms of proper names for reference and address. By understanding these terms, anthropologists can also begin to understand the sociocultural kinship system in which they are used.

Consanguinality and Affinality

Human kinship links individuals and groups together through two principle ties, consanguinality and affinality.

Consanguineal kin are literally "blood kin." Colloquial English calls these kin "blood relatives," or "relatives by blood." This recognizes that the kinship connection is one of begetter, bearer, and begotten, or biological kinship.

Affinal kin are kin whose relationship is one of marriage. Colloquial English calls affinal kin "relatives by marriage," or "in-laws." This recognizes that the kinship connection is one assigned by the culture when two people have been joined together in a relationship which the culture recognizes as "marriage."

The pattern of consanguineal and affinal kinship forms a skeletal structure of the kinship system. But the meaning and nature of an individual's life within this framework depends upon a number of interacting processes, including that of descent, which will be discussed later.

Status and Role

Status is a social category, or cultural "pigeon-hole" that entails a set of expected behaviors. The expected behaviors appropriate to given social categories are *roles*.

For example, the *status* of "college student" entails the expected behaviors of coming to class, taking examinations, and following a plan of courses that will result in a degree. Individuals who indeed do come to class, take examinations, and take courses needed to graduate are fulfilling the *role* of student. These are the *formal* status and role of "college student." The *informal* status of student has the expected behaviors of socializing with other students, grumbling about required courses, and having a somewhat casual manner. People who appear casual as they grumble about certain courses while socializing at a student "hang-out" are fulfilling the informal role of student.

Status is of two types: ascribed and achieved. *Ascribed status* is assigned by the culture, usually at birth. An individual receives the ascribed status and then learns the appropriate role (behavior) for that status. Prince Charles of England was assigned the ascribed status of "Prince" at birth. Later, he received the ascribed status of "Crown Prince" and "Prince of Wales," meaning that he is expected to receive the ascribed status of "King" someday. As he grew up he learned the language, court etiquette, and other role behaviors appropriate to his ascribed statuses.

Achieved status is a social position one must earn, often with the help of others. "President of the United States," and "Prime Minister of Canada" are achieved statuses, as are "star baseball pitcher," "leading television actress," and "college graduate." In each case, the appropriate behaviors are learned before the status is achieved.

If a person with achieved status does not fully show the expected behaviors for the role, the society may alter that person's status. For instance, baseball players who do not perform well in the major leagues are sent down to the minors, and thus are demoted to a lower status role. When a Crow couple have their first child, the grandmothers (mother's mother or father's mother) will take the child away to raise it if they feel that the parents are too immature for the job. Thus, Crow parents who have not yet learned the behaviors appropriate to the achieved status of "Crow parent" are not allowed to raise their own child.

Kinship Maps

Kinship diagrams map relationships and serve as a basic tool for analysis and comparison of kinship systems. Anthropological kinship diagrams use a standard notational system to show individuals and how they are connected. Kinship diagramming is a useful tool. But, as with any tool, "practice makes perfect." To understand kinship diagrams, systematically study the individuals one by one, and see how each is connected to others in patterns of relationship. Think of the individuals in the diagram as real people. Write out kinship diagrams for your own family, and for friends' families. As you become fluent in its use, you will find that kinship diagramming is fun and interesting.

Symbols for Individuals

Three geometric symbols, the triangle, circle and square, serve to designate individuals. Each of these symbols has a special association with the type of individual it represents.

Mars, the ancient Roman god of war, carried a spear whose point was triangular. Thus, a triangle △ symbolizes a male. Venus, the ancient Roman goddess of beauty, often used a mirror. Roman mirrors were circular in shape, and a circle ○ symbolizes a female. Unopened square boxes hold mysterious, unknown contents. Thus a square □ symbolizes an individual whose sex is unknown or is irrelevant to the discussion. The symbols normally appear in outline form. But a solidly filled-in symbol ▲ ● ■ indicates *Ego*.

Ego is the Latin word meaning, "I." In anthropological kinship studies Ego indicates the single individual with respect to whom a given set of kinship relationships or a given set of kinship terms is defined. Thus, if I am Ego, then my male sibling is my brother, and my female sibling is my sister. But if Ego is my mother, then my male sibling is her son, and my female sibling is her daughter.

Many anthropological kinship terms, like Ego, derive from Latin and others derive from Greek. Figure 9.1 lists these Latin and Greek words with their English meaning. Remember that until World War II, Latin and Greek were standard languages studied by college students. Students easily understood Latin and Greek scientific terminology. This classical background also appears in the anthropological diagramming symbol for death.

Death comes to all of us, be it peacefully or otherwise. In ancient warfare, a spear thrust often ended lives. Thus the symbol for a dead person is a slanted line / piercing the triangle of a male, the circle of a female, or the box of

Term	Root and Meaning
lineal	*linea* (thread)
lineage	*linea* + *age* (belonging to)
unilineal	*unus* (one) + *linea*
bilineal	*bi* (two) + *linea*
ambilineal	*ambi* (both) + *linea*
matriline	*mater* (mother) + *linea*
patriline	*pater* (father) + *linea*
descent	*descendere* (to climb down)
clan	*clann* (offspring, tribe) (from Irish)
matriclan	*mater* (mother) + *clann*
patriclan	*pater* (father) + *clann*
natal	*natus* (born)
cognatic	*co* (together) + *natus*
consanguineal	*com* (with) + *sangunis* (blood)
affinal	*affinis* (adjacent)
conjugal	*com* (with) + *jungere* (join)
nuclear	*nuculeus* (nut, kernel)
corporate	*corpora* (to make into a body)
corporate clan	*corpora* + *clann*
endogamous	*endon* (within) + *gamos* (marriage)
exogamous	*exo* (without) + *gamos*
monogamous	*mono* (single) + *gamos*
moiety	*medietos* (the middle)

Figure 9.1. Roots of kinship terms

an unknown. The slashing line represents a lethal spear piercing the dead person. Figure 9.2 summarizes the symbols described above.

Symbols for Relationships

Lines drawn between two individuals indicate the manner in which those two people are related. Each of these lines also symbolizes the nature of the relationship. In a kinship chart, the two basic spatial dimensions are horizontal and vertical.

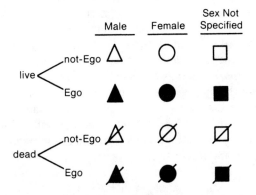

Figure 9.2 Kinship symbols

Individuals on the same horizontal line are genealogically in the same generation. Siblings (brothers and sisters) are all genealogically in the same generation. Thus, a horizontal line placed above two symbols indicates a sibling pair or a group of siblings.

A married couple is also in the same generation genealogically. Thus horizontal lines indicate the marriage relationship. The most common way of indicating marriage is an equal sign = placed between the two married individuals. Another way of indicating marriage is a horizontal line placed *below* the two married people. The equal sign will be used for diagrams in this book.

Divorce is the death of a marriage. To indicate divorce, place the slanted line symbolizing death through the symbol for marriage.

Individuals on different horizontal lines in a kinship diagram are in different generations. Thus a long vertical line | indicates relationships of ascent and descent. The basic ascent-descent relationship is that of parent and child. Parents are the ancestors of their children—parents are in the ascendant generation. Children are the descendants of their parents—they are in the descendant generation. The relationship symbols discussed above are summarized in Figure 9.3.

On roadmaps, the convention is to place "North" at the top of the map. In kinship maps, the convention is to place ascendant generations above descendant generations. Thus, the generations descend from the top of the chart to the bottom, and the generations ascend from the bottom to the top. So, as with stairs and ladders, when you go to the top you ascend and when you go to the bottom you descend. Imagine a ladder of generations reaching up and down the chart.

Each rung of the generational ladder is identified by a special number. Ego's generation is placed at about the center of the ladder and receives the generation number zero. Generation is abbreviated "G" so Ego's generation receives the designation "G 0". Ascending

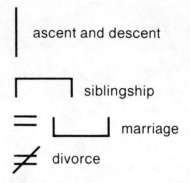

Figure 9.3 Symbols used to indicate relationships

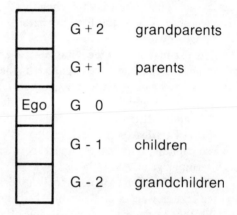

Figure 9.4 The ladder of generations

generations receive positive numbers. Ego's parents are in "G +1," Ego's grandparents are in "G +2" and so forth. Ego's descendants receive negative numbers. Thus Ego's children are in "G −1" and Ego's grandchildren are in "G −2" and so on. Figure 9.4 shows the ladder of generations of an anthropological kinship diagram.

Labels

Kinship charts tend to become crowded, leaving little room for labels. In order to label charts without overcrowding them, anthropologists use abbreviations for English kinship

Fa = father	Wi = wife	Au = aunt
Mo = mother	Hu = husband	Un = uncle
Da = daughter	Ch = child	
So = son	Pa = parent	
Si = sister	GP or GrPa = grandparent	
Br = brother	G CH or GrCh = grandchild	
Gr = grand or great	GrGrPa = great grandparent	

Figure 9.5 Kinship term abbreviations

terms. Figure 9.5 lists some of the common abbreviations. These are easy to remember because most consist of the first two letters in each English word.

The list in Figure 9.5 capitalizes the abbreviations. When they are capitalized, they can be written right next to one another. For example, great-grandchild can be written GrGrCh and Father's brother's daughter can be written FaBrDa. Some anthropologists do not use capitals; they leave a space between each term: gr gr ch and fa br da.

The abbreviations are commonly used in written text as well as in diagrams. They are helpful when taking field notes, which is often done under difficult conditions (as when many people are talking at once while sitting together during a bad storm).

Special Mappings

Thus far, the kinship diagrams you have encountered have shown relationships of marriage, siblingship, ascent and descent. However, when anthropologists want to focus on certain of these relationships, they diagram only the specific relationships of concern. Sometimes, siblings or spouses are omitted from the charts. When the marriage tie is not shown, a line linking one parent with the child indicates descent and ascent (Figure 9.6).

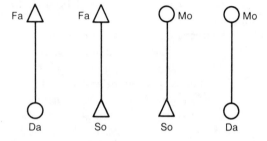

Figure 9.6 Mapping descent and ascent

Simplified kinship diagrams which omit some of the relationships effectively bring out patterns which would be obscured in a fuller diagram. For instance, Figure 9.7 shows only the males of the kinship group and their male children. This might be useful if the anthropologist wished to determine the positions of male heirs to a political position, and the relationships might not be apparent in a fuller diagram.

The relative position of the sibling symbols on kinship diagrams usually has no special meaning. But sometimes, the relative age of siblings is of key importance and needs to be indicated. In Chinese families, for example, elder and younger siblings have very different statuses and roles. The eldest and youngest sons particularly have special roles within the family. When the relative age of

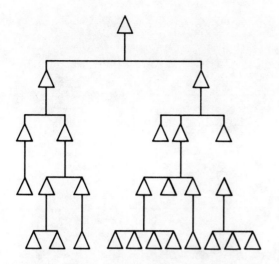

Diagram showing descent and siblingship of males only.

Notice that the marriages are indicated only by the presence of male descendants, thus marriages which were childless or had only female offspring do not appear on the diagram.

Figure 9.7 Simplified kinship diagram

siblings needs to be indicated, the siblings may be ordered on the chart with the eldest at the left and the youngest at the right, or numbers may be assigned to indicate their relative age. In either case, a special note is made on the chart to explain the way relative sibling age is being indicated. Figure 9.8 shows rank-ordered siblings.

During fieldwork special kinship situations often appear which must be indicated in a diagram. Since there is no convention for diagramming unique cases, the anthropologist must decide on a format. It is important to use a consistent way of diagramming, and to make a note on the kinship chart of what the special diagramming means. Road maps which show special features, such as national parks, airports, or motels, always include a key to help the reader. Kinship diagramming, like mapping, is a flexible tool which can be adapted and altered to meet special needs.

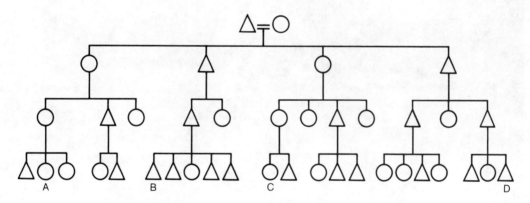

Note: in each of these sibling pairs, the eldest sibling is farthest to the left, and the youngest farthest to the right, with the others rank-ordered accordingly in between.

Thus A is the eldest Da of an eldest Da of an eldest Da
B is the eldest So of an eldest So of an eldest So
C is the eldest Da of an eldest Da of a youngest Da
D is the youngest So of a youngest So of a youngest So

Figure 9.8 Kinship chart with relative ages

135

Figure 9.9 Two Navajo siblings are sharing a burro-ride in the desert. (Photograph by Harry Teller)

Some Diagrams

The symbols and abbreviations described above form the basic tool kit of anthropological kinship diagramming. Their value becomes apparent as they are used to illustrate nuclear and extended families.

The *nuclear family* of parents and children is a basic kinship unit. Figure 9.10 shows two nuclear families. In Figure 9.10a, Ego is a male parent and in Figure 9.10b, Ego is a female parent. Remember that Ego is the individual with respect to whom all other kinship relationships are indicated. In Figure 9.10c, Ego is a female child, and in Figure 9.10d, Ego is a male child. Analyze what relationship each relative is to Ego, and what relationship Ego is to each relative. This basic two-way analysis of all individuals with respect to Ego is the type of study that should be done on all kinship charts. Figure 9.11 is an abstract form of the diagram. It shows the shape of a nuclear family without any specific Ego and without any numbering of generations.

The extended family is an important kinship unit in many cultures. Figure 9.12 shows the extended family of a male Ego. Figure 9.13 shows the extended family of a female Ego. Try to diagram other extended families with male and female Egos. Place your Egos in different generations, in different marital statuses, make them alive or dead, and place them in as many different kinship relationships as you can. Remember that in any one kinship diagram there can be only one Ego. You need to make a new diagram for each new Ego (or shade Ego in with pencil and then erase to create a new Ego). Practice with the extended family diagrams given in the figures above, and with ones you create yourself, until you become accustomed to seeing the relationship of individuals to one another. You will find that

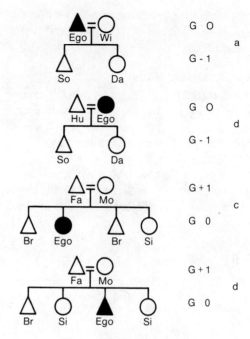

Figure 9.10 Ego positions

Figure 9.11 A nuclear family

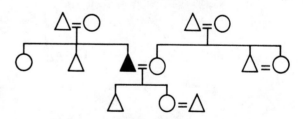

Figure 9.12 Extended family of a male Ego

after you have practiced awhile, kinship diagrams will become easy to draw and understand.

Larger Kinship Maps

Larger kinship diagrams follow the same principles as smaller ones. The only difference lies in the fact that more individuals are involved and that their relationships may be more complex.

Figure 9.14 shows a large extended family. It is similar to Figures 9.12 and 9.13, but shows more individuals. Figure 9.15 also shows a large extended family, but note that no Ego is indicated. To understand this chart, designate one individual as Ego, then trace the relationships to and from that Ego. Repeat the analysis, choosing various individuals as Ego. Remember that whatever Ego you select, that individual will be in "G 0" and all other generations should be numbered accordingly. Continue your analysis until you can easily interpret all aspects of the diagram.

In some Moslem countries, a man may be married to four women simultaneously. First cousins can marry, too. The resultant chart

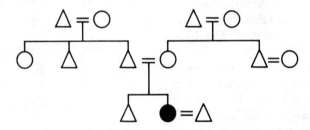

Figure 9.13 Extended family of a female Ego

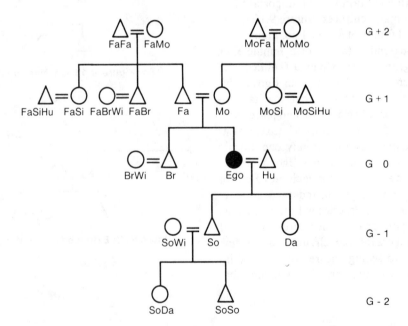

Figure 9.14 An extended family: Ego's relationships

138

(Figure 9.16) is complex. Study this chart in the same way suggested for the large extended family chart in Figure 9.15.

Whenever you encounter a kinship chart, study it step by step with care. If an Ego is indicated, study and analyze the relationship of that Ego to every individual indicated on the chart. If no Ego is indicated, select an individual as Ego and study the chart from Ego's perspective (and remember to number the generations correctly). Kinship charts are road maps of human relations. You can become skilled in finding your way around on them, and will find pleasure in doing so.

When Lines Cross

The kinship charts in books are carefully drawn for clarity. But anthropologists in the field have to take genealogical information in whatever order it comes. This often means sloppy-looking working diagrams with lines criss-crossing everywhere. To minimize conflict in such situations, anthropologists use the same convention that electrical engineers use when they draw wiring diagrams. When one line must cross another, draw the second line as a semi-circle at the place where it crosses the first line. Should a line cross two or more

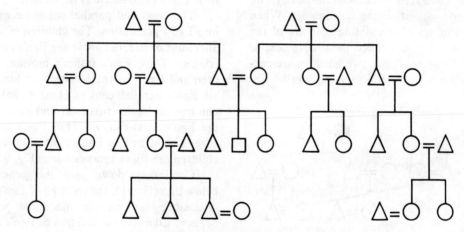

Figure 9.15 An extended family: no Ego

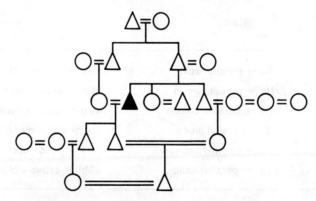

Diagram showing an extended Muslim family of first-cousin marriages and multiple wives.

Figure 9.16 Extended Muslim family

other lines, draw a semi-circle each time the lines cross. Figure 9.17 shows the use of crossing lines.

Diagramming as a Path to New Concepts

Kinship diagrams make visual interpretations of new concepts possible. Anthropologists abbreviate the terms for cousins just as they do other kinship terms, in order to have a convenient notation to use in the field and to make charts readable. Figure 9.18 shows the abbreviations used. Refer to them when you read the charts associated with this discussion of cousin terminology.

To understand cousin terminology, we must first look at sibling terminology. When both members of the sibling pair are of the same sex, they are called parallel in sex, or *parallel siblings*. Thus, two brothers are parallel siblings and two sisters are parallel sib-

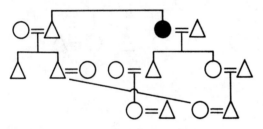

Figure 9.17 Diagramming crossing lines

lings. But if a pair of siblings consists of one sister and one brother, they are of the opposite sex, and are called a *cross-sibling* pair. Figures 9.19a and 9.19b show sibling relationships.

The same pattern holds true of sibling pairs in Ego's parents' generation (G +1). Father and father's brother are parallel siblings, thus father's brother is Ego's *parallel uncle*. Likewise mother and mother's sister are parallel siblings, and mother's sister is Ego's *parallel aunt* (Fig. 9.19c). But father's sister is his cross-sibling, and she is Ego's *cross-aunt*. And mother's brother is her cross-sibling, and he is Ego's *cross-uncle* (Fig. 9.19d).

The cross and parallel pattern continues into Ego's generation. The children of a parallel aunt or parallel uncle are Ego's *parallel cousins*. Thus, Ego's father's brother's children and Ego's mother's sister's children are all Ego's parallel cousins (Fig. 9.19e). The children of Ego's cross-aunt and cross-uncle are Ego's *cross-cousins*. Thus Ego's father's sister's children and Ego's mother's brother's children are Ego's cross-cousins (Fig. 9.19f).

Continuing down into the generation below Ego (G −1), the children of Ego's parallel sibling are parallel niece and parallel nephew. Likewise the children of Ego's cross-sibling are cross-niece and cross-nephew.

Au = aunt	//Au = parallel aunt	xAu = cross-aunt
Un = uncle	//Un = parallel uncle	xUn = cross-uncle
Co = cousin	//Co = parallel cousin	xCo = cross-cousin
Ni = niece	//Ni = parallel niece	xNi = cross-niece
Ne = nephew	//Ne = parallel nephew	xNe = cross-nephew
Si = sibling	//Sbl = parallel sibling	xSbl = cross-sibling

Figure 9.18. Abbreviations for cross and parallel kin

Notice that Ego's cross-niece and cross-nephew are Ego's children's cross-cousins. Ego's parallel niece and parallel nephew are Ego's children's parallel cousins.

Notice how diagramming makes the cross and parallel kinship patterns clear. Figure 9.20 summarizes these cross and parallel relationships. Anthropologists are careful about how they use the terms "aunt, uncle, cousin, niece" and "nephew," because each of these terms subsumes a chain of kinship linkage. For example "niece" means both brother's daughter and sister's daughter. "Uncle" means both mother's brother and father's brother. "Cousin" means only parent's sibling's children. The cross and parallel distinctions make the reference more precise. Thus "maternal cross-cousins" are mother's brother's children, and "paternal parallel cousins" are father's brother's children. Anthropological descriptive kinship terminology thus overcomes much of the built-in bias of Standard English kinship terminology, and provides a precise descriptive vocabulary for anthropological kinship studies.

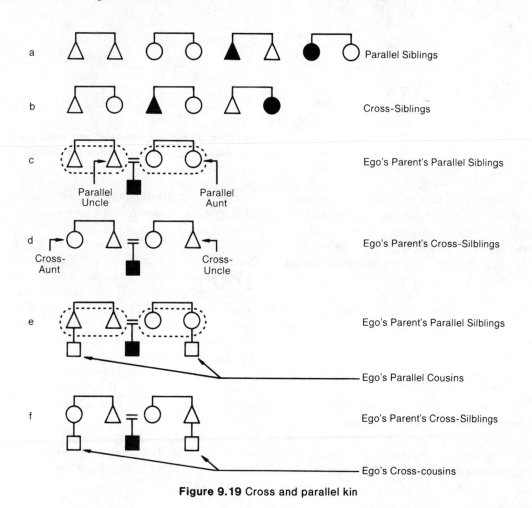

Figure 9.19 Cross and parallel kin

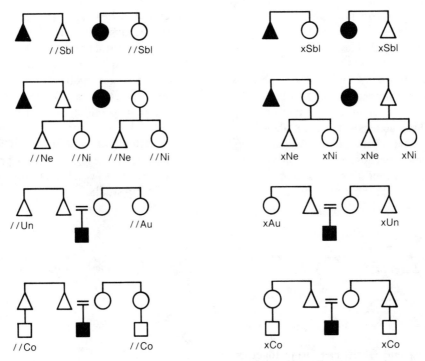

Figure 9.20 Summary of cross and parallel relationships

Anthropologists distinguish between cross-cousins and parallel cousins because in many cultures these distinctions are of crucial importance. People such as the Crow, whose kinship system places great importance on the distinction between cross- and parallel aunts and uncles and on cross- and parallel cousins, do not understand how the English kinship system could be so "stupid" as to not make these distinctions.

Reckonings of Descent

Kinship is active, not static. One of the active principles of kinship is the reckoning of descent. Several basic patterns of descent occur frequently throughout the world. Understanding these basic descent patterns is essential to understanding the general principles of the particular kinship systems in which they occur.

The majority of people in the United States use the bilateral principle of descent. In *bilateral descent,* both the mother's and father's families are equally important in inheritance and descent. In a bilateral descent system, a person is equally descended from both mother and father, and when mother dies, Ego inherits from her. When father dies, Ego also inherits from him. The individual traces descent and inheritance through all possible combinations of males and females on both sides of the family (Fig. 9.21).

Relatives linked to Ego through the father are referred to as paternal relatives, or relatives "on the father's side." Relatives linked to

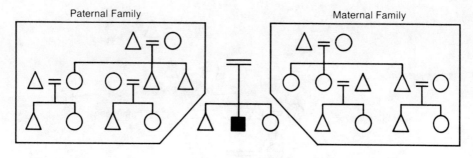

Ego is equally related to the maternal and paternal families.

Figure 9.21 Schematic diagram of bilateral descent

Ego through the mother are referred to as maternal relatives or relatives "on the mother's side." The bilateral kinship group also includes affines and their relatives. Thus, the term "aunt" can be applied equally to parent's sibling or to parent's sibling's spouse. Family reunions and major holiday feasts, such as Thanksgiving and Christmas, bring together the bilateral family group.

Many people mistakenly assume that the bilateral model is universal because we use it in Western society. But this is not so. A different type of descent, unilineal descent, occurs in many cultures throughout the world.

A *unilineal descent* system restricts the tracing of descent and inheritance to one single line only. The descent line consists of either males only or females only (Fig. 9.22). Those who are in the direct line of descent are *lineals* and all those not in the direct line of descent are *collaterals* (Fig. 9.23).

Descent traced through the female line only is *matrilineal,* "mother line" (Fig. 9.24). The Crow Indians have matrilineal descent. In matrilineally organized societies, each individual belongs to their mother's lineage. Since mother's brother is part of grandmother's lineage, his inheritance goes to the children of his sister, not to the children of his wife.

His biological children are in their mother's lineage and would inherit from her brother.

Descent traced through the male line only is *patrilineal,* "father line" (Fig. 9.25). In patrilineally organized societies, mother and mother's brother inherit from their father. A man's inheritance goes to his biological children.

Unilineal societies differ in their treatment of affines. A Chinese woman upon marriage ceases to be a member of her father's patrilineage and is incorporated into her husband's patrilineage. By contrast, in late-medieval Florence, Italy, a woman always remained a member of her father's patrilineage. This meant that if she became a widow after 40 years of marriage and had no son to support her, she would leave her husband's house and return to her own natal patrilineage. If her father were no longer alive, she would move into the house of her brother or her brother's son (Estell, pers. comm.).

Some descent systems count two lines. In *double descent* or *bilineal descent,* both the matrilineal and the patrilineal lines are used. An individual traces descent matrilineally for some purposes and patrilineally for others. The Ashanti of West Africa have matrilineal clans and patrilineal groups (Rattray 1923, 1927).

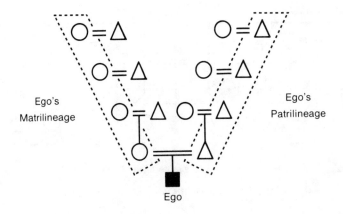

Ego's Matrilineage

Ego's Patrilineage

Ego

Bilineal Descent or Double Descent	Ego uses matrilineal descent for some purposes and patrilineal descent for others.
Ambilineal Descent	Ego chooses to be associated with either the matrilineage or the patrilineage, but cannot be associated with both.
Unilineal Descent	Matrilineal—Ego belongs only to the matrilineage. Patrilineal—Ego belongs only to the patrilineage.

Figure 9.22 Unilineal, ambilineal, and bilineal descent

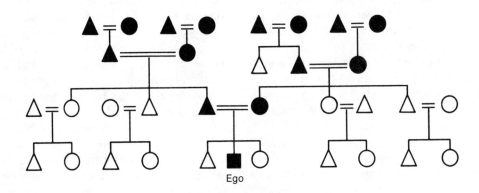

Ego

All shaded figures are lineals.

All blank figures are collaterals.

Figure 9.23 Schematic diagram of lineals and collaterals

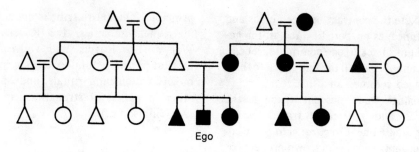

All shaded figures are members of the same matrilineage.

Figure 9.24 Schematic diagram of matrilineal descent

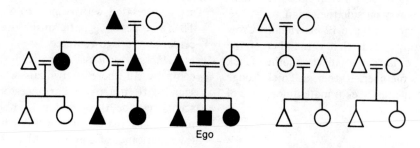

All shaded figures are members of the same patrilineage.

Figure 9.25 Schematic diagram of patrilineal descent

Ambilineal descent means that the culture recognizes both matrilineal and patrilineal descent, but an individual uses only one, either matrilineal or patrilineal, but not both. New York City Jews use ambilineal descent as a way of preserving traditional close family ties in the face of modern economic and social pressures (Haviland 1982).

Lineage

A lineage is a group which consists of all the unilineal descendants who can be traced directly back to a single ancestor. In a *matrilineage*, descent is traced through female lines to the common forebear. In a *patrilineage*, descent is traced through male lines to the common forebear.

A lineage whose members customarily cooperate with one another in order to further the best interests of the lineage as a cohesive social or economic unit is a *corporate lineage*. Lineages often act as a cooperative unit which forms an economic or political component within a cultural group. Crow matrilineages have considerable political power, and serve as lobbying units within the tribal council. Inheritance of land, the most important form of modern Crow wealth, takes place within the matrilineages.

Clan

A clan consists of one or more unilineal kinship groups, all of whom acknowledge common descent from a mythical or legendary ancestor. Note the contrast between clans and lineages. Lineages purport to trace all the genealogical links back to one common forebear. But clans cannot trace all the links back to their acknowledged common ancestor.

Matriclans trace descent through the female line, and *patriclans* trace descent through the male line. *Corporate clans* are cooperative organizations which own property or material goods, or both. Clan members usually refer to one another by kinship terms.

One of the most important functions of clans is the regulation of marriage. Clans are usually *exogamous,* which means that members must marry outside their clan.

The Crow now have 12 matriclans. Crow clan exogamy means that a member of the Thick Lodge clan cannot marry another Thick Lodge clan member. Rather, a Thick Lodge clan member must seek a mate among one of the 11 other clans.

Moiety

Reciprocity is an important aspect of kinship relations. Reciprocity is exchange, or give and take. Reciprocity means a two-way flow or passage of goods, services, and other items. Almost all societies have some form of reciprocity. The institution known as a *moiety system* is one form of reciprocity. (The term "moiety" derives from the French word for "half.")

Some societies are divided into two exogamous social units based on kinship. Each of these exogamous social units is a moiety. In a moiety system with institutionalized reciprocity, each moiety supplies the other with marriage partners and other goods and services, such as gambling partners, mortuary duties, and athletic opponents.

The Tlingit Indians of the northern Northwest Coast in Southeast Alaska have a system of reciprocity based on the moiety principle. The entire tribe is divided into two matrilineal moieties, the Ravens and the Wolves. The Ravens and Wolves exchange marital partners, fulfill a set role in the other moiety's mourning rituals, and oppose each other in games of strength or in gambling (McGinnis, n.d.).

Cognatic Kinship Systems

Some kinship systems do not focus on lineality as such. *Cognatic kinship* operates on the principle that individuals who are all related with respect to some particular person are also related with respect to one another. The two types of cognatic kinship are ancestor-centered and Ego-centered.

Ancestor-centered cognatic kinship groups comprise all those individuals who are descended from a particular ancestor. The descent may be through any combination of males and females. In North America, when the inheritance of a multi-millionaire is left to "all my descendants," it is being left to that individual's ancestor-centered cognatic descent group. The members of that group can promptly begin to squabble over division of the inheritance.

An *Ego-centered* cognatic kinship group, also known as a *kindred,* contains all those individuals who are related to a particular Ego, through any combination of males and females. The Ego-centered group is the functional one for large family gatherings among most Americans who practice bilateral descent.

Brunei Malay kinship illustrates the point that one culture may use many different kinship reckonings. Brunei Malays are patrilineal and follow the Moslem pattern of inheritance. However, the inheritance of fruit trees, kitchen goods, and certain specialized knowledge is through the matrilineage. The active functional group in preparing for and attending weddings is the Ego-centered cognatic group of the bride and groom. Brunei Malays also recognize ancestor-centered cognatic groups. Two individuals who can both trace descent to a common ancestor, through any combination of males and females, will consider themselves to be related. Also, people sometimes identify "all the descendants of Famous Ancestor" as a special group.

The Six Basic Kinship Systems

The people of each culture feel that theirs has the "correct" kinship system, and that all others are flawed somehow. But anthropologists disagree. For the anthropologist there is no "correct" kinship system. There are only different systems, each of which should be understood.

A useful viewpoint for understanding kinship systems is the examination of pattern and process. *Pattern* is the formal structure of the kinship system. *Process* is the way a kinship system works, how it might be especially useful for an individual or group.

Hundreds of different kinship systems exist among the cultures of the world. By categorizing the systems according to their basic structural properties, or patterns, we can look at the process of the system more easily. Anthropologists have identified and categorized six main structural types of kinship which occur frequently. Each kinship type is named after a well-known group in which that particular structure occurs. The kinship systems of other cultures are categorized in terms of these six types: Hawaiian, Eskimo (or Yankee-Eskimo), Iroquois, Crow, Omaha, and Sudanese.

Hawaiian

The pattern of the Hawaiian system is a generational one (Fig. 9.26). Thus, in the parental generation, the term "mother" includes mother, mother's sister, and father's sister. The term "father" includes father, father's brother, and mother's brother. In Ego's generation, "brother" includes brother, and all male cousins. "Sister" includes sister, and all female cousins.

Anthropological terminology separates into two categories the relatives which the Hawaiian system groups together, labeling these categories "real" or "own," and "classificatory." *Real* means that the relatives are what their name identifies them as. Thus, biological

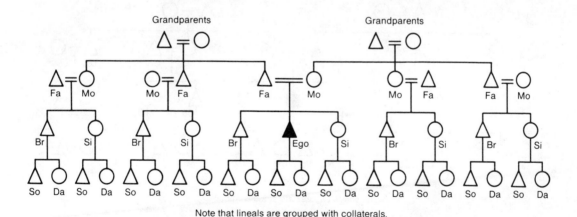

Note that lineals are grouped with collaterals.

Figure 9.26 Hawaiian Kinship Terminological Pattern

mother, father, brother, and sister are all labeled as real or own. *Classificatory* means that the blood relationship of the individuals is different from what they are called. They are being "classified" as what they are not, biologically. Hawaiians, of course, do not make the distinction between "real" and "classificatory" parents and siblings. Anthropological terminology reflects the built-in bias of the English kinship terminology it uses. This is understandable. Every language in the world has a bias toward the kinship terminology used by the speakers of that language.

The Hawaiian generational system is terminologically the least complex of the six types of kinship system. It uses fewer kinship terms than any of the others. This is just the pattern of the Hawaiian system, though. The life of the system lies in its day-to-day effect on human lives—its process.

The process of ambilineal descent often accompanies Hawaiian terminology. Under ambilineal descent, Ego can affiliate with the kinship group of any mother or father. Flexibility of group membership is an important survival asset in situations where massive de-struction is all too frequent. The Hawaiian system occurs in Hawaii, Samoa, and other areas of Polynesia. Life has a peculiar precariousness in this region because typhoons often ravage large areas. It is useful to have many mothers and fathers to go to for refuge.

The Blackfoot and Cheyenne traditionally lived in precarious situations. Warfare and raiding often swept over large areas and harsh winters, with temperatures reaching $-40°$ F could decimate a group. They too used a Hawaiian kinship system.

Eskimo (or Yankee-Eskimo)

Eskimo kinship has a bifurcate pattern. To *bifurcate* is to separate the kinship terms into two branches (Fig. 9.27). The Eskimo system bifurcates parent from parent's sibling. It classifies all male siblings of parents as "uncle" and all female siblings of parents as "aunt." In Ego's generation, the bifurcation of the parental generation appears in the terms for their descendants. Ego's siblings (children of Ego's parents) are "sister" and "brother." In this system, however, all the children of

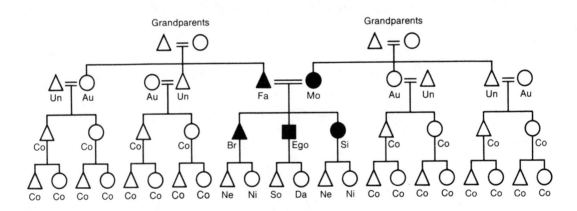

The shaded figures are a nuclear family.

Figure 9.27 Eskimo kinship terminological pattern

148

Ego's parents' siblings are grouped under the term "cousin." In Ego's children's generation are "son" and "daughter," "niece" and "nephew." The Eskimo kinship pattern thus clusters together only parents and children, separating off everyone else.

The structural clustering of parents and children encourages the process of the nuclear family as the active functional unit. Among the Eskimo, this means that a nuclear family can preserve the food it obtains for its own use. Only members of the nuclear family can casually "raid the refrigerator." The lack of strong ties outside the nuclear family also makes mobility comparatively easy, a factor important for Eskimo hunting-gathering life.

The alternate designation of the Eskimo system is the "Yanke-Eskimo" system. The British called settlers in North America "Yankees" to distinguish them as colonials, a group apart from the British on the home island. Mobility to open farmland and to take advantage of other economic opportunities played a key role in colonial survival. The Yankees had, and still have, the Eskimo pattern of bifurcate kinship terminology which isolates the nuclear family. Patterns of present-day North American socioeconomic life continue to emphasize the self-contained nuclear family which moves about in response to economic fluctuations. Because the Yankee and Eskimo kinship patterns are almost identical, the system is often called Yankee-Eskimo.

Kinship processes often interact with other processes. In North American frontier settlements where concerted defense action might be necessary, and where cooperation among nuclear families was vital for survival at times, the process of "neighborliness" arose. Neighborliness was cooperation and mutual help between families living close to one another, and occurred whether they were related or not. Women helped with household chores and fed a family when the mother was ill or in childbirth. Men cooperated at house-raisings and barn-raisings. Neighbors also helped one another at harvest.

In residential areas of towns and cities in North America today, local groups attempt cooperative endeavors based on a new interpretation of neighborliness. Groups can be found in cities in the United States where several related and unrelated nuclear families may pool economic resources and services such as child care and laundry. In many rural areas of the United States there is a pattern of related nuclear families living close together and cooperating for the benefit of the larger family. In these places, other factors partially override the divisiveness of Yankee-Eskimo terminology.

The terminological pattern is thus seen as a flexible structural framework. The many kinship processes and other factors at work determine the nature of the actual kinship system and how it will operate at any given place and time.

Iroquois

Iroquois kinship has a bifurcate merging pattern. To *merge* is to associate different categories of relatives under one term as classificatory kin.

Iroquois terminology merges parallel cousins and their parents with Ego's siblings and parents. Thus, Ego's parallel aunts and uncles are classed as "parent." They are merged with "parent" (Fig. 9.28, 9.29). Similarly, Ego's parallel cousins are classed as "sibling." They are merged with "sibling." Study the Iroquois terminology first from the diagram with an Ego of your sex, after you understand this, study the diagram with Ego of the opposite sex.

Iroquois terminology also bifurcates. Cross-aunts and cross-uncles are separated off as "aunt" and "uncle." Cross-cousins are separated off as "cousin."

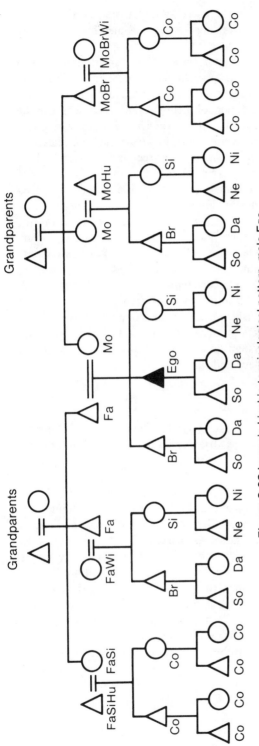

Figure 9.28 Iroquois kinship terminological pattern, male Ego

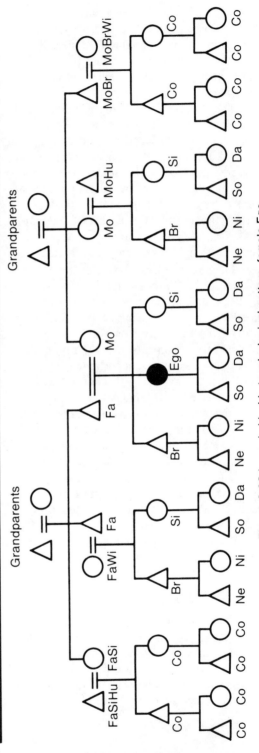

Figure 9.29 Iroquois kinship terminological pattern, female Ego

150

One of the processes often encountered in societies which use Iroquois terminology is sororate or levirate marriage. If Ego's father dies, then Ego's classificatory father (father's brother) may marry Ego's mother in a *levirate marriage*. So when a man dies, his brother marries the widow. By the same token, if Ego's mother dies, then Ego's classificatory mother (mother's sister) may marry Ego's father in a *sororate marriage;* when a woman dies her sister marries the widower.

An advantage of the Iroquois system in aboriginal North America was that if a group was raided or decimated by disease or famine, there were close classificatory relatives to whom one could go for shelter. Also, the alliance of two kinship groups through merging meant that there was extensive hunting territory available to each man because he could use the territory of all the individuals who were classified as "sibling." Alliance could also be extended to groups linked through connections in previous generations. Thus there existed the potential for large-sized offensive and defensive groups.

Iroquois kinship terminology has no strong patrilineal or matrilineal bias because all paternal and maternal cross-aunts and cross-uncles are separated off as "aunt," or "uncle." All cross-cousins are separated off as "cousin." By contrast, in the Crow and Omaha systems, to be discussed next, a special merging of one set of cross-relatives provides a matrilineal bias in the case of the Crow, and a patrilineal bias in the case of the Omaha. Lacking a patrilineal or matrilineal bias, the Iroquois terminology can and does occur with both types of descent. The Iroquois, Seneca, and Mohawk have a matrilineal system of descent and use Iroquois terminology. But the Algonkian have a patrilineal system of descent and also use Iroquois terminology.

Crow

The terminological pattern of the Crow system is bifurcate merging. However, the Crow system is structured to work with the process of matrilineality. Notice that the Crow kinship terminology is slightly different for male and female Ego. First study the diagrams (Fig. 9.30, 9.31) for Ego of your own sex, then study it for Ego of the opposite sex. As you read the following account, study the relevant parts of the kinship diagrams until you have a real understanding of Crow kinship. On the paternal side, the Crow system merges father's brother with father. This means that in father's matrilineage there is always a "father" available to undertake levirate marriage, keeping the alliance intact between the matrilineages of Ego's mother and father. Because the man making the levirate marriage to Ego's mother is already "father" to Ego, there will be minimal behavioral adjustments to make. Ego has already interacted with "father" according to his classificatory kinship status.

On the maternal side, Ego has certain responsibilities toward special individuals within his or her own matrilineage (Fig. 9.31). A female Ego has special responsibility toward those individuals in her matrilineage who are in the status of "child" with respect to her. She is mother to her own children, and to her mother's sister's daughter's children.

A male Ego also has special responsibilities. The Crow "father" (father or parallel uncle) is a "nice guy" who listens to Ego's problems. Each man is responsible for the child of his sister, and of classificatory sisters in his matrilineage. He will pass on his inheritance to those children. The Crow cross-uncle, that is, the mother's brother, is also the authority figure and disciplinarian. This means that male Ego will be the authority figure and disciplinarian to those individuals within his own matrilineage who stand in the relationship of niece

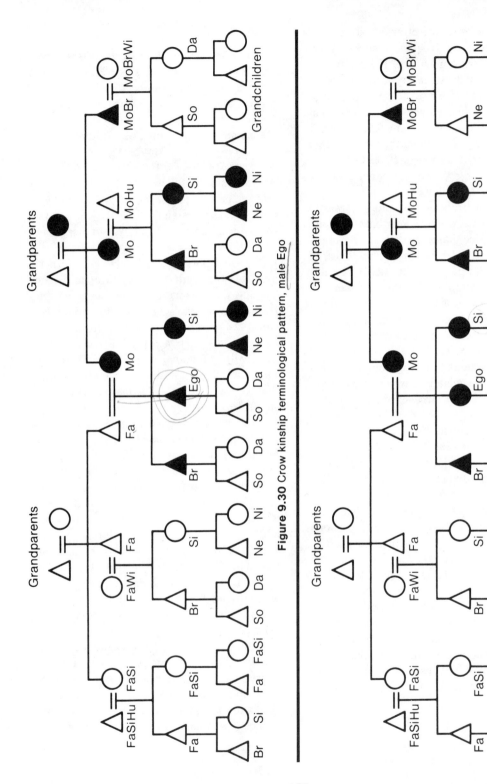

Figure 9.30 Crow kinship terminological pattern, male Ego

Figure 9.31 Crow kinship terminological pattern, female Ego

and nephew to him; these will be his sister's children and his mother's sister's daughter's children.

The Crow system effectively separates out the mother's matrilineage as being of primary importance. It also clearly sets apart the father's matrilineage from all other lineages. This separation delineates those relatives to whom Ego has strong kinship obligations. Ego's primary kinship obligation is to the maternal matrilineage, and Ego has secondary obligations to the paternal matrilineage. Obligations to all other matrilineages are minimal.

Among the Crow there are also close kinship ties between affinal relatives. For example, brothers-in-law are expected to be close friends and loyal to one another. In traditional times, brothers-in-law often rode into battle together and remained side-by-side to face the enemy. If one of them was unhorsed the other was obligated to rescue him by pulling him from the ground and placing him on the back of his horse. If such a rescue was not possible, the mounted brother-in-law had to dismount to join his unhorsed brother-in-law. On foot they faced the enemy together, even if it meant that both brothers-in-law would die.

Among the Crow sisters-in-law are also close friends, and are expected to assist one another in times of need. For example, sisters-in-law help one another after the birth of a child or after the death of a matrilineal relative.

The Crow were originally horticulturalists. Prior to 1750, they lived with the Hidatsa on the Low Plains and gardened, raising corn, beans, and squash. When the Crow moved out onto the High Plains, about 1750, and became the Crow, they gave up farming with one exception, tobacco. The Crow believe that annual planting of tobacco regenerates the tribe. So long as there is tobacco there will be Crow; should there ever be no tobacco, there will be no Crow. Only women who are members of the Sacred Tobacco Society can store and care for

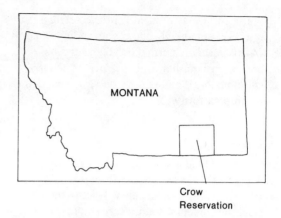

Figure 9.32. Crow reservation

the seed. Only these women can do the elaborate preparation needed before the seed can be planted. When planting time comes, the woman dibble-sticks a hole in the earth, preparing the womb of the earth to receive the seed. Her husband, who is also a member of the Sacred Tobacco Society, puts the seed into the hole and covers it over. Once the seed is planted, the Crow identity is renewed. Great importance thus attaches to mother, the gardener and renewer and sustainer.

In traditional times Crow women widowed during their childbearing years were quickly remarried. But old widows often remained unmarried, and if no one was willing to support them they soon died. Men often died in war, and women in childbirth. Death was a common visitor who left orphans behind. Hence, classificatory parent's rearing of children was important for Crow survival.

The relationship of classificatory parent in one's own matrilineage remains important today. Crow women say that you should always cook more food for a meal than your household alone will need, because you never know who will be coming to dinner. A woman's mother's sister's daughter's child (classificatory "child" to the woman) may drop by the house in mid-afternoon, raid the refrigerator to make a sandwich, and then wander outside. In this perfectly normal behavior for a child in her or his mother's house, performed by a classificatory "child," can be seen the Crow kinship pattern at work.

Omaha

The Omaha system is bifurcate merging. The Omaha system is structured to work with the process of patrilineality. On the maternal side, the Omaha system merges mother's sister with mother. There is always a "mother" available to undertake a sororate marriage which keeps the alliance intact between patrilineages of Ego's father and mother. Because the woman making the sororate marriage to Ego's father is already mother to Ego, there will be few adjustments for Ego to make.

Note that in both the mother's patrilineage and the father's patrilineage, parallel cousins are called "brother" or "sister." But the system bifurcates the cross-cousins, treating maternal cross-cousins differently from paternal cross-cousins (Fig. 9.33, 9.34).

The Omaha system separates out the father's patrilineage as the one of primary importance. It also clearly sets the father's patrilineage apart from all other patrilineages. This separation tells Ego that the primary kinship obligation is to the father's patrilineage, and the secondary obligation is to the mother's patrilineage. Obligations to all other patrilineages are minimal.

The Omaha and the Sioux of the North American Plains had Omaha kinship terminology. Both the Omaha and Sioux were far-ranging hunters whose economy centered around the buffalo. Cohesive male hunting and warring groups were essential for survival. Sororate marriage was a way to provide replacements for women who died, keeping marriage alliances intact between the two patrilineages.

Comparison of the Crow and Omaha kinship systems shows that they are partially mirror images of one another. In each system, lineality is emphasized. The presence of clearly defined kin to undertake sororate or levirate marriage ensures continuance of alliances between lineages. In both systems, also, one lineage is stressed as being of primary importance and the lineage of the other parent is of secondary importance.

But it is essential to note the differences between the two systems. Recall that among groups using the Crow system, mother's brother is the disciplinarian, and father is the "nice guy." Among the Omaha, this relationship is reversed. Father is the disciplinarian, and mother's brother is somewhat like the figure of "uncle" in Euro-American culture. Among some patrilineal groups of East Africa who have an Omaha type of kinship system, mother's brother has a special "joking relationship" with male Ego, a relationship of practical jokes, friendship, and comraderie.

Sudanese

Sudanese kinship terminology is the most descriptive, that is, least classificatory, of the six kinship systems. This system has a separate and distinct term for most relatives, but it still is not completely descriptive. The Sudanese system has terms to distinguish aunts and uncles according to whether they are on the father's or mother's side, and to distinguish cross-cousins and parallel cousins from brothers and sisters. The Sudanese system does classify kin in one case, though. Parallel cousins on both the mother's or father's side are called by the same term. Likewise, cross-cousins from both sides are called by the same term. They are distinguished by sex (Fig. 9.35). This one classificatory category is very important to the people who use the Sudanese system because they practice cousin marriage.

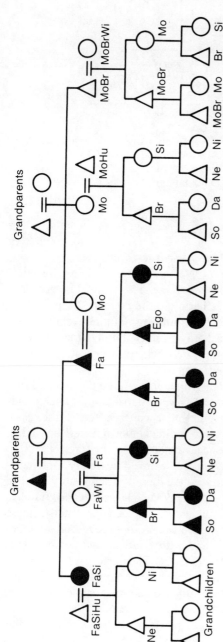

Figure 9.33 Omaha kinship terminological pattern, male Ego

Shaded figures are members of Ego's patrilineage. Note that maternal and paternal cross-cousins are classified differently.

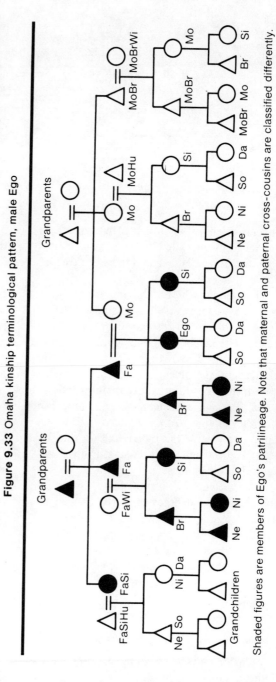

Figure 9.34 Omaha kinship terminological pattern, female Ego

Shaded figures are members of Ego's patrilineage. Note that maternal and paternal cross-cousins are classified differently.

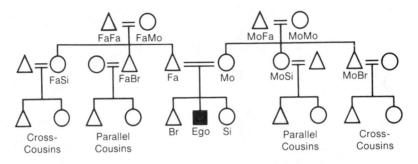

Figure 9.35 Sudanese kinship terminological pattern

Anyone called by the cross-cousin term can be married. Anyone called by the parallel cousin term cannot be married, and these are treated differently.

The groups who use the Sudanese system tend to have complex political systems with differing opportunities for each member of the society. The kinship terminology they use reflects their need to distinguish among all the relatives in the lineage (usually a patrilineage) who have different occupations and opportunities. Sudanese nomads divide up cattle and other mobile possessions according to the status and role of the individuals in the lineage, as reflected in the different kinship terms. Agricultural Sudanese and the Iranians, who also have Sudanese terminology, divide up land, houses, and other property as well as herds, according to the individual's place in the social system. When someone dies, groups with Sudanese terminology know who ought to receive each share of the inheritance, though this does not prevent disputes over the actual apportionment.

Some Uses for Kinship Studies

Kinship plays a central role in human life. Understanding the kinship pattern and the processes associated with it in any particular culture provides a basic background for understanding larger aspects of the culture. For this reason, kinship studies form a major area of anthropological research.

Many North Americans today are interested in genealogy. They want to trace their family's heritage, their "roots." The anthropological kinship diagramming technique is a practical way to draw family trees. In some cases, these may help settle genealogical or inheritance disputes.

The "immediate family," a small extended family seldom reaching beyond grandparents and first cousins, forms the basic kinship unit for many North Americans today. People accustomed to keeping track of kinship only within the "immediate family" find it difficult to read the literature and history of other times and places when large extended families linked numerous people. Traditional Chinese novels, Tolstoy's *War and Peace,* and other fiction abound with relatives and complex kinship connections. The history of Europe is difficult to understand unless the relationships among royalty are known. Complex kinship is found in Greek and Roman mythology, and in religious scriptures including the Bible, the Koran, and the Rig Veda.

To make history and classic literature more readable, diagram the kinship relations as they are mentioned. In this way you can see the type of complex genealogical structure that readers of other times and places have easily carried in their heads.

According to this kinship chart, being my father's sister's daughter's son...you're my dad!

Figure 9.36 (Refer to the Crow kinship diagrams for explanation.) (Cartoon by David Flemming)

Political and economic dynasties still have great power in the modern world. Analyzing kinship to discern the pattern and process of kinship in foreign countries can be useful to business and government in dealing with modern dynasties.

SUGGESTED READINGS

Schneider, David M. *American Kinship: A Cultural Account.* 2d ed. Chicago: University of Chicago Press, 1980.
This work attempts to deal with American kinship apart from familial roles.

Schneider, David M. and Kathleen Gough, eds. *Matrilineal Kinship.* Berkeley: University of California Press, 1961.
This book contains a series of chapters on nine different matrilineal systems and an analysis of the variations these systems exhibit.

Schusky, Ernest L. *Variation in Kinship.* New York: Holt, Rinehart and Winston, 1975.
This book is designed for the beginning student of kinship and attempts to remove some of the abstraction that often confuses the beginner.

Social Structure and Organization

Humans are social beings who constantly interact with other human beings in a variety of social settings ranging from ritualistic religious ceremonies to informal conversations. *Social structure* is the underlying structural pattern of cultural behavior in social interaction. It serves as a guideline which sets patterns and limits for social interaction, while allowing for individual variation. Each culture also has its own *social organization,* the way individuals behave; and the organization of this behavior rests on the ability of an individual to anticipate the behavior of another individual. It is the guidelines set by a particular culture that allows one individual to anticipate the behavior of another individual. For example, within the culture of the United States, when two people are introduced to one another they often extend their right hand and clasp the hand of the other person in a "hand shake"; this ritual is anticipated by both parties involved. However, if one of these individuals is not from the United States, but is a man from Saudi Arabia greeting an American man, the Arabian man may expect a kiss on the cheek rather than a handshake. Social organization is the way in which social structure is actualized in daily life.

In looking at social structure, anthropologists examine what the formal properties of the system are, how the system works, and the ways it changes over time. In looking at social organization, anthropologists examine the way structured human relationships are conducted in daily life, the nature of the interactions, and how behavior alters over time.

Viewpoints

Social groups and social identity form the core of social structure and organization. Social structure and organization can be considered from two separate viewpoints. The *individualist* viewpoint considers how an individual operates within the social structure and how the individual manipulates the social structure.

The *structuralist* viewpoint takes social structure and organization as a single patterned system, and examines the nature of the formal patterning and the way it functions.

These viewpoints provide two different perspectives from which to consider social structure and organization. A brief consideration of *curanderismo* in Mexico and matrilineages among the Crow will help illustrate how the same structures can be looked at in different ways.

The structuralist view notes that *curanderismo* is a folk-healing system found among lower class Mexicans and Mexican-Americans. *Curanderismo* provides an alternative to "modern" medicine. The *curandera* is the practitioner who heals by treating the illness and re-integrating the individual into society. The healer and the patient are usually known to one another. The *curandera* treats each case as unique, has respect for the patient, and considers the patient's entire life as important. The *curandera* asks no fee, but accepts whatever the patient may give as a gift. It is clear how different, and perhaps appealing, this system is in opposition to Western medical systems.

The individualistic view examines *curanderismo* from another perspective, the interpretation and meaning which an individual gives to a particular event. This can be seen through consideration of why a *curandera* takes up that occupation, and what it means to the individual healer. The healer may feel "called" to serve her people and her God. Perhaps the individual feels a psychological need for the enhanced status and prestige the role conveys. Or the individual may be a *curandera* in order to manipulate the system to obtain economic survival. From the individualist view, a combination of these factors may be used to explain why an individual becomes a *curandera*.

A structuralist view of the Crow clan views the clan as comprised of several matrilineages. Each matrilineage is an aggregate of individuals organized together on the basis of shared matrilineal descent. The clan in turn is an aggregate of matrilineages grouped together on the basis of descent from a common ancestor, though the exact relationships cannot be traced. This structural view is analogous to an automobile mechanic doing a structural analysis of cars in general and seeing a piston as one component of an internal combustion engine which in turn is one functional unit within a car.

An individualist view is somewhat analogous to a mechanic "trouble-shooting" a particular problem in a given engine. Here the unique specific functioning and relationships in that one particular engine are important. An individualistic view of the Crow clan system may take the perspective of a particular woman or man seeking financial support to attend community college. The individual will first approach his or her matrilineage with the appeal. The matrilineage will seek help from the clan. The clan uses its political influence in the tribal council to obtain the financial support necessary to send the individual to college.

The individualist and structuralist viewpoint differ markedly. But they are complementary. Taken together, the two viewpoints can lead to a better understanding of the social structure and social organization of a particular culture.

Social Identity

Every individual has a social identity. This identity has many facets, including being a member of a cultural group, speaking a certain language, having a certain age, sex, and personality, and having particular status and role within the culture. The status and role of any individual or group are defined by contrast with the status and role of other individuals or groups. A skilled basketmaker is defined by contrast with unskilled basketmakers. A prosperous village is defined by contrast with poor villages. The elite of a stratified hierarchy is defined by contrast with the non-elite.

As discussed earlier, status and role enable individuals and groups to know, in general terms, what behavior to expect of themselves and of others in social situations. Young children in traditional North American households were taught that when guests are present, "children should be seen and not heard." Young children in traditional Chinese households were taught to scurry away into the private family quarters, because children should not be seen or heard when guests were present. In both cases, the status of "child" demanded a certain role behavior when guests were present.

An individual's status and role define her or his place in the social structure. Wife, hunter, bishop, youngest son, head of the Poro society, trance-medium for El Niño Fidencio, doctor, shaman, farmer, all are descriptions of social identity.

Different cultures place different values on ascribed and achieved statuses. In medieval Europe, the ascribed status of a person's birth

Figure 10.1 A Navajo woman and her horse symbolize millenia of human-animal companionship. (Photograph by Harry Teller)

virtually dictated the course of their life. But in China of that same period, both ascribed and achieved statuses were important. The Emperor and royal family had ascribed statuses, as did low-status boatmen and entertainers. But entrance into the civil-service bureaucracy was by competitive examination, and subsequent advancement depended on performance. In the United States and Canada today, wealth and power are largely achieved statuses, but birth into a wealthy well-connected family will ease achievement of high status, while birth into a impoverished urban ghetto hampers or prevents achievement of high status.

Another aspect of social identity is membership in social groups. Social groups are important components of social structure, and many of the activities of social organization center around social groups.

Social Groups

A *social group* is an organized collection of people who share a group identity, interact with one another to varying degrees, have implicit rules of behavior, and perceive themselves as being a special category of people.

Anthropologists study groups both because groups are interesting in themselves, and because groups often can give insight into the social structure and organization. Groups are entities which, like people, have a beginning, a flourishing, and an end. Some groups last only a short time, while others have long duration. Anthropologists are interested in the precise nature of each group. Why is a particular group important or unimportant at a given time and place? What is the life history of a group? How does a group compare with similar groups in other cultures?

Anthropologists see kinship as a primary organizing principle of social groups. The fact of being born ties every individual to a kinship group. In American society, birth gives an individual ties to maternal and paternal kin groups. Birth ties a Crow to a particular matrilineage and a Chinese to a particular patrilineage.

Kinship, however, is not the only organizing principle of social groups. Residence, age, sex, and common interests are also important organizing principles of social groups. Many times social groups cut across kinship lines. For example, a father may belong to the Benevolent Paternal Order of the Elks and his son belong to the Lion's Club. The fact that many times social groups do not follow kinship alignments makes it possible to establish loyalties between an individual and other members of the community who are not related to him or her by kinship; these non-kinship alignments promote solidarity within the community as a whole.

Residential Groups

Residential units provide clues to the social structure of a group. The band is the smallest territorial unit, and giant nation states are the largest territorial groups. Bands, villages, neighborhoods, tribes, cities, states and nations are all residential units.

Co-residential groups, such as the village or camp, frequently act together. The members of residence groups recognize that they share the same space. In coming together as a social group they lay claim to that common locality. Members of nomadic groups, such as hunter-gatherers and pastoralists, reside together temporarily at a particular time and place. Sedentary groups, such as farmers, remain in one locale for longer periods of time. Shifting cultivators may move to new locales every few years. Among sedentary people, social identity becomes tied to the residential group identity.

Brunei Malays identify themselves as residents of a particular village. Many British and Chinese families trace their lineage back a thousand years or more in a particular place. In North American culture, an individual living in the black district of Seattle, Washington, might lay claim to being black, a Seattlite, a Washingtonian, and an American. Yet, if that individual had been born elsewhere, the place of birth, say Texas, might be more important to social identity.

Sometimes an individual lays no claim to a residential group. One of the characteristics of suburban areas in the United States has been the frequent lack of residential groups which act together. Yet even in urban areas, where the nature of housing itself with small self-contained apartments creates a barrier to residential groups, people sometimes act together in building or neighborhood associations.

Age Groups

Kinship is the basic principle of social organization, and the family is the basic unit of social organization. The family normally encompasses two or more generations. In some cultures, age groups rather than the family, are principle organizing groups. An age grade or age set is a group which is formed on the basis of age, and not on the basis of kinship (Eisenstadt 1956).

An *age grade* is a cultural category related to specific stages in the biological life cycle, such as infant, toddler, adolescent, teenager, young adult, adult, and elderly person. An *age set* is an actual group of individuals who share the same age grade. In some societies members in an age set pass from one age grade to another together. Ideally an age set grows old together.

Among the Nyakyusa of Tanzania, 10 to 11 year old males who are members of a particular age set move off to found their own village in one phase of an initiation cycle. They later bring their brides to the age set village and raise their families there. Sons of the age set village will form their own village at some point, continuing the pattern (Wilson 1963).

In the United States, retirement communities are age group residences. Many of them have formal patterns of activities in which the residents interact as a group or as small subgroups.

An excellent example of an age set is children's play groups. The Bushman boys' play group was a place to learn the elementary skills of hunting and tracking which would be needed for survival. The girls learned elementary gathering skills which would later provide the bulk of Bushman diet (Draper 1975).

Groups often have an obvious function, such as the education and socialization which occurs in children's play groups. But groups may also have important functions which are not obvious. Hitler's youth groups were indoctrinated into Hitler's ideology, giving them a strong sense of social identity, prestige, and power, which allowed Hitler to use the youth against their parents.

Gender Groups

One of the more obvious functions of groups is the separation (and identification) of the sexes. The sexual gender of an individual may allow him or her entrance into certain associations such as men's groups, women's groups, secret societies, and military societies.

However, sex alone is not always the key to membership. Factors such as wealth, rank, power, and supernatural intervention often are needed to open the association doors.

Before the 1970s, anthropologists often disregarded women's groups, or explained them in biological terms. Women, however, are important social actors and come together in exclusive groups based on politics, economics, and religion as well as pregnancy, childbirth, and childrearing. In cultures where women move away from their families at marriage, women's groups are sometimes a form of near kinship.

Women's associations, by stressing women as a collective group different from men, give the women a sense of female solidarity and provide a means to power and influence. Women's groups can range from church clubs to brothels, from tea parties to trading associations, from sororities to political action committees.

West Africa is well known for its prestigious female political and religious societies, such as the Aba women's group of southern Nigeria and the Sande Mende women's group of the Sierra Leone (Leis 1974). Among the Igbo women, membership in the women's trading groups allows an individual to regulate the products sold, their price, and who might sell them in the markets. However, economic control is not the sole issue of these groups. Each village has a women's council which protects women's interests, keeps peace in the village, determines sacrifices to be made, passes laws to protect crops, and polices its own members. The market network serves as a communications channel to pass information among women in outlying villages (Sanday 1981).

The power of the Igbo women's associations can be seen in history. The Igbo women rioted against the British in 1929. The British were implementing a new policy which would

Figure 10.2. Japanese woman

count women, children, and domestic animals as taxable wealth. The Igbo women's trading group met, and decided to protest. A palm leaf, a symbol of trouble and a call for help, was sent to all women in the region. The British quelled the riot after 20 days and implemented their tax policy, but they now knew that the women's societies were a force to be reckoned with (Sanday 1981, Leis 1974).

Women's secret societies are often the source of female social identity. Among the Mende of Sierra Leone, a woman cannot marry until she is initiated into the Sande, the secret society. The Sande protects women's rights, wields religious and economic power and influence, and guards the traditional knowledge associated with being female (Hoffer 1974).

Men also bond together in various groups to establish their social identity by creating and reinforcing male role and status, and by enhancing and supporting male solidarity. The male individual is defined socially through involvement in associations. Military societies reinforce the male role as protector and guardian of the people while investing members with a certain amount of prestige and power. Lowie (1935, 1963) and Hoebel (1954) have described the Plains Indian military societies. In military societies, men come together in warfare and combat. Among the Masai of Africa, most males must pass through a warrior age grade (Forde 1963).

The Zulu *impi* consisted of males in the same age grade who were given the ascribed status of warrior. This military unit not only went to war, but also herded the king's cattle and tilled his fields (Gluckman 1940).

Military societies among many of the Plains Indians served to reinforce the male role as a protector and guardian of the people; the military societies also functioned as a social club, much as the American Legion does today within the United States. The members of a military society were all fighting men. They seldom went to war as a fighting unit, but after battle gathered together in their lodge to relate past war experiences and to enjoy good fellowship.

Plains Indian military societies have been classified into *ungraded* and *graded* associations. The ungraded occurred among the Crow, Cheyenne, Kiowa, and Wind River Shoshone. The ungraded societies were open to any mature male within the tribe. The only requirement was that the proposed new member have a sponsor within the military society.

Among the Arapaho, Blackfeet, Gros Ventre, Hidatsa, and Mandan the military associations were graded in a hierarchy based on age and prestige. Movement from a less prestigious grade to a more prestigious grade was accomplished by a collective purchase of the rights and symbols of the grade above the previous grade. The Hidatsa provide one example of this. A group of Hidatsa young men would band together and offer to buy out the Kitfoxes, the lowest grade military society. When the Kitfoxes accepted the young mens' offer, they, the former Kitfoxes, were without an association until they succeeded in purchasing the next higher grade, the Half-Shaved Head Club, who themselves then had to purchase from the Dogs, who in turn had to buy out the Lumpwoods. This pattern continued up the ranked hierarchy until the oldest men became members of the Bull Club which the Hidatsa considered to be the most prestigious of all the military societies.

Both men and women may join the United States military associations, the Army, Navy, Marine Corps, Coast Guard, and Air Force. Women have only recently been allowed into the prestigious military academies, such as West Point, and at present only men are allowed into combat.

In some cultures, women have been warriors. Women took an active part in warfare among the Dahomeans of West Africa during the nineteenth century, and were organized on the same lines as the male army. These women warriors, named "Amazons" by the Europeans, were the king's guardians. The Fanti company, the elite corps, consisted of famed elephant hunters, the boldest and toughest of the Amazons (Sanday 1981).

Group membership can bring with it certain rights, privileges, and power. Among many African and New Guinean cultures, men's societies allocate to men the power to control marriage, prestige, and economics. This power is vested as their right through the acquisition of sacred knowledge and history. Murphy (1980) in studying the Poro, a men's secret society of the Kpelle of Liberia, concluded that their knowledge of history validates land rights and political claims, giving them economic and political power.

Entrance into the elite of men's associations is often based on power and wealth. Most societies have men's clubhouses which are off-limits to females and uninitiated males. Mythologies, demons, and sacred instruments uphold the men's power. Many of the men's societies in Melanesia build large men's clubhouses. These are on sacred ground, and here the men relax, have fun, create and reinforce social bonds and tell stories.

In many societies of highland New Guinea, the men spend little time with their wives. The men prefer to do men's chores, guard against raids, or hang around the clubhouse. The clubhouse is the center of male life, the focus of male activity in the village, and the source of male identification.

In the United States, upper class clubs for men provide the same focus for activity and identity. Men's secret societies, which have components of mythology and sacred instruments, meet often in the United States. Such societies, such as the Freemasons and Knights of Columbus, are often based on forms of Christian mysticism. Special buildings are used for meetings, and special symbols help members identify one another in the world outside. Many of these groups, like men's groups elsewhere, contribute to charitable community work.

Common Interest Groups

People in many cultures join together to form common interest groups. These voluntary associations may be based on mutual aid, healing, and other shared goals. Fraternities and sororities in Western societies are groups whose common interest is socializing and mate selection.

Some common interest groups center around a particular economic activity. Malay fishing teams, station (ranch) hands in the Australian outback, and members of oil exploration expeditions are all common interest groups centered around an economic activity. A main channel of interaction among adults in the United States are work groups, and many times the work group is a social outlet as well as an economic pursuit. Because the work group has both social and economic importance retirement, or loss of a job, is often traumatic, because the individual is severed from the work group and falls into economic and social decline. Many workplace groups are not cohesive. In the assembly-line factory, workers are viewed as interchangeable parts of the total assembling machine, and are shifted around and treated accordingly. This contrasts sharply with the traditional crafts enterprises where sustained interaction continued over long periods of time. Some of the newer models for factory production, in use in Japan and becoming more popular in the United States, are partial returns to the crafts pattern of sustained interaction.

Social Identity Groups

In a sense, the elite of stratified cultures represent social identity groups. In many countries, the elite of government bureaucracy form social identity groups. In others, royalty and the wealthy have groups which function to provide social networks, business relationships, and marriages.

The social identity of an individual is related to the social identity of the group of which that individual is a member. Ethnic groups are an excellent example of this. In America, individuals may claim allegiance and loyalty to their nation state residence group as Americans. But they also claim an ethnic identity based on shared culture, language, economic position, and occupation. Ethnicity is a prime factor in the formation of groups. It allows the individual to feel a sense of self-worth, validation and power as well as a sense of solidarity (Gluckman 1961). There are many ethnic groups in America, such as the Chicanos, Blacks, Chinese, Irish, Scots, German, Japanese, and Filipinos. Each group has members who identify strongly with their ethnic background.

Rank Groups

Another principle of group organization is hierarchy or rank. Membership in rank groups depends upon an individual's class, caste, wealth, occupation, and ascribed or achieved status. The crown heads of Europe in the century preceding World War I were an elite rank group. They were heads of state living an oppulent lifestyle. They intermarried and constantly interacted with one another. They were above, and apart from, other people.

At the opposite end of the social scale were the informal associations of thieves and fences in Whitechapel, the center of London's criminal world. These often centered around a shop run by the fence, or around a particular tavern. Members exchanged information about where the "pickings" were good. These associations centered around an economic activity. The London underworld of the time had its own social rankings, with pickpockets, safe crackers and thieves having different status.

In many Northwest Coast Indian tribes status was defined according to the class an individual belonged to. Each of these hierarchical statuses was a rank group: nobility, commoners, and slaves.

Caste, the social system found even today in most of India, is a ranked category assigned at birth. India's caste system contains four main categories, Brahmins, Warriors, Merchants, and Farmers/Laborers. Below these are the people who have no caste, and are called outcastes or untouchables. Each caste is a rank group, as are the untouchables. Every Indian person is born into a certain caste, which regulates who may be talked to, eaten with, associated with, and worked with. An individual must also marry within his or her caste, caste endogamy; individuals are locked into their caste and do not have social mobility from one status to another. Each caste is further divided into jatis. A *jati* is usually a group within a caste who have the same name and occupation. There may be 100 to 1000 jatis in each caste. Jatis themselves are ranked within each caste depending on the prestige of a particular jati in the local area. While individuals can increase their status within a jati, they can never move to a higher status jati. And while jatis may increase their status within a caste, they can never move to a higher caste.

Groups reflect and manifest the social structure and organization of a culture. But they also are part of the larger cultural setting. Shifts in social, political, technological, and economic circumstances affect the nature and function of groups.

Changing Groups

Groups may exist over long periods of time or may die quickly. The Roman Catholic Church is a group which has survived for over 1,500 years, changing in certain ways the whole while. At the other extreme are the cliques of high school students which may exist for only a few weeks and professional conference groups which may have solidarity lasting only a few days. Most groups have a duration which falls somewhere between these extremes.

Perhaps the oldest groups of all are children's play groups. They change dramatically over time, and no child belongs to one for very long. But as some children leave a play group, others enter it. Wherever children join in a play group, they continue the unbroken string of children's play groups stretching far back into human history.

Humans form many types of groups, some of which have been described here. Each person lives out a part in the social structure and organization in many ways, one of which is participation in groups. Thus, the study of groups and how they function provides valuable insights into a culture. This study is of scholarly interest to anthropologists. It is also a practical tool for coping with the workplace and other situations in daily life.

SUGGESTED READINGS

Eisenstadt, S. N. *From Generation to Generation: Age Groups and Social Structure.* Glencoe, Illinois: Free Press, 1956.
This work is a comparative study of age grades as well as youth movements in both small-scale and complex societies.

Hammond, Dorothy. *Associations.* Reading, Massachusetts: Addison-Wesley Modular Publications 14, 1972.
This is a review of past and present anthropological thinking on associations and age groups.

Goodenough, W. H. *Description and Comparison in Cultural Anthropology.* Chicago: Aldine, 1974.
This book examines theoretical and methodological issues encountered in the anthropological study of social structure.

Homans, G. C. *The Human Group.* New York: Harcourt Brace, 1950.
A classic work on the structure of human groups.

Merton, Robert K. *Social Theory and Social Structure.* 2nd ed. Glencoe, Illinois: Free Press, 1957.
This work is a modern day classic and presents a thorough discussion of structure and function as used by the social scientist.

Power and Its Uses

11

Power appears in different guises, including political, economic, and religious. Political power deals with law and war, with the ordering of relations so as to maintain reasonable harmony. Economic power has already been discussed; it is related to control over resources and rights to their use. Religious power centers around special connections to other (non-human) beings, or involves formal control of the hierarchy or apparatus associated with religion, and will be discussed later.

Smith (1960:18–19) defines power as "the ability to act effectively on persons or things, to take or secure favorable decisions which are not of right allocated to the individuals or their roles." He defines authority as "the right to make a particular decision and command obedience."

Power is structured and used in different ways, but it basically involves the relationship between one individual in control and another under control. Power involves the control of resources, manipulation of people, creation of and influence over public decisions, the ability to award negative and positive sanctions, and the exercise and legitimacy of force with its inherent possibility of warfare. Control is the key word in the understanding of power.

Anthropologists focus on political power as a viewpoint from which to examine the general topic of power. *Politics* refers to the governing of a body of people, or a society. When large numbers of humans interact in close proximity there is often a perceived need for them to be ordered somehow. Politics is thus a major aspect of social structure and organization.

Political systems are a form of social control. The system is governed by leaders who maintain control over public resources and labor through legitimacy and coercion. In many cultures, power over the public is further enforced by laws. Laws are rules controlling social behavior, purportedly for the good of all. They are used to resolve conflicts and to deal with deviant behavior, however it is defined within a particular culture.

Rationale for Power

Every political system has a rationale which justifies its existence. Anthropologists find that Weber's (1958:1–12) typology of power provides a useful analytical scheme. Weber identified three main rationales for power; these are bureaucracy, traditional authority, and charismatic authority.

In *bureaucracy* officials who are appointed by the ruler, or by the ruling power structure, administer laws; everyone is expected to obey these laws. Bureaucratic power is impersonal, "Its basic idea is that laws can be enacted and changed by formally correct procedure" (Weber, 1958:1).

Federal and state laws in the United States are examples of bureaucratic legal authority. The particular office-holder is irrelevant to the duties of the office. The rules and regulations

Figure 11.1 Military-industrial complex, traditional Pacific style. Construction and operation of the war-canoe consumed significant portions of available resources and man-power; and the sea-borne military contingent was bent on violence and destruction.

which represent abstract norms allow very little room for the consideration of individual differences as to why the law or laws were broken. An example of this is when a law enforcement officer issues a speeding ticket, and the offender argues that the citation is unfair because he had a justifiable reason for speeding. The police officer may counter with, "I don't make the laws, I just enforce them."

Traditional China was a bureaucratic society, with the Emperor as the head of state and the legitimating authority for the laws which were administered by the civil servants. The Emperor had the Mandate of Heaven to rule, but this mandate lasted only as long as the kingdom flourished. When times grew difficult, the people interpreted natural disasters such as earthquakes, successive poor harvests, plagues, and floods or droughts as signs that the Mandate of Heaven had been withdrawn from the Emperor; and they took this as an indication that the time was ripe for revolt. Thus, the strength of the emperor depended upon his grasp on the economic and political structure. China was so large, and communication so slow, that provincial governors often served in effect as absolute rulers within their regions.

To prevent them from becoming entrenched, they were shifted to new posts every few years. But when times were troubled, local warlords arose, seized local power and passed it on to their sons. Suppression of the warlords meant killing them and all members of their extended family; the Chinese euphemistically described such mass killings as, "exterminating the enemy root and branch." Chinese inheritance law required that a man divide his land equally among all of his sons, which effectively prevented the building up of large hereditary estates. But when a dynasty weakened, the inheritance law was ignored, and the warlords built up vast feudal estates. In reality China was so large that no one man could oversee it all, and much of the actual governing was in the hands of the bureaucrats. The emperor might make a decision and issue an order, but the bureaucrats could stymie it by their slowness in implementing it.

The modern equivalents of this rule by the bureaucracy are referred to as "Bureaucratic red tape" and "proceeding through the proper channels." Interestingly, the expression "red tape" comes from the red-colored ribbon-like cords the English used for tying up official files.

In *traditional authority* the rationale for power is "the belief in the sacredness of the social order and its prerogatives as existing of yore" (Weber 1958:12). Traditional authority is impersonal in that its rationale is allegiance to a perceived past; but it is also personal in that people obey whomever is personally in charge because his authority is sanctioned by tradition and perhaps also by divine right. Under this type of authority, the ruler or administrator bases many of his decisions on purely personal considerations, also taking individual differences into account.

In traditional India the king was believed to be a god, and therefore had the right to absolute rule. The same rationale was applied in Egypt and in Rome. When Roman emperors proclaimed themselves as gods, they were following a pattern which contact with the Egyptians had made acceptable in Rome.

One special type of traditional authority is theocracy. A *theocracy* is a state whose political leaders are also its religious leaders. Until the Communist take-over in 1958, Tibet was a theocracy headed by the Dalai Lama. Iran today is a theocracy headed by an Ayatollah, "religious leader." Iranians are Shi'ite Moslems, and justify their theocracy by saying that according to Shi'ite Islam it is the Will of Allah that the religious leader should also hold political power.

Political acts and the taking of political power are often done "in the name of religion." The great medieval monastic estates, and the former papal estate in Italy, used the "Name of God" to justify the concentration of enormous economic and political power in the hands of a few.

In *charismatic authority* the rationale for power is the ". . . effectual and personal devotion of the follower to the lord and his gifts of grace (charisma)" (Weber 1958:12). Charismatic authority is personal. An individual has charismatic authority because of special personal traits, which may be such things as magical abilities, heroic actions, receipt of special revelations, and outstanding powers of mind, speech, and personality. The purest types of charismatic authority are the rule of the prophet, the war hero, and the great demagogue. Ghengis Khan was one such leader, Joan of Arc was another; both of them were in command and given obedience exclusively as personalities, not because of an appointed office or because of traditional sanctions.

Charismatic leadership is strong only so long as the leader strongly exhibits his or her personal powers. For this reason, what begins as charismatic authority often becomes transformed into something else. Ghengis Khan built the Mongol Empire through charismatic leadership, and his sons who continued it also had an air of charisma. But even in Ghengis Khan's time traditional authority and bureaucracy were used as additional rationales for power and authority.

Multiple rationales for power are often at work. In the past, when the Crow Indians were a significant power in the Great Plains, legitimate power among the Crow was a combination of traditional authority and charismatic authority. Historically, leaders of the Crow Tribe and those people in positions of authority were dependent on acts of heroism, power of medicine received during vision quests, and oratorical abilities. Also, there is historical evidence to suggest that certain matrilineages were hallowed by tradition, and that the members of these matrilineages were consistently accorded more positions of leadership than were members of other matrilineages. Crow leaders retained their position of authority only as long as they could demonstrate their powers to the Crow people. "A camp chief served as long as the tribe enjoyed good luck under him . . ." (Lowie, 1935:6). "At present on the reservation, the Crow select leaders using the charismatic and traditional method, which results in tension between the introduced bureaucratic civil service pattern of the Bureau of Indian Affairs and the Crow Tribal Government" (McGinnis 1981:55).

Bureaucracy is a major rationale for, and instrument of, power in most nation-states today; the late twentieth century is a bureaucratized world. But other power factors and rationales, including substitution of military *fiat* (arbitrarily decided upon and completed action) and international economic manipulations for civil law-and-order, often cross-cut bureaucracy. Strong religious and cultural beliefs can be powerful currents battling bureaucracy. "Personalistic, culturally determined loyalties to kin and local groups often defy the more nationalistic ideologies that underlie bureaucratic rationality" (Lomnitz 1988:42). Nor should it be taken for granted that bureaucratic rationality is always the *summum bonum* (highest good, best thing).

Political Anthropology

Political anthropology is the study of comparative political systems world-wide. This study seeks to elucidate how each individual political system is perceived by the individuals directly concerned, and whether there are hidden operative principles functioning. Some anthropological studies examine political systems as sources of social and cultural continuity. Others focus on how political systems change through time.

Political systems vary from culture to culture. Many anthropologists have found it useful to view them as points on a continuum. At one end is the informal political organization found among groups so small that everyone knows everyone else (also called *face to face groups*). Gathering-hunting bands are often of this type. At the other end of the continuum are the large, highly complex political systems of modern nation-states.

The face to face group, or the *band,* is the smallest functioning human group. Among the !Kung Bushmen of the Kalahari Desert, this was traditionally the only type of group. In a band, power is shared; there is no fixed hierarchy. The Inuit of northern Canada and Alaska were also a band society.

Both the !Kung and the Inuit lived in areas where survival is difficult and which cannot support a large concentration of people in one locale. Because it is believed that the earliest humans were also gatherer-hunters, some anthropologists believe that those groups too were band societies.

The *multi-band* political system is more complex than the face to face band. The multi-band has been well documented in aboriginal Australia, where the basic social structure was one of complex kinship ties and clans linked to specific totems. People normally lived in face to face bands, but at certain times of the year several bands gathered together to hold ceremonies. Certain individuals in the multi-band group held power. A man gained access to power by becoming a member of certain male societies. The highest ranking individuals in these societies were the ones who had power.

The aboriginal Australians lived in a harsh environment, but one which periodically had concentrations of food available, thus making possible temporary multi-band encampments. A similar environment probably existed in prehistoric Eurasia and North America during the time of the big game hunters. Thus, some anthropologists who tend toward an ecological-determinist view, believe that these big game hunters probably had a multi-band organization.

The traditional political organization in many parts of Melanesia centered on the *Big Man,* which was an acquired status. The Big Man is economically the central figure of his group. He manipulates social ties and economic obligations in such a manner as to have many people in debt to him. Usually he begins with the support of his kin group. Using their resources and his, he does favors for other people, thus enlarging his group of followers. People follow a potential Big Man because they can see that he is a "mover"; he may be rich some day, and he may make them rich. After he has built up a reserve of favors owed him, he calls in all these debts at once in order to hold a big feast which will shame all his opponents by its size and abundance. Having feasted his entire village, and sometimes members of other villages as well, his status is greatly increased, and he is informally acknowledged as the leader of the group. But the position of the Big Man is inherently unstable. So long as he is the last person to have given a feast, and so has not been bested by someone else, he is the Big Man. But as soon as someone gives a bigger feast, he becomes the new Big Man.

In a *ranked hierarchy* power and leadership depend upon inherited or ascribed status. An ascribed status is one which is assigned at birth, usually by virtue of being born to a particular family at a particular time and place. In a ranked hierarchy, certain families are considered to have a rank higher than that of others. A person born to a family of lower rank can never achieve a higher rank. In contrast, a person who is ascribed a higher rank has access to the power and influence inherent in that rank, but whether she or he actually wields that power or influence depends largely on her or his own efforts and life circumstances. The best-known example of a ranked hierarchy is the caste system of India, in which everyone is ascribed a caste status at birth, and this status cannot be altered. This ranking of social status can be seen in the naming of the castes, as set forth in the Laws of Manu; the name of a Brahmin, the priestly caste, should be auspicious; the name of a Ksatriya, the warrior caste, should relate to power and protection; the name of a Vaisya, the merchant caste, should refer to wealth and prosperity; and the name of the Sudra, the lowest caste, must reflect his despicable menial condition (Polomé, 1989, personal communication).

Nobody's ever seen him, but he sure sounds all powerful!

Figure 11.2 (The cartoonist is making a strong statement about modern American culture.) (Cartoon by David Flemming)

Many African groups have *complex ranked hierarchies.* But the example familiar to most Americans is that of medieval Europe. Here, one was born a serf, a freeman, a low-ranked noble, a high-ranked noble, an aristocrat, or royalty. With very few exceptions, one associated with, and married people of, one's own rank. The majority of the people were serfs and freemen. At the top of the hierarchy was the king who, in theory, had indirect rule over all of the country through the intermediation of the ranks of royalty, nobility and aristocracy. But the lower level units, especially the aristocrats, often acted as *de facto* independent rulers.

Another type of ranked hierarchy was that of traditional China, which operated on a bureaucratic system for nearly 2000 years. In this system, status and rank were achieved through success in competitive examinations, but ascribed status determined eligibility for the examinations. Thus, neither the low-caste people nor their descendants were permitted to take the civil-service exams. In times when the dynasty was strong, the exams did in fact provide a way of upward mobility, and failure to pass them meant downward mobility. As was the case in traditional China and in medieval Europe, complex ranked hierarchies are usually associated with traditional kingdoms.

The *nation-state,* as opposed to a kingdom or an empire, is a phenomenon of comparatively recent times. The Roman Empire was an early nation-state in that territorial boundaries took precedence over all other boundaries, and that massive engineering works ensured rapid communication and movement of troops and goods over long distances. Rome also provided civil engineering for the benefit of the populace, such as public baths, aqueducts, stadia for entertainment and assembly, massive public buildings for government, and markets. Also akin to modern nation-states was the importance of a literate bureaucracy using one standard language, and a standardized military organization. But the Roman Empire differed from the modern nation-state. The emperor was deemed a god, and the central government interfered little in the lives of individual citizens.

The modern nation-state is based upon a concept of territorial unity, fierce delineation and protection of boundaries, and the welding of all those living within the boundaries into a homogenous unit whose prime loyalty is to the nation-state or to its official national ideology. This loyalty is to take precedence over loyalty to kinship groups, residential locale, subculture, religion, or any other type of grouping. Such loyalty is enforced, and all the accoutrements of modern communications technology are brought to bear upon it. For example, in order to leave the town or county in which they live, citizens of the U.S.S.R. must have an internal passport stamped by the police. In Canada the Inland Revenue, and in the United States the Internal Revenue, have intimate details of most individuals' finances. This information is used to ensure payment of the requisite amounts of taxes, which are intended to support the nation-state. And in many countries, such as Malaysia, every citizen over the age of twelve years is issued an identity card which must be renewed periodically. An individual is required to carry the card at all times, and can be fined or jailed for not doing so. The cards provide a way for the government to check on people's movements, to ensure that no non-Malaysian can pretend to be Malaysian, and to prevent people from hiding behind an alias.

Unit Analysis

Another anthropological perspective on political organization looks at the units involved and how membership in those units is determined.

One of the basic units is territory. Territorial units include the territory of gathering-hunting bands, the environmental range of pastoral nomadic groups, tribal areas, villages, towns, cities, kingdoms, empires, and the territory of a nation-state.

Another basic unit is groupings or alignments of people, such as secret societies. In some east African cultures, secret societies such as the Leopard Society keep the power of the king in check. And it was specific power alignments, many of them secret, which resulted in the present rulers of China coming to power some years after the death of Mao Tsetung. Usually, there are standards which one must meet in order to become a member of such a group. In some groups, membership is hereditary; in others, it must be achieved.

Today the nation-state has become the dominant international unit; defense of arbitrary map-lines has become paramount, as has bending the will and resources of the majority to the wants and needs of the ruling group. Since the ideology of any nation-state is an abstraction, rulers face the problems of motivating the loyalty of the people. Often, such loyalty is motivated by the use of coercion. Coercion can be covert, such as the use of flags to symbolize the nation-state, or it can be an overt use of force, such as the threat of legal retribution against any male of legal age who does not register for the draft.

Membership in nation-states is determined in various ways. In the United States, citizenship is by birth within the United States or by naturalization. In France, a person is a citizen by virtue either of being born in France, or of being a woman who has married a Frenchman. In Indonesia it is determined by the citizenship of one's father. As can be seen, the rules vary, but there is always a way to determine the insiders (citizens) and the outsiders.

Checks and Balances

It is not enough to look at the structure of a political system, for this tells us little of how it actually works. In order to understand the operation of a system, we need also to investigate the ways in which various elements in that system function together.

Power, and especially political power, is not static. It waxes and wanes, it alters and shifts. A power structure must have a base of support; in the case of politics, that support usually comes from those who are ruled. If power becomes excessive, the will of the people to provide that base may be sapped, and the power structure either erodes gradually or is overthrown violently. An extreme instance of such erosion was noted in the case of the Indians of Central Mexico. After the Spanish Conquest, chroniclers related that the Aztecs and others were so dispirited by being conquered and forced to work as slaves that women and men refused to sleep together, because they did not want to bring other humans into the world to suffer their fate (Taylor, pers. comm.).

In order to fully understand a political system, one of the most important aspects to be examined is the ways in which the balance of power is maintained, because political systems can be as complex as the myriad power relationships involved in maintaining the balance of the political system. This is especially true in the case of nation-states, which often have formalized means of maintaining such a balance. These means are sometimes referred to as "checks and balances."

The United States' Constitution formalized the system of separate executive, legislative, and judiciary branches to keep the government in check. The military, for example, is under the ultimate command of the President, but the military budget is determined by the legislative branch. This is to prevent militarism and military take-over.

Almost everyone today lives in a nation-state. The current nation-states carefully demarcate their boundaries and control the flow of people across those borders. Control of borders is not a new phenomenon. The Great Wall of China formerly served to keep invaders out of China, and to keep peasants in. (This was to prevent peasants on marginal farmland in the north from succumbing to the temptation to become pastoral nomads.) Today, double rows of barbed wire and electronic systems surround all the land borders of the U.S.S.R. These guarded boundaries are indeed a defense against invaders, but they also serve to prevent citizens from leaving the country illegally. The U.S. does not prevent people from leaving its territory, but it does maintain border patrols and customs officials to prevent people from entering the country illegally and legally.

"Coyotes," a Mexican term for one who smuggles people illegally across the Mexico-U.S. border, earn their living by playing games with the border officials. Even a U.S. citizen can be denied entrance, if she does not have a passport or other proof of her American citizenship in her possession when she tries to cross the border; and she will be scrutinized with special care if she speaks Spanish and does not have a white skin.

The world is indeed turning into a mutually suspicious armed camp, with nation-states constantly hostile to one another, just as the feudal entities of medieval Europe were constantly hostile to one another.

Politics must serve two countervailing purposes. It must maintain group cohesiveness to a working degree, while at the same time providing enough outlets for differences so that dissidents do not fission off. In the modern world many regimes refuse to tolerate any dissent. In these cases, there is no system of checks and balances on the power structure, except by natural attrition. When there is no room for differences, dissidents are forced to eventually overthrow the government or to set up a separate government of their own.

By studying political systems, anthropologists achieve a greater understanding of the lives of people who live within certain social structures. The application of insights gained by political anthropologists can help in the search for world harmony and peace.

SUGGESTED READING

Bohannan, Paul, ed. *Law and Warfare, Studies in the Anthropology of Conflict.* Garden City, New York: Natural History Press, 1967.
This work contains a collection of articles dealing with conflict situations in various cultures and problems of how these conflicts may be evaluated and handled through the process of governance.

Fallers, Lloyd. *Bantu Bureaucracy.* Chicago: University of Chicago Press, 1965.
This book deals with the political development of tribal society in Uganda and focuses on tribal social organization in relation to political organization of the people of Uganda.

Fried, Morton. *The Evolution of Political Society: An Essay in Political Anthropology.* New York: Random House, 1965.
The author applies evolutionist theory to the development of governance systems.

Mair, Lucy. *Primitive Government.* Baltimore: Penguin, 1962.
This work deals with the subject of law and order in small societies. The writer demonstrates the importance of kinship and lineage to governance in a small society.

Nader, Laura, ed. *Law in Culture and Society.* Chicago: Aldine, 1969.
This work is a compilation of articles dealing with law in various societies throughout the world.

Religion

12

As humans we face the mysteries of birth, life and death, all of which help mold humans into cultural beings. Humans use symbols as one way of giving meaning to existence. Religion can be seen as a symbolic statement which helps to explain the unexplainable and to justify human existence, through use of belief systems, rituals, specialists, and certain "sacred" objects.

Religion as a cultural symbol is intertwined with all areas of culture, including economics and politics. The nature of religion varies widely from culture to culture. This makes it difficult to define religion adequately, and even more difficult to arrive at a definition which reflects the importance of religion in the social system as well as the importance of the specific aspects of a given religion in a specific culture.

Geertz's (1979:79) definition of religion is "(1) a system of symbols which acts to, (2) establish powerful, pervasive and long-lasting moods and motivations in men by, (3) formulating conceptions of a general order of existence, and (4) clothing these conceptions with such an aura of factuality that (5) the moods and motivation seem uniquely realistic." This definition is discriminating, yet it is broad enough to be used as a definition of religion as a cultural system.

Anthropologists have used four major approaches to the study of religion: (1) evolutionary or the search for origins, (2) functional, (3) structural, and (4) expressive or symbolic. Regardless of the approach used, the comparative anthropological study of religion helps us to understand the meaning of religion and the meaning given to religion by its participants in human societies.

Evolutionary Approach

Much of the intellectual ferment of the nineteenth century centered around the concept of evolution. It seemed to many that if plants and animals had evolved from earlier, more "primitive" forms, human culture and society must also have followed a course of evolution from early "primitive" forms to the modern, complex, "advanced" forms. Scholars sought to establish what the origins of particular cultural features had been, and to trace their evolution to the present.

Working within the evolutionist framework, the British scholars Edward Tylor and James Frazer sought to trace cultural features such as religion, economics and politics through a series of evolutionary stages. They assumed, as a matter of course, that "civilized man," such as the Englishman, was at the apex of evolution, while "primitive man," such as the Australian aborigine, occupied the bottom rung of the evolutionary ladder. And women, of course, were not included in the scheme at all. Anthropology during this time used the concept of "primitive" versus "civilized" to study the customs and traditions of "others." Ultimately evolutionists sought to find out how human culture had been at the very beginning of time.

Figure 12.1 These Brunei schoolchildren are gathered on the greensward for a special celebration near a district mosque. The helicopter in the distance could use the green for a landing-field. (Photograph by L. A. Kimball)

Tylor maintained that religion had passed through four major stages, beginning with animism and animatism, and continuing on to polytheism. The final, most "civilized" stage of religion was monotheism. Tylor argued that along this continuum one could plot all the variations and gradations of religion. Tylor gave "belief in spirit-beings" as his definition of religion. Though anthropologists have rejected his "evolutionary" scheme, Tylor's view of religion was radical in its own time. As Europeans encountered many different people throughout the world, many of them assumed that the people they found were not human because they had no belief in the Christian God. Tylor's definition allowed Europeans to see religion in a different way. However, even in the twentieth century there are those who still believe that anyone who does not believe in one particular religion's specific concept of God are condemned to endless suffering after death.

Animism attributes the concept of "soul" to animate and inanimate objects. Animism populates the earth with spirits. These spirits are held to be the cause of many of nature's puzzling phenomena. Animism perceives unusual rocks or trees as having some sort of spirit living inside. Hills and mountains may have spirits, as they do in the Shinto religion of Japan.

Totemism is found among groups which practice animism. Totemism recognizes a special relationship between humans and certain animals or natural phenomena. Kinship is assumed between a social group and the mystical animal or phenomenon. Among the Northwest Coast Indians, clans traced their ancestry, special privileges, powers, and rights to their totems. Thus, if a Tsimshian belonged to the Eagle Clan, that individual claimed the powerful Eagle as first ancestor, and had the privilege to wear the dress and sing the songs of one who belonged to the highest class of leaders. Totemism is associated with ranked societies. Emile Durkheim, the French sociologist who studied the religion of Australian aborigines, argued that totemism was the origin of religion because of the social functions of totemic ritual.

Many cultures believe that spirits can possess either inanimate or animate objects, that spirits can freely run in and out of objects. Possession is a widespread cultural phenomenon which occurs in some form in all the major religions. Judaism and Christianity believe that the "devil" can possess people; religious specialists must perform rites of exorcism to expel the devil. Among many Hindus, spirit possession is a valid sickness and must be handled in the appropriate religious manner, involving a Brahmin priest, offerings, rituals and prayer.

Fetishism involves the manipulation of the spirits for an individual's advantage through the use of special objects. Charms, talismans, and amulets are fetishes. The fetishes are believed to attract the spirits and influence their actions in an individual's life. A rabbit's foot in American culture is thought to bring the wearer good luck.

In *idolatry,* the fetish object is changed into an idol. An idol is a physical object which serves as a permanent dwelling place for a spirit. Each idol has its own personality or spirit. Thus, the statues of the Buddha in some monasteries represent a manifestation of the Buddha to a devout Buddhist. The statue of a deity in Hindu temples is an idol, venerated as being a physical manifestation of the god, and receives regular worship as the god.

The early Christian missionaries thought it their religious duty to destroy "pagan" idols, images of peoples' gods, in order to spread Christianity. In Mexico, the rich legacy of cultural artifacts associated with the Aztec religion was destroyed by the Spanish in their religious and colonial zeal. But some of the

That amulet not only keeps away evil spirits, but also everything else.

Figure 12.2 (Cartoon by David Flemming)

Spanish friars were interested in Aztec culture and wrote descriptions of it. Because religion is a people's philosophy of and for life, an invading or dominant group who wish to subjugate a people does so in large part by forbidding them their religion. Thus, the Moslem Mughul conquerors of India destroyed many Hindu temples in order to forcibly subjugate and convert the Hindu populace.

Animatism is the belief in an impersonal power or force that is inherent in certain phenomena. This sacred power does not have physical form itself, but can be contained in or can inhabit physical forms such as rocks, priests, rivers, or can reside in events and natural phenomena.

Mana is a Polynesian term given to an unseen power or force which may inhabit physical form or may manifest itself in events

Figure 12.3. Japanese Buddha

and natural phenomena. Mana is a strong power, an unseen impersonal force that can be either evil or good. It must be treated with great care if ordinary people are not to be harmed by it. In this respect, mana can be seen as analogous to electricity. Ordinary people who handle high-power electric lines will be harmed, but skilled electricians can handle these lines safely, though there is always the danger of harm through carelessness. An ordinary person contacting someone or something inbued with mana will come to harm, but those who are properly qualified to deal with mana can contact the mana safely.

Mana is not always permanent. Polynesian chiefs who suffered defeat in battle were believed to have suffered defeat because they had lost their mana. A chief needed mana, so a defeated chief was replaced by another who did have mana. Inanimate objects such as rocks may contain mana. A peculiarly shaped rock lying in a garden which produces lots of yams is assumed to have mana. However, if the yams do not grow as well next time, then the rock has lost its mana.

Many cultures have a concept of mana. Among the Crow, this unseen power was called *maxpe*. *Maxpe* was a vital life force and the sun was the ultimate symbol of *maxpe*. To acquire *maxpe*, a Crow had to be very close to nature and have a vision. The Sioux call the power *wakandaa*, the Iroquois know it as *orenda*, and when Moslems of North Africa speak of *baraka*, they refer to mana.

According to the evolutionary view of religion, the generalized spirits of animism become a specialized species of deities which constitute a pantheon of beings. This is *polytheism*. The supernatural beings each have special qualities, powers, and functions related to their relationship with human individuals. The pantheon of deities may be organized along kinship lines which mirror the kinship system used by their believers. The social structure and ordering of the gods, spirits, and lesser spirits often parallels the social structure and order of their supplicants; in effect, the social structure is a microcosm of the cosmic structure.

Brunei Malay folk belief shows this paralleling of the human and non-human world. The Brunei Malays are devout Moslems, but like most Malays, they also recognize a world of spirits.

Just as humans have different lineages, Brunei Malay folk belief recognizes that spirits have lineages. The lineage descended from the devil includes illness-causing *hantu* and other evil spirits. The non-devil descent line bifurcates. One descent line contains various giants, the other the inhabitants of the Kingdoms in the Clouds.

The deities made kingdoms and had royal lineages in the Kingdoms in the Clouds, just as humans in Borneo made kingdoms. The chief rulers of the Kingdoms in the Clouds were Batara Kala and Batara Indra, two brothers sired by an unknown father. Batara Kala and Batara Indra are able to pour out great force and energy, even intervening in human affairs. They are the grandfathers of the great god-kings: thus, they are the distant ancestors of the earthly kings. The folk belief is that kings are special beings and have a portion of deity-power because at least part of their distant ancestry is divine. When people refer to the Brunei Sultan as Batara Indra, they mean that he is the supreme ruler of all the Brunei Malays. Some old people say that the Lord sent a Prophet to destroy the Kingdoms in the Clouds. Others say that perhaps the Kingdoms are still there.

Just as humans are sometimes mischievous, so too are certain spirits. Deity-like *diwa* spirits and *mambang*, the trickster spirits, often had sexual relations with women on earth. A favorite trick of the mambang spirits was to put their children into an edible fruit. A woman who ate the fruit became pregnant, even though she was a virgin, and gave birth to the mambang child. Thus, humans give their gods human attributes, the capacity for love, hate, war, and even sex.

According to the evolutionary study of religion, the final and highest stage is monotheism. *Monotheism* is the belief that one supreme being created everything and is the one and only deity. Christianity, Judaism, and Islam are all monotheistic religions.

But even cultures which practice monotheism do not fully relinquish belief in other spirits. In Christianity, the Christmas tree, yule log, and many other celebrations surrounding Christmas have pre-Christian roots. Similarly,

Easter eggs trace back to pre-Christian fertility symbols. Many Christian beliefs about ghosts, spirits and good-luck charms are non-Christian items incorporated into active folk belief which can have a powerful influence on behavior. In the 1950s in the Republic of Ireland, a road crew refused to continue work on a road which would go through a fairy castle. The engineers had to revise their plans, and detour around the castle. Today, the road makes a sudden curve to avoid what appears to be an empty field to those who do not know of the castle.

Functional Approaches

Why is religion important to humankind? What is its function in human society? How does it structure human behavior and thought? These questions were asked by functional anthropologists in their comparative anthropological studies of religion. Durkheim of the French sociological school focused on religion as a unified system of beliefs and practices relative to sacred things. He stated that the function of religion was to foster and perpetuate the kinds of human behavior necessary to social existence. He saw religion originating in the moral order of society itself.

Functionalists such as Malinowski analyzed religion in terms of what it could do for and to individuals. Malinowski's (1948) *Magic, Science, and Religion* looks at those three systems and their interrelatedness. Malinowski defined religion as a response to the needs of cultural survival. A classic distinction made between magic, religion, and science is made by looking at how humans attempt to control the world. Magic is an attempt to control the supernatural by manipulation. Religion is an attempt to control the supernatural through supplication. And science is an attempt to deal with *natural* phenomena by controlling things

and events in the external world. But in reality magic, science and religion overlap, and the distinction is blurred. Religion is viewed as being the belief in supernatural forces combined with particular ways of behaving because of such beliefs, and this is an adequate description of magic. It is worth noting that in the systems of knowledge of the Western world, many things that were once viewed as supernatural are now thought of as natural phenomena, explainable through science. For example, people who found old stone hand axes in the eighteenth century presumed they were thunderbolts cast down from heaven during the battle between God and Satan. Now they are interpreted as early tools made by prehistoric people. Saint Elmo's Fire is no longer considered a ghostly haunting of ship's rigging, but is known to be the flicker of static electricity.

In general, the functionalists looked for examples of how religion worked for the individual and for society as a whole. The modern functionalist Wallace examined the intention of the performer and the ritual. Looking at these intentions, Wallace argues that religions have five basic functions. The first is the control of nature. The Hopi rain dance was a religious ceremony designed to control the weather. Second, religion functions to make people sick or well. Shamans in West Africa can cure sickness and Voodoo doctors in Haiti can cause illness. Third, religion serves to organize human behavior. Islam regulates the dietary, prayer, and social habits of its followers. Fourth, religion can change pathological, or abnormal, behavior. Mexican *curanderas* act as indigenous psychiatrists through ritual and ceremony. And fifth, religion can revitalize a society through messianic cults or revitalistic cults, such as the Ghost Dance religion of the Plains Indians in the nineteenth century. Wallace (1966) maintains that these five functions can be used to explain almost all aspects of religion.

Myths are the oral or written narratives of a cultural group. The schemings and jealousies of the gods in Greek and Roman myth mirrored the schemings and jealousies in society. For the non-literate religions, myths reveal that all things have a supernatural origin and history. Through ritual, a category of behavior associated with belief, the myths acquire a sense of being. For example, the enactment of creation myths by specially costumed men during male initiation rites in aboriginal Australia taught the myths to the new initiates. But it also made the myths real to all the participants and observers. This sense of reality with its sacred connotation and validation is applied to all areas of human life, and gives those areas meaning. Thus, as Eliade (1976) says, the very acts of eating, sleeping, working, playing, and having sex are colored and valued as being sacred. The couple in a Hindu wedding walk around a sacred fire just as the gods did in their weddings. A woman baking puffed rice for her son may think fondly of Krishna's mother making puffed rice for him when he was a boy. Myths can be social charters and sacred narratives.

Structural Approaches

Structuralists approach the study of religion from another perspective. Structuralists seek to elucidate how the elements of one system, such as religion, relate to the elements of another system, such as politics or economics. Claude Levi-Strauss (1976) has analyzed myth and ritual in an attempt to determine how cosmological myths mirror the ordering of society. The structuralist analysis of religion and the social structure reveals that religion is thoroughly a part of politics and economics.

Another structuralist approach is that of Van Gennep (1960). He looked at the way rituals cluster about certain stages of life, and discerned that the transition from one life stage to another is often accompanied by ritual which he called a "rite of passage." Rites of passage marking birth, initiation into adulthood, marriage, and death occur in many cultures.

Symbolic Approaches

Religion may be seen as a symbolic statement of social order which includes thought and behavior. Symbolic analyses of religion look at the symbolic constructs of belief, ritual, symbols, and their cultural meanings. Two concepts which have been explored by symbolic anthropologists are the sacred and the profane.

Sacred and Profane

Sacred and profane, holy and unholy, clean and unclean are concepts used to order the religious conceptual universe. Sacred deals with the extraordinary, and profane with the mundane. A church is sacred, an office is profane. Attitudes toward the profane reveal an acceptance of things on a basis of common familiarity, and attitudes toward the sacred reveal a sense of awe and mystery. In India, Hindus hold the cow sacred, and will not eat beef. Moslem men consider menstruating women unclean, and forbid them to pray or fast. Hindu men deny menstruating women entrance to temples and forbid their attendance at weddings.

Men who have returned from killing on a hunt are often considered profane and unclean until they have gone through a ritual purification. Among the Papago, men who brought home a scalp were considered "ripe," and as dangerous as a menstruating or post-partum woman. They had to undergo a ritual purification that defused their potential malevolent power into a benevolent power (Niethammer 1977).

Sacredness may indicate a special connection to power and therefore the need for careful handling. Traditionally, churches are

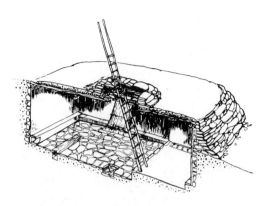

Figure 12.4 The Hopi ceremonial kiva symbolizes the Hopi cosmology, in which the Hopi came from the bowels of the Earth up to the Fourth World where they now live. A hole in the floor of the kiva links the present world with the spiritual world.

sacred ground in Euro-American culture. Graveyards too were sacred, thus, people spoke of being buried in the church's "hallowed" or holy ground, and burial was denied there to suicides and others who had transgressed certain religious laws or mores. To have a profane burial outside sacred ground meant disgrace and disfavor in the afterlife.

Most cultures have a way to set off certain spaces as sacred, apart from the profane. However chaotic the everyday space may be, sacred space is well-ordered. The segmenting of space into sacred and profane allows an individual to step outside the boundaries of the mundane into an area where the supernatural is closer. In many cultures, sacred temples are miniature replicas of the world, a form of temporal symbolism (Eliade 1961). Thus, among the Crow the sacred lodge represented the worldview and cosmological ordering of the world.

The Navajo make a particular area of ground sacred for one healing ceremony. The medicine men chant and sprinkle corn flour on the ground to purify it. They then use colored sands to make a sandpainting on the ground.

The painting establishes a special connection between humans and the world of spirits. After the ceremony is complete, the sand is carefully taken up again and ritually disposed of. The ground then reverts to its profane daily use as the floor of a hogan (the Navajo six-sided house).

Objects are often imbued with sacredness. In Christianity the Bible is a sacred symbol of divine revelation and truth. Swearing on the Bible in United States law courts has the meaning "If I tell an untruth, may God strike me dead," because the Bible is sacred. Followers of El Niño Fidencio, a Mexican folk saint, regard the pirul tree (California pepper) as sacred and having special curative powers. The pirul tree is where El Niño Fidencio is said to have received the divine revelation that he was to be the "healer of healers."

A Marxian concept, "celestialization," refers to the use of the sacred to achieve political and economic power. Celestialization uses myth and ritual under the symbolic sanctions of pollution, purity, danger, duty, and sacredness to mystify political and economic reality. Thus, the power of many religions' elders is validated through their knowledge and use of the sacred. Many religions' elders and leaders have been able to dictate their social controls over the group as a result of their "divine right." The power of the mullahs (religious officials who also hold secular rule) in Iran is an example of celestialization. The Ayatollah Khomeini, as head of the mullahs and the country, justifies his position through celestialization.

Sometimes, a person becomes vested with a special power that consecrates that individual as a representation of the sacred. The crowning of the English monarch, who is also head of the Anglican church, has the symbolism of being conducted in a religious ceremony. The monarch rules by divine right, that is, by special dispensation from a god. This is symbolized by the monarch holding the scepter of a leader and a golden vessel for consecrated oil. On the monarch's head is placed a crown, and the crowning by the Archbishop of Canterbury, the religious leader of England, symbolizes the special connection between the monarch and the deity.

In ancient Egypt, Pharoahs were manifestations of the ruling deity. The people worshipped the Pharoah not merely as their ruler, but as their god on earth. The Inca rulers also were believed to be living manifestations of their deities. Many African tribal groups, such as the Ashanti, considered their kings, queens, or leaders as mediators to and representatives of their deities. Power under the guise of religious sanction is a predominant theme in many cultures, one that may be explored through the symbols of the sacred and the profane.

Elements of Religion

Religion is a belief system. As with any system there will be the firm believers, the tagalongs, and the doubters. In many cultures, religion permeates everyday action and thought, as Christianity did in medieval Europe. In such situations, one must accept the religious code or there will be ramifications in other areas of life. An individual who openly breaks the religious code may be ostracized by society at large and by the kin group. Religious tagalongs obey the system's demands, but without deep emotional commitment. Doubters may seriously question the truth of the religious system, or deny it outright, but they may observe religious demands to avoid ostracism or the consequences of being wrong.

In cultures where religion is not important to daily life, many attitudes toward it may exist. In these cultures, other activities may carry near-religious significance. The Queen's Birthday in England, Independence Day in the United States, and May Day in the Soviet Union are ritual ceremonies affirming nationalism. In American culture, football draws

Figure 12.5 At the turn of the century this Franciscan friar went to the ruins of an old Spanish mission in Arizona to say a special prayer in memory of those who had gone before him. (Photo by Harry Teller)

large crowds on weekends. The functions and rituals of sports in many places might be seen as religious.

Belief Systems Concerning the Dead

Many beliefs and rituals surround death. The rites for the dead serve to conduct the deceased into the realm of the dead and to help reestablish the social fabric of the living, to restore society to an integral whole. Every culture has distinct beliefs regarding the fate of the dead.

In many cultures, there is a belief that the dead inhabit another world. Tylor (1979) categorized beliefs about life in another world into continuance and retribution. Continuance in the other world means that life continues on in a manner similar to life on earth, but in a different place. The Crow believe that their dead cross the Slippery Log and live as they did before in a camp with all the other dead Crow. Retribution means that an individual will be rewarded or punished after death, depending upon his or her actions during life. The Christian and Islamic beliefs hold that there will be a final judgement day when the world ends forever. On that day all the dead will be judged according to their life and religion on earth. The judgement will either condemn them to hell or raise them up to heaven. The ideal afterlife in the Christian and Islamic traditions is eternal residence in heaven.

Another widely occurring belief about life after death is that the essential essence of the person will be reincarnated (*re,* "again" and *incarnate,* "made flesh") in a new body. Depending on how the individual lived in the last life, the new birth will be better or worse than the one before. Hinduism and Buddhism believe in reincarnation after death. The ideal life after death in the Hindu and Buddhist traditions is release from the endless round of rebirth, an escape.

Nature of Humans

Most religions believe that all humans consist of the physical body and the spiritual body, or soul. The spiritual body, the soul, is often considered the breath of life. The Hindu tradition speaks of *prana,* "breath of life." Some cultures believe that the soul may consist of several parts. The Egyptians of ancient times believed that there were two different souls, *ba* and *ka.* Each went by different roads to the underworld (Gardiner 1961). The Tztozil-speaking Maya Indians in South Mexico believe that there are two kinds of souls, *chu'lel,* "personal soul" and *chanul,* "animal familiar soul." The *chu'lel* is said to have 13 parts. One of these 13 parts may wander off while a person is sleeping, and what that wandering soul experiences are dreams. Sometimes one of the 13 parts of the inner soul gets lost or is stolen by a witch. The treatment for "soul loss" illness consists of finding the lost part of the soul and restoring it to the person. The *chanul,* the animal familiar soul, is revealed to the village priest by supernatural beings at a child's birth. The ancestral gods water, feed, and care for the *chanul* soul. The Tztozil believe that whatever happens to the animal familiar soul also happens to the person (Vogt 1970).

Literate and Non-Literate Religions

Most humans who ever lived had non-literate religions, which did not have or depend on a written body of texts. However, they had access to an effective oral tradition. The religious beliefs and rites were preserved in song, dance, and story. The history and lore of a people could be recited by a religious practitioner in the manner that other practitioners had recited before.

Rituals are reenactments of the original sacred acts. "Thus the gods did; thus men do" (Eliade 1976, citing the *Taiiriniya Brahmana,* I5, 9, 4). Sacred dances often told a story related to the rituals taking place—marriage, death, healing, and initiation. Followers of the Bhakta devotional worship cult express their dedication to and love of God through the medium of song and dance.

The stories and myths were cultural treasures, keys to the sacred past and examples for incorporating the sacred into the temporal world. Recitation of the myths was usually the prerogative of certain specialists, such as shamans, priests, and religious leaders of secret societies. "It is the specialists in ecstasy, the familiars of fantastic universes, who nourish, increase, and elaborate the traditional mythological motifs" (Eliade 1976:9). In pre-Norman Ireland, the responsibility of telling stories and myths belonged to the bards, who studied for years to become proficient. While these bards were not religious specialists, they did have special powers as judges.

Not until the beginning of writing in Egypt and Mesopotamia in the third millenium B.C. do written religious texts appear. It is significant that many of the earliest writings are religious verses and tax records.

Religious authority resides in many locales. For non-literate religions, authority resides in oral myths and legends. Religious authority among the traditional Crow resided in myths and legends of the elders because they were the oldest and held the traditions, and with the shamans because they had received information directly from the supernatural. For the literate religions, authority resides in both religious specialists and in the body of texts itself. The Torah and the accepted bodies of written commentary on it are the religious authority of Judaism.

The authority to interpret or re-interpret oral or written religious texts resides in a person or persons, in a particular caste or class, in the wisdom of the living elders, or in *dogma* ("opinion, decree"), a body of commentary about sacred texts and religious practices. In the Roman Catholic system, the Pope is the supreme religious authority residing on Earth. In India the Brahmin caste is the holder and interpreter of the sacred Vedic texts of Hinduism. Among the Kpelle of Liberia it is the elders of the Poro, the men's secret society, who hold the oral wisdom of the tribe.

Many of the major literate religions believe that theirs is the "true" key to ultimate salvation. Each has its own elite corps of teachers, ritualists, and intellectuals who have the authority to transcribe, interpret and teach the "truth." These religious practitioners set the moral code of society. In the Roman Catholic church, the clerical hierarchy are the religious elite. They transmit and interpret the received truth, and tell believers how they should behave in all aspects of life.

However, when the dogma of the dominant religion, the ideal version, becomes intolerable or when it neglects the everyday reality of life, change occurs. The common folk reinterpret the ideal ideology and practices so that they are compatible with and applicable to the realities of life. The reinterpretations of the great religions become *folk religions*.

The Fidencismo of Northern Mexico is a folk religion which is a synthesis of Catholicism and belief in possession by spirits. The Mexican folk healing system, *curanderismo,* is a major part of this folk religion. Craig (1984) investigated the origins and practices of Fidencismo. Fidencismo was founded in the 1920s. At that time, the dominant religion, Roman Catholicism, neglected the realities of everyday life. The Catholic belief is that if an individual wants God to grant a favor, such as healing a sick person, a special ceremony or ritual must be held by a priest. However, most of the villages in Northern Mexico were too poor to build a church and support a priest. Thus there was no priest available to perform these services, and had there been, the people were too poor to pay for the rites. In addition to this, the Mexican government had effectively disempowered the Catholic Church. If a couple were married in the Catholic Church, the state did not officially recognize the marriage until a civil marriage had been performed. Thus, in effect, the Mexican people were left bereft of religious specialists and had no spiritual recourse available to handle the frequent troubles of life.

Then El Niño Fidencio received his revelation under the pirul tree that he had been blessed by God with the gift of healing. He

Figure 12.6. Hindu dancing temple woman

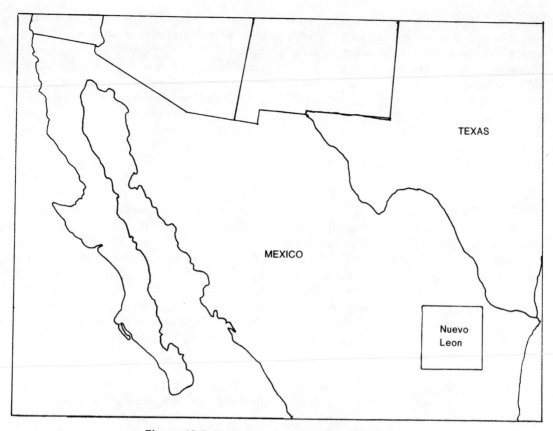

Figure 12.7. Nuevo Leon: home of El Niño Fidencio

came to fulfill the priestly role of intermediary between the people and God, and performed rites to help the people. Other "divine" healers also appeared throughout Mexico during the 1920–30's.

Northern Mexican culture already had the beliefs, reaching back to pre-Catholic times, that a soul could be lost from a person and another would take possession of that person, and that an ordinary individual might receive special revelation which would elevate him to a high spiritual status and role. Thus, El Niño Fidencio fulfilled a need which the dominant religion did not. After his death, the people canonized him as a saint because of the many miracles he had performed, but the Catholic Church refused to do so. He is thus a folk saint,

recognized by the people but not by the official hierarchy. The Fidencismo movement continues today, for the same reasons that it succeeded in the past.

Today trance-mediums are possessed by El Niño at special ceremonies. El Niño, acting through the trance-medium, heals people and performs rites of baptism, marriage, and shriving. El Niño is an accessible intermediary between the people and God. Devotees follow the "road" of Fidencio in hopes of receiving eventual spiritual salvation. But the path is not easy, and followers repeat over and over, "The road of Fidencio is very hard." Used within a religious context, the metaphors of "road," "path," and "ultimate way," imply a journey toward spiritual attainment (in Christian terms, salvation). Through Fidencismo the people have an intimate and immediate interaction with the supernatural because El Niño Fidencio's spirit can be present helping them in the here and now. The Fidencismo cult was not an isolated phenomenon. Similar folk saint cults developed elsewhere in Northern Mexico, for the same reason that the people lacked access to an intermediary with God. Many of these folk saint cults remain active today.

Religious Practitioners

Religious practitioners are technicians of the sacred (Eliade 1976). These technicians cure sickness, direct communal prayer and ritual, help guide the souls of the dead, and protect the community from spiritual harm. There is a certain amount of magico-religious power inherent in the status and role of religious practitioners. Often, the religious practitioners are the intellectuals of the community, the storehouses of history and lore as well as sacred knowledge.

Religious practitioners may be non-specialists, prophets, priests, shamans, healers, medicine men or women, or others. Prophets claim to foresee the future and to make predictions. Many prophet's voices ring out in the Old Testament of the Bible. Priests are full-time specialists. They are usually associated with complex societies, social ranking and hierarchy, and the advanced food production technology that allows individuals to participate in specialized fields. Healers and medicine women or men are specialists who concentrate on maintaining the spiritual and physical health of their people. Shamans are medicine men or women, priests, and spirit guides. All religious practitioners act as mediators and play an intermediary role between supernatural powers and the ordinary people.

The word "shaman" is of Tungus origin, *saman*. The Tungus shamans of Siberia are experts in curing and divining. An individual can become a shaman in three ways: by inheritance, by divine call or election, and by personal quest. A shaman must acquire techniques of ecstasy in order to play the role. The shaman must be able to leave the physical body at will in order to wander over the earth and to spiritual realms.

Among the Eskimo, the novitiate shamans must be able to see their bodies as skeletons, divested of all flesh. They must then meditate on and number all their bones while searching for their meaning (Eliade 1964).

Shamans deal with the spirit realm. They make a formal voyage to the spirit world in an effort to bring back a human spirit that has been captured, and so to heal the person who is sick because the spirit has been stolen. Apprentice shamans make formal voyages into the spirit world to learn how to be a shaman. Shamans often have a familiar spirit or spirit helper, one particular spirit who helps the shaman in his or her endeavors.

Trance-mediums may or may not be shamans, but they are individuals who can be possessed by one or more spirits. In many cultures, if an individual receives the call to be a trance-medium and rejects it, she can expect to go crazy or become severely ill unless she makes the appropriate appeasing rituals to the spirits. This was so among the Brunei Malays until trance-mediums were outlawed after World War II.

Most trance-mediums are women. Being a trance-medium brings with it a certain amount of prestige, status, and power. Thus in Haitian voodoo cults and the Mexican-American spirit-possession cults, women appear to be the dominant actors (Craig, 1984).

The familiar spirits who possess trance-mediums may make mischief, but usually they are invoked to help cure illness. In Fidencismo, certain healers take on the spirit of El

Niño to cure or bless their followers. During religious fiestas celebrating the Niño's birth, death, and saint's day, the spirits in the guise of their trance-mediums walk among the people. The saint's presence in the trance-medium is usually signified by a change of costume and behavior. Behavioral change in possession trance state is common cross-culturally (Bourguignon 1976).

Daily Life

In daily life, many people attempt to apply religion to solve their problems. What is labeled "superstition" in English is religion from an anthropological perspective. Rubbing a rabbit's foot to ensure good luck on an exam is a type of religious practice, because it is an attempt to make the unseen force of "luck" favor the person taking the exam.

One and the same event may be interpreted differently in various cultures. In the United States, a black cat crossing one's path is considered bad luck. But for the Brunei Malays it is good luck, because the black cat is the "cat taught by the gods." In certain areas of the United States, if an individual were to start speaking "nonsensical talk," some would say he was "touched" by the Holy Spirit. But many people do not share this religious belief, and would place a different interpretation on the performance.

Religion is important not only when religious rituals occur. Religion permeates culture. The belief systems associated with religion contribute to an individual's world view or world philosophy. Thus, all activities will be measured and tested against religious attitudes. The concepts of sacred and profane, clean and unclean, polluted and dangerous, address daily occurrences. These concepts, when codified and justified by a religious belief system, are reinforced through ritual behavior and thought. The concept of sacred ground and sanctity has allowed the Christian church since medieval times to be a refuge or sanctuary from outside forces. During the 1980s, this religious concept is being tested in the political arena in the United States as various churches declare themselves sanctuaries for the Central American political refugees in opposition to current government policy.

Many Mexican-American and Mexican families, especially among the lower class, have home altars. These altars, often just a little shelf or small table in a corner of a room, are decorated with statues and pictures of Virgin Mary, Jesus and other personages of the Catholic pantheon, candles and an assortment of other items. Women are the mediators at these home altars. They act as informal intermediaries between the Catholic pantheon and the family. Extra candles and incense may be lit, promises made, prayers sent, and hopes sent forth at this altar for such things as good luck on an important exam, proper functioning of the family car, or guidance and protection of the family.

Function of Religion

Religious observance often has key social functions. Malinowski (1948), as noted above, stated that religion is a response to the needs of cultural survival. But what of the function of religion for the individual, not society? Religion serves to make order out of chaos. It is the ultimate explanation and answer. Through religion an individual has access to power and seeks control over life. Humans are symbolic animals and, next to language, religion is the ultimate symbolic system. Through religious beliefs and philosophy the individual creates a world view and a working model of the universe.

Figure 12.8 This Moslem woman is saying one of her five daily prayers.

Religion functions to alleviate the damage to the social system when death or disaster occurs. It allows the living to go on living, knowing that the dead will be taken care of in the afterlife. And it gives succor and help to those who must cope with unexplainable illness, hunger, poverty and war.

Religion functions as a form of social identity. An individual's religious identity may close or open doors in other areas of life, such as marriage, politics and economics. The traditional pattern in small town America was that young people in a church would often become husband and wife, finding their spouse within the religious group. In Fiji today, a strong element of social identity is first, whether one is ethnically of Fijian ancestry or of Indian or other ancestry, and among those of Fijian ancestry one's religious affiliation is a strong matter. It will determine with whom one socializes and identifies.

It is certain that humans will always face the mysteries of life and death, and seek to cope with them. In this respect, humans always have had and always will have those patterns of behavior and thought which anthropology calls "religion."

SUGGESTED READINGS

Lehmann, Arthur C. and James Myers, eds. *Magic, Witchcraft, and Religion: An Anthropological Study of the Supernatural.* London: Mayfield Publishing, 1985.
This book contains a collection of articles by some of the better known anthropologists in the field of magic and religion. The articles range from traditional to non-traditional themes.

Less, William A. and E. Z. Vogt, eds. *Reader in Comparative Religion.* New York: Harper and Row, 1972.
This reader is the most well-known in the field of anthropology. The book deals with a wide variety of religious and magical phenomena. The articles discuss magic and religion as a response to human needs.

Malinowski, Bronislaw. *Magic, Science, and Religion, and Other Essays.* Garden City, New York: Doubleday, 1954.
This is a classic work on belief systems in small societies. The author covers such subjects as religion, magic, faith, and death with a convincing and readable style.

Norbeck, Edward. *Religion in Human Life: Anthropological Views.* New York: Holt, Rinehart and Winston, 1974.
This book presents a comprehensive view of religion from an anthropological perspective. The work is clearly written and is recommended for the beginning anthropology student.

Food

13

Food sustains human life and society. Serving, preparing, sharing, discussing, and manipulating food involves many different aspects of culture. By analyzing and understanding the symbolism of food in all its cultural applications, we can enhance our holistic understanding of culture.

The technological aspects of getting food are directly connected to the major strategies humans use to produce things to eat. There are five basic categories of economic strategies for survival: hunting-gathering, agriculturalism-horticulturalism, pastoral nomadism, peasant and non-peasant farming, and industrialized technology. (These were discussed in Chapter 5.)

The practical techniques of obtaining food vary with specific details of ecology and environment. Is the food grown or harvested from the land or sea, or through gathering or hunting on land or sea? The Indians of the Pacific Northwest Coast had a saying, "When the tide is out the table is set" (Johnson, pers. comm.). At low tide there were so many types of food to be gathered from the tidal flats, such as clams, mussels, seaweed, and sea urchins, that one could make a meal of them. Practical techniques of obtaining food include the manufacture and use of items associated with procurement, preparation, serving, and storage of food. Such items range from boats, plows, and windmills to spears, baskets, cooking pots, plates, and eating utensils.

But there is more to food than practicalities of economics, technology, and material culture. Food has symbolic importance in culture, an importance which touches on many aspects of culture, including religion, pollution beliefs, sex roles, status, mediation, and global hunger.

Food Selection

What is considered food in one culture may not be appreciated or recognized as food in another. Instant, fried witchity grubs would not sell well in the United States, but on the Pitjantjara Reserve in Australia they might be a hot best-seller. The Japanese eat a lot of seaweed, but most Americans do not, except in hidden form as an ingredient in commercial ice cream. Each culture has distinct flavor preferences. One person's spice is another's poison. English diners accustomed to rather bland cuisine do not appreciate the explosively spicy curries of the Sri Lankans. Americans who delight in Roquefort and other strongly-flavored cheeses disdain Southeast Asian fish pastes.

The stereotypical American is a "meat and potatoes" person. But to a Brunei Malay, food is rice and rice is food. "Makan sudah nasi kah?" ("Have you had rice?") means "Have you eaten?" At one wedding feast, as a special treat (because "White people like grilled steak") the visiting anthropologist was handed a five-pound grilled steak to have for a snack. After eating until she was full, and sharing it with several others, she staggered up, only to hear the old women say, "You poor thing, you

Figure 13.1 Navajo women rub two ears of corn together in order to remove the corn grains from the cob. They then grind the grains of corn to make flour. (Photo by Harry Teller)

must be starving, you haven't eaten yet!" The solution was to take and eat a little rice. Only then had she really eaten.

Every culture defines what is or is not edible food. Moslems and Jews find pork repulsive, and Hindus are revolted at eating beef. These food taboos are validated and justified by religious belief systems. To Moslems pork is offal and filth; to Hindus the cow is sacred. Mary Douglas's symbolic analysis (1966) of the food taboos found in the Old Testament in Leviticus revealed that those creatures considered abominations and unfit to eat are those anomalous animals that the ancient Semites could not fit into their defined animal classification. These included pigs, and fish without scales.

Anomalies of the plant and animal world, those that cannot easily fit into a defined category, are usually the objects made sacred or taboo by people. Sometimes food that is scarce or dangerous to obtain is made sacred. Only individuals holding particular status, such as royalty or shamans, are able to eat the food without violating its sacredness. Anyone else eating the food will die or come to harm.

Food taboos often accompany those liminal events in life where the transitory state of the individual is considered potentially harmful to the general welfare of society. The food taboos associated with pregnancy, birthing, menstruation, initiation, death, and warfare symbolize the cultural concerns and beliefs regarding these potentially dangerous and status-changing situations.

Food as Status Marker

In ordinary life, the food eaten often makes a statement about social status. Beans and corn tortillas form the staple diet of Mexicans of lower socioeconomic class. Members of the higher classes seldom touch such food; they eat a diet more like that of the upper class in Spain. Middle-class Mexicans eat beans and corn tortillas as a staple, but supplement them with Spanish-style food. Different foods are associated with different statuses. Filet mignon has a high status in North America, and hamburger does not. For the Chinese, wonton soup is average food, but bird's nest soup and shark fin soup are prized and very expensive delicacies.

Prime rib is a desired meat in the United States, but peanut butter sandwiches are a basic protein staple food for many people. The United States Government subsidizes food through Food Stamps. The allotment and use of these stamps is a status marker. A woman who buys prime rib cuts and brie cheese with Food Stamps may be accused of misusing them. Food Stamps are supposed to be used for the basic foods necessary for lower-class life, not for luxury food items associated with the middle or upper class.

How a culture allots tasks related to the production of food provides the anthropologist with valuable insights into the social structure and other cultural factors such as sex differentiation and social ranking. In North America today, as in many cultures, everyday preparation and serving of food is considered women's work. In hunting-gathering societies such as the !Kung Bushmen and the Crow, women are the primary providers of staple vegetable foods. In sedentary groups, food preparation becomes more complicated, and the sexual division of labor with respect to activities associated with food is marked. Grains must be brought in from the field, dried, milled or pounded into flour or meal, and then cooked into bread or some other grain-based dish. Much of this is considered women's work in many societies.

Men and women do not always eat the same foods. In many cultures only men are permitted certain cuts of meat or access to certain foods. These prestige foods function as markers of sexual differentiation. Among

Figure 13.2 Pueblo woman grinding corn on a large stone metate, her grinding instrument is a stone mano (roller). The window of another apartment in the pueblo is visible through the doorway.

the Mbum Kpau of southwestern Tchad in Africa, a class of prestige food—white porridge, beer, and meat, particularly chicken and goat—is accompanied with eating prohibitions and unequal food distribution (O'Laughlin 1974). Women are forbidden to eat chicken or goat under the penalty of pain or death in childbirth, or sterility. Beer and white porridge are allotted to the men first. In Fiji, only upper status men were normally allowed to eat fishheads (Dauunica, pers. comm.). In traditional Brunei Malay households, the men are served first; only after the

men have eaten do the women eat. This pattern of serving food is found in many cultures where the role of women is culturally defined as subservient to the male role.

The sharing of food is often an important cultural item. The functions of food sharing are intimately intertwined with the kin and non-kin relationships. Food sharing serves to cement relationships. "I feed you, you feed me," is the basis for sharing food in all the basic subsistence economies. Among the !Kung, a woman shares food with her kinswomen, thus cementing kinship ties and ensuring that if food is scarce, the kinswomen in turn will share their

Figure 13.3 Pounding rice is a hard chore which women must do every day in Borneo. Rice is "the staff of life," and the rice mortar and pestle also symbolize the creation of life. (Photograph by L. A. Kimball)

resources with her. "Wining and dining" is a modern version of food sharing, as are pizza parties.

Food sharing often serves as a marker of group identity and membership. Among many North Americans, being invited to dinner by people of higher social status marks success for the "social climber." Dining at the "right" or "in" restaurant also serves to indicate group identity or membership. In similar fashion ethnic communities hold dinners to serve as status reminders and boundary markers that reinforce an individual's ethnic identity and loyalty to the ethnic group.

Food serves as a status marker and mediator. "Breaking bread together" has a rich Southwest Asian meaning of being guest and host, and therefore friendly, and of being fortunate to have enough to eat, which is carried over into European culture. Food has affected the course of battle. En route to the Battle of Copenhagen, Admiral Nelson had a falling out with his commander. To smooth things over, he had one of his sailors catch a delicate whitefish. Nelson sent the fish to his commander who was inordinately fond of it, and the commander relented and restored amicable relations with Nelson (Warner 1958). The provisioning of armies has always been crucial, as Napoleon's words, "An army marches on its stomach" express.

Status and other cultural statements also appear in the types of utensils used in serving and eating food. Status and formality of occasion appear in the silver service for North American dinners. Figure 13.5a shows the ordinary place setting for a daily meal.

This place setting alone is a considerable comment upon the culture. The presence of a plate shows that the food will be eaten from a plate. It will not be eaten from a banana leaf as it would be in southern India, nor from a rice bowl as in China. Each individual person has a plate. Food is not to be taken from a common wooden dish as it was in farm households of Europe until recent times. Hard crusts of bread will not be used to hold food, as they were at the tables of important personages in medieval Europe. And, whatever the food is, it is something that needs a plate to hold it, as the tortilla-wrapped beans of a Mexican peasant do not. The cup or glass shows that each individual has a separate container for drinking beverages. A common dipper or jug will not be passed around as it often was in medieval Europe. The liquid will be consumed with the meal. A glass of water at one's place in a traditional Brunei Malay house, though, is meant not to be drunk but to be used for hand washing.

Figure 13.4 Kitchens and cooking habits are specific to each culture. This Brunei woman is using a three-foot long *parang* (machete) as her kitchen knife. She is preparing goat-meat for a special feast. Note the kerosene lantern in the background; at night it provides the only light for cooking.

The knife, fork, and spoon are European eating utensils. Traditional Chinese would think them most uncouth, saying that the work of cutting up meat and other food is something that ought to have been done by the cook in the kitchen. Solid food can then be eaten with chopsticks and one need only use a porcelain spoon for soup, though it is acceptable to eat the solids from soup with chopsticks and then to drink the liquid from the bowl. In India or in the Indonesian world, the right hand is the traditional eating utensil, and there is an elaborate and detailed etiquette of the proper way to eat with one's fingers.

Most Americans today sit down to meals with small and utilitarian place settings. The elaborate American place setting uses many more plates, liquid containers, and eating utensils (Fig. 13.5b). A century ago, many upper middle class households used such a service quite commonly, but they had household servants to lay the table, serve, and clear away. Servants also did the cooking, washing, and other chores such as shining the silver, sharpening knives, cleaning and mending the table cloths and napkins. Few people have servants today, and few women do the arduous chores necessary for elaborate meal service. The need for economy of labor has led to a simplification in place settings.

Consumption of food in ritual circumstances varies widely. Eating at banquets on the international diplomatic circuit is expected to be dainty and almost more of a tasting of many courses than a vigorous consumption of any of them. Ritualized overeating characterizes the United States

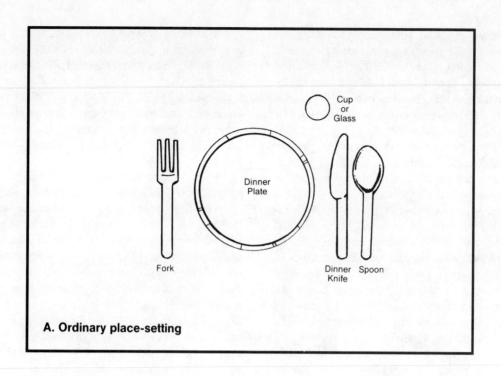

A. Ordinary place-setting

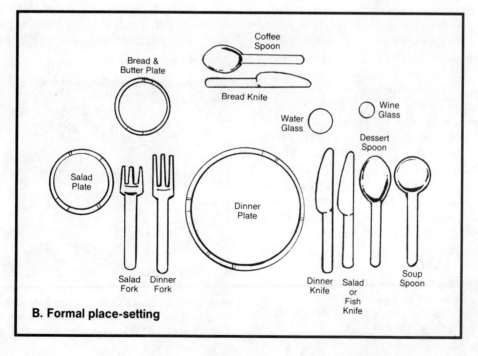

B. Formal place-setting

Figure 13.5

Thanksgiving feast, where hostesses often feel insulted if the guests are not literally groaning with satiation. Muruts in Brunei feel insulted if guests have not gorged until they physically cannot stand up. This is particularly true at a funeral feast, where eating beyond surfeit is a sign of proper mourning.

Preparation of food is a major task. Farmhouses in colonial America had spring houses, either as part of the basement or as a separate house built into the side of a hill. Here, cool spring water kept butter at a constant temperature winter and summer. Many colonial houses had two basements, one beneath the other, each used for storing different kinds of food. Luxury in a colonial house was having a spring house opening off the lower basement. Meats and many vegetables hung in rows in the kitchen to be cured and preserved by the smoke from the wood cooking fire.

In the tropics, spicing and sun-drying is a frequent preservative. Indians of the Pacific Northwest Coast fileted and sun-dried or wood-smoked the fish they caught during the salmon runs to preserve it for year-round use. Medieval Europeans controlled spoilage to convert milk to cheese, which can be stored for long periods of time. Controlled spoilage of protein as a preservation technique produced Chinese fermented bean curd, Malay belachan shrimp paste, and the fish sauces of Thailand, Vietnam, and the Philippines. Salting and pickling are two other traditional preservative methods. Modern preservation techniques include freezing, refrigeration, gamma radiation, and the use of assorted chemicals. Until the 1950s, fresh citrus fruit was an expensive and prized winter treat for people in the northern United States.

Obtaining food, sharing and eating it, or lacking food, are major factors in human life. Prolonged insufficiency of food causes lethargy and susceptibility to disease. Protein calorie malnutrition in the early years of life can cause life-long mental retardation. A prominent problem in the industrialized world today is over-nutrition, prolonged excess of food consumption. Over-nutrition, too many fatty and highly refined foods, aggravated by lack of exercise or by spurts of excessive exercise alternated with lethargic inaction, causes serious health problems in the industrialized world today.

Humans in many times and places have faced dietary difficulties. Early sailors often suffered from scurvy, caused by lack of vitamin C due to the shortage of fresh fruits and vegetables in their diets. Victims of scurvy became weak and bled easily. Old wounds reopened, their teeth loosened and fell out, and their bodies became masses of sores. Finally, if the disease continued, they died. British sailors have the nickname "Limey" because the British Navy discovered in the late 1700s that a regular ration of lime juice prevented scurvy. American Indians of the Midwest often had excessive tooth wear because of the grit in their corn diet. This grit came from the stone grinding instruments used to make the meal.

Figure 13.6 "The old and the new." Traditional Brunei Malay brass cooking pots sit beside a modern steel bucket and a small aluminum cooking pan.

Medieval peasant diets in Europe often lacked adequate protein, while the diets of the rich were excessive in protein and fat, but inadequate in fruits and grains. American settlers in the Midwest often suffered from goiter because their crops grew on soil lacking iodine, and they ate only fresh-water fish which lacked the iodine of sea fish. Goiter formerly was common in interior Borneo for similar reasons. Today iodized salt provides the trace amounts of iodine needed to prevent goiter.

Equitable sharing and distribution of food has always been a problem, and remains so on a global scale today. The comparative anthropological analysis of food getting and sharing strategies provides a tool which can be used in solving our global food problems.

SUGGESTED READINGS

Farb, Peter and George Armelagos. *Consuming Passions.* Boston, 1980.
This work attempts to show the relationship between how people eat and other qualities of their society. The authors employ a cross-cultural approach to the analysis of the selection, preparation and consumption of food in various societies of the world.

Kuper, Jessica, ed. *The Anthropologists' Cookbook.* New York: Universe Books, 1978.
A presentation of global gastronomy in a cookbook format that includes cultural insight as well as intriguing recipes.

Bates, Marston. *Gluttons and Libertines: Human Problems of Being Natural.* New York: Random House, 1980.
The pursuit of pleasure through food and other areas is discussed in this informative book.

Health and Illness

14

Illness and suffering form part of every human life. This is why the ultimate goal for Hindus and Buddhists is release from the endless cycle of rebirth which they believe an individual otherwise suffers. People in every culture experience illness, injury, or incapacity; but they try to prevent such events, and to treat them when they occur. This is the subject of medical anthropology—how people in different cultures deal with illness, injury, and incapacity.

Current anthropological theory is based on Western modes of thought and investigation. One main purpose of anthropological concepts and theory is the systematization and understanding of non-Western modes of thought. Medical anthropology examines all phases of medicine cross-culturally, including definitions of health and illness, etiology of illness, epidemiology, and treatment of illness.

Definitions of Health and Illness

Health and illness are culturally defined. For many people illness means the inability to continue with their daily round of activities. Modern Western medicine recognizes incapacity to work as being illness. But modern Western medicine also classifies as "sick" an individual who is able to continue work but who has certain bodily processes which deviate from a standardized norm. For example, a person can have blood sugar levels or blood pressure levels which are considered too high or too low, and they can continue to work.

Modern hygiene and medicine enable many people in modern Western society to enjoy an unprecedented level of wellness and freedom from physical discomfort. For example, good nutrition, sanitation, and clean laundry help prevent chronic skin ulcers and abcesses that once were a part of life for many. A degree of bodily discomfort and lack of abundant energy that Americans would call sickness or ill health is an everyday state of being for much of the population in Third World countries. But people in those countries would say that they are "healthy" because they are able to keep on with daily life. According to their definition, only absolute incapacitation constitutes "sickness." Feeling unwell is a normal state of life. When individuals, for whatever reason, can no longer continue with daily activities, then their culture will deem them sick.

Etiology of Illness

"Etiology" comes from two Greek words, *aitia* meaning "cause" and *logia,* "description." Thus, the etiology of illness can be seen as the cause assigned to a particular disease or condition. Every culture has its own set of etiologies, and treats illnesses primarily on the basis of their etiologies. Many cultures believe that witches or sorcerers can send harm, illness, or even death to an individual. Many of the peasants in Mexico blame all illnesses on witchcraft. These Mexican peasants then treat the disease by hiring a sorcerer, or *brujo,* to

Figure 14.1 Tlingit shamans used masks, such as this one, in healing ceremonies to invoke the supernatural in aid of healing.

counter the power of the other *brujo* who sent the illness. When the power is effectively countered, the patient will recover.

Another widespread belief is that evil spirits cause illness. The way to treat the illness is to drive away the evil spirit. Prevention consists of avoiding places where such spirits lurk, and wearing amulets so that even if people do encounter an evil spirit, it will not harm them. According to this etiology, evil spirits sometimes strike violently. One old man in Brunei spent his days crouched on the back porch of his house. His wife said that he had been perfectly normal, a father happy to see his grown children well-married. One day he went down to the river and he must have met an evil spirit because when he returned home he no longer talked to people but just sat hunched in a corner. He spent more than a decade crouched up on the porch, fed and bathed regularly, but otherwise isolated.

The traditional Brunei Malays fumigated baby clothes over the kitchen fire so they would smell smokey and evil spirits attracted to the "sweet" smell of a baby would be repelled. In the Mediterranean world there is a belief that certain people can harm others by looking at them. These people have an "evil eye." Many people wear charms to ward off the evil eye. In Mexico, children wear a charm called an *ojo de venado,* deer's eye, which is said to ward off the evil eye. The charm is not an actual deer's eye, but a special nut threaded on a red string. The color red has the meaning of protection. Often, they put the picture of a folk saint or the Virgin Mary on the string too, to add extra protection.

Imbalance is commonly held to be a cause of illness. Traditional Chinese medicine attributes illness to an imbalance in the flow of vital energy through the body. The medicines of India and medieval Europe both attributed illness to an imbalance of "humors," emotional substances thought to exist in the body.

"Immoral" behavior, however it is culturally defined, can also be seen as a form of imbalance. In this case, balance is often thought to be restored through "paying for one's sins." Thus, during the Reformation in Europe, a common explanation for disease was that it was visited upon a group or individual in retribution for their sins. In the 1980s, Acquired Immune Deficiency Syndrome, with its accompanying homophobia and moral censure, is also being attributed to retribution for sins.

Until recently, Western medicine dealt with illness in terms of a mind-body duality. For this reason, mental illness was viewed as distinct from physical illness. Western medicine has now begun to recognize the interconnectedness of mind, body, and the total life environment. In many other cultures, however, mental illness is perceived as one of many sicknesses (including physical) which incapacitate people.

Many disorders which would be classified as mental illnesses in Western medicine are culture-specific. "Running amok" is a Malay illness. A person who runs amok breaks into a sudden homicidal rage, grabs a weapon, and attempts to kill everyone in sight. The only way to stop the person is to kill him, or less often, her. Among the Eskimo an individual (most often a woman) may in the middle of the long winter night see terrifying spirits. Suddenly, she will run naked into the blizzard outside, a lethal behavior. Sometimes the person can be restrained or brought back, but often she dies.

Cultural change and stress often cause mental or physical illness, or both. For example, among Southeast Asian refugees in the United States, there are cases of vigorous men in the prime of life who die suddenly in their sleep. They simply wake up, yell, and then die. And American folk wisdom recognizes that a recently widowed person may sicken and soon follow their spouse in death, and that too much happiness and excitement can make one ill. The phrase "too much of a good thing" expresses the concept that balance is necessary for health.

Figure 14.2 Navajo medicine man creating a sand painting

Treatment of Illness

When a person falls ill in any culture, the first treatment is usually "home remedies." If these fail, more formal outside help is sought. In all cultures certain individuals are recognized as best able to treat illness. For example, every traditional Mexican woman knows some basic herbal remedies. If these do not work, an elderly woman is called in to contribute her herbal and healing knowledge. If the patient still remains sick, a local folk healer (*curandera*) is brought in. As a last resort, the regional *curandera* is consulted. She may go into a trance and be possessed by a folk saint or helpful spirit who treats the illness through her.

People in many cultures use local herbs and plants to treat illness. The traditional Chinese developed a sophisticated pharmacopoeia of herbs and plants, used in skillful combinations to treat particular illnesses. Many of the substances used in modern Western medicine either have a plant origin, or are a synthetic production of the active principle in certain plant medicines. For instance, using the "blueprint" of quinine, a naturally occurring drug which combats malaria, Western scientists developed synthetic antimalarials.

The Brunei Malays traditionally had two types of healers. Those in the intellectual tradition massaged broken bones, reset dislocated bones, used herbs, and had manuscript prescription books. In the other tradition were the healers who went into trance, were possessed by helping spirits, and prescribed medicines or drove evil spirits out of the patient.

Massage and manipulation are commonly used to deal with swollen or painful joints and cracked or broken bones. The Brunei Malays massaged broken or cracked bones to keep them in proper alignment for healing. The Japanese used a semi-mobile bamboo splinting system. Ayurvedic medicine of India uses special massage techniques and medicinal rubbing oils. The Chinese combined massage techniques for bone alignment with acupuncture to restore proper vital energy flow.

Cultural variation is also evident in the treatment of mental illness. In most cultures there are people who simply do not fit in with normal expected behavior. They may be violent, withdrawn, irrational, or any combination of these.

Each culture has a different way to deal with these situations. Many groups hold ceremonies for the person, seeking to remove the evil spirit causing the condition, and then to reintegrate the person into society. For example, after the Vietnam War many Chicano and Native American soldiers underwent purification and exorcism rites in order to leave their wartime experiences behind them and fit once more into their societies.

In other cultures, the person may be initiated into a special group which at ritually approved times performs the abnormal behavior in an acceptable social context, such as the Iroquois False Face Society. And all cultures recognize that there are some people whom nothing will help; in that case, they are restrained if they are violent, and are often put under custodial care.

Epidemiology

Illness affects particular individuals, but patterns of illness affect groups of people and geographic regions. Epidemiology is the study of how diseases and accidents affect different populations and different geographic regions. For example, epidemiological study of car accidents in North America shows that a high percentage are associated with drunken drivers. Acting on this information, the Province of British Columbia has enacted, and enforces, very strict laws against drunken drivers. The term "epidemiology" derives from "epidemic." *Epidemic* (*epi*, "among," *demos*, "the people") diseases are diseases which come suddenly and infect large numbers of people in a particular area.

Until the development of the polio vaccine in the 1950s, summer epidemics of polio were common in North America. The great typhoid, diptheria, and cholera epidemics are a thing of the past in North America, but until World War I they occurred frequently, killing thousands. In areas of the world where clean drinking water is not available, and where public sanitation is poor, these illnesses remain a real threat.

An epidemic which affects people over a significant portion of the globe is known as a *pandemic* (*pan,* "all," *demos,* "the people"). At the end of WWI, the "Spanish influenza" broke out in Europe and soon spread worldwide. It was the worst pandemic of modern times, killing more people than WWI had done. In the Middle Ages the Black Plague was a pandemic that swept over Eurasia and altered the course of history.

Another major category of disease is endemic disease. *Endemic* (*en,* "in, native to," *demos,* "the people") diseases are those which are constantly present within a population. Various forms of hepatitis and parasitic infestations are endemic in many tropical countries. Smallpox was once endemic in Europe; "having the pox" was an expected trial encountered in life. Many died from smallpox, and others were severely disfigured or blinded by it.

Diseases may also be classified as acute or chronic. Acute diseases are of fairly sudden onset, rage furiously, and then either kill or go away. Influenza and typhoid fever are two examples of acute diseases. Chronic diseases often have a slower, even insidious, onset, and can linger on, often for years. Heart disease and diabetes are two widespread chronic diseases in North America today. People in many cultures also recognize "lingering" or "wasting" diseases which kill a person gradually.

Medical Anthropology

In order to understand an indigenous medical system, that system must be viewed within its own cultural context. In other words, it must be comprehended in terms of its own concepts and patterns of reasoning. Medical anthropologists seek to do this, and then to look at the traditional medicine from various anthropological perspectives.

Many societies have medical specialists who are shamans. The Tungus shamans of Siberia are experts in the diagnosis and curing of illness. According to Tungus belief, the shaman goes into a trance in order to enter the spirit world to fight off the evil spirits causing the illness. However, both in Western and Tungusic terms, Tungus shamans are mentally abnormal. Part of the training for Tungus shamanship involves channeling wild and aberrant trance behavior into the socially acceptable function of diagnosing and curing. Thus, anthropologists view Tungus shamanship as a role which permits some deviates to fulfill a useful role in society rather than being outcasts (Bourgignon 1976).

Chinese traditional society has spirit mediums who go into trance to diagnose and in some cases treat illness. But in contrast to the Tungus case, the Chinese spirit mediums are not the sole diagnosticians and treatment experts. Rather, treatment is specialized according to the nature of the illness. Thus, the trance medium may treat some illnesses (by driving out or appeasing the causative evil spirit), while other illnesses are treated by herbalists or acupuncturists.

Medical anthropologists also look at various facets of the relationships between the role of the patient and the role of the traditional medical practitioner. In this type of research, many kinds of questions may be asked. For example, do certain types of patients who use traditional Chinese medicine consult spirit mediums more often or over longer periods of time than do others? Is there perhaps a relationship between the wealth of the patient and the type of practitioner consulted? Do people originating from certain geographical areas or certain cultural backgrounds consult traditional medical practitioners more often than do others?

Equally important is the contribution of medical anthropology in pointing out instances where Western cultural bias has resulted in the overlooking of valuable native treatment. Such bias was clearly manifest in the last century when Europeans vehemently denied the effectiveness of native Chinese medicine. Yet research in the last two decades, primarily in mainland China, has shown clearly that traditional Chinese medicine has much value and effectiveness. Similarly, the Malay treatment of rolling a pepper seed under the fingernail of the patient is dismissed as useless by most Westerners. In the Malay view, this painful treatment causes the body to become an uncomfortable place for the illness-causing spirit, encouraging it to leave. Most Westerners disagree with the Malay etiology that evil spirits cause illness (although the Western belief in micro-organisms might be seen as anthropologically similar). Yet the treatment works for Malays. One (Western) explanation is that the body may react to the painful stimulus by releasing hormones, enzymes, or other chemicals which play a role in countering disease. In short, even though the etiology of a particular disease may be in dispute, the method of treatment may still have medical value. And the mere fact of treatment often gives the patient some psychological comfort.

Local-level synthesis of Western and non-Western medical systems is occurring in many parts of the world. For example, the rural Malays in some areas still believe that all illness is caused by evil spirits. Yet they seek medicine from Western medical practitioners.

These Malays explain that the Western anti-evil spirit medicine is more effective for certain sicknesses than the traditional Malay medicine. On the other hand, these same rural Malays maintain that their traditional practices are effective for mental illnesses, whereas Western medicine is not. Thus, these Malays have switched to new treatments for physical ailments while retaining the traditional Malay etiology.

Not only are non-Western people adapting to Western medicine; Western medicine is also adapting to them. A good example of this is found at the Medical Center for Aborigines of West Malaysia. When the patients are evacuated by helicopter from their jungle homes to the Medical Center, part of their family comes too. This is counter to most Western hospital practice, but fits in with the cultural practice of the aborigines, who never leave an ill person alone. If the Medical Center did not have this enlightened policy, the sick aborigines would either refuse evacuation for treatment, or, once evacuated, would languish for want of the necessary psychological support afforded by having relatives at the bedside.

One of the directions of the future is the combination of Western and traditional medical treatments to provide maximal benefits to patients. Many African countries, for example, are beginning to use traditional practitioners as integral parts of the national health care system. India has successfully integrated the Ayurvedic, a traditional medical system, into the public health system. Thus Ayurvedic medicine acquires the veneer of modernism. Within the United States several pilot programs involving traditional healers and the modern medical system have proven the value of this approach. In Washington and Texas *curanderos* are actively involved with physicians in diagnosing and treating Mexican-American patients (Craig 1989, personal

Figure 14.3 Each culture has its own ideas about the best ways to sit, move, and sleep. This Borneo bed has a thin cotton mattress laid atop hard boards. The brass bedstead was a deluxe wedding bed nearly half a century ago. Most people in this house sleep on the wooden floor; but they sleep soundly and well. In the daytime this bed serves as a sitting and socializing place for the family.

communication and survey). Non-Western medicine, such as that of traditional Chinese, is also becoming more important in industrialized countries. Each of these medical systems comes from a particular culture, and needs to be modified in some ways to fit new circumstances. The Malaysian Medical Center's practice of bringing in family members with the patient is an example of this. Medical anthropologists are well-qualified to suggest such modifications because their long and intense fieldwork experience uniquely attunes them to cultural subtleties and differences.

The cost of health care is always a factor in health care systems. Among some hunting-gathering groups in the Amazon, a person who is seriously ill or injured is left behind with food and water when the group moves on, as the group cannot stay and there is no way to carry

the person. Among the Eskimo, an old person or an injured one who could no longer contribute to the group would be exposed to the elements to die. Many groups neglect or expose infants who are deformed or handicapped; thus, the group does not have to use scarce resources to support them. In American culture health-care costs are prohibitive to many individuals, especially to the elderly and those who live at or below the poverty level.

All cultures recognize the importance of diet for maintaining health, and each has its own conceptions of nutrition. For example, the Brunei Malays feel that food eaten without rice is not a meal. It is just a snack, regardless of how much food is eaten. Sick people are expected to follow special dietary precautions; they should not eat chicken, pineapple, or shrimp. Chicken and pineapple are considered "harmful" foods that will make one sicker, and shrimp, because they jump about, will make the illness recur. Many Americans, on the other hand, believe that chicken soup is an excellent food for sick people.

Many international nutritional guidelines are based on the diet thought to be necessary for people of European or North American descent who live in a temperate climate. But people of African or Asian descent, for example, or those who live in other climates, may have different nutritional needs.

Protein calorie malnutrition is a problem in much of the world. Often men are given the choice foods, so that malnutrition particularly affects women and children, especially girls. Infants weaned from their mother's milk and put on a high-starch, low-protein diet will fall ill with protein deficiency diseases. The selling of powdered-milk infant feeding formulas by American and European companies in Third World countries has caused many babies to be sickly and has contributed to economic problems. The mother loses her breast milk and has to spend money she often does not have to buy the powdered milk; she then over-dilutes the powdered milk to make it last longer, and the baby receives inadequate nutrition. Medical anthropological study of diet and varying dietary needs should lead to better dietary guidelines for specific regions.

Medical anthropology studies both Western and non-Western medical systems and their interrelationships with the culture as a whole. Any scientific study of a Western or non-Western medical system should include one or more anthropologists. Anthropologists can make three especially pertinent contributions to the scientific study of any given medical system. First, anthropologists can show points of hidden cultural bias in a Western-oriented study of non-Western medicine. Second, they can point out where Western cultural bias may result in overlooking valuable native treatment. And third, anthropologists can point out ways that synthesis of different medical systems may be accomplished with minimal conflict and difficulty.

SUGGESTED READINGS

Horacio, Fabrega. *Disease and Social Behavior.* Cambridge, Massachusetts: MIT Press, 1974.
A cross-cultural account of disease and healing in various societies around the world.

Horton, Robin. African Thought and Western Science. In *Rationality,* edited by B. Wilson. New York: Harper and Row, 1970.
The author points out that many times in a traditional society disease is thought to be linked to disruptions in the social fabric and must therefore be treated with this in mind.

Kimball, Linda A. *Borneo Medicine: The Healing Art of Indigenous Brunei Malay Medicine.* Ann Arbor, Michigan: University Microfilms International, 1979.
This work is an in-depth account of Brunei folk medicine, its remedies, practices, and cures.

Turner, Victor. *Lunda Medicine and the Treatment of Disease in the Forest of Symbols.* Ithaca, New York: Cornell University Press, 1967.
The author points out that many times therapies or curing rituals are woven into the social fabric of a given culture.

Sights and Sounds—Art, Music and Dancing

15

If culture is seen as an intricately patterned tapestry, then art forms several of the vibrant-colored threads woven throughout it. In many cultures, art is intricately and intimately interwoven with other cultural themes such as religion and social ordering. The isolation of art as a separate entity for study is a Western construct.

Art as a cultural category includes visual art, the performing arts, and folklore. Visual art takes many forms, ranging from painting and sculpture to pictoral decoration and ornamentation of utilitarian objects. Theater, music, dancing, mime, puppetry and recitation are some of the performing arts. Poetry, myth, storytelling and song are genres of folklore. Folklore is also a performing art if two or more individuals participate in a folklore event.

All art conveys a cultural message, for art is a form of symbolic communication which mirrors culture. Anthropologists seek to understand the cultural message art conveys. Anthropologists study both the particular art form itself, and the specific cultural context in which it occurs. The study of masks, for example, includes description and comparison of the physical objects "masks." It also includes the context in which those masks are used. For example, when Eskimos perform the swallow dance, they use quietly colored and sparsely decorated masks, which are sacred symbols connected with religious ceremonies important for the continued survival of the group.

But when Mardi Gras celebrants in New Orleans dance on Fat Tuesday, they wear wildly ornamented masks which provide anonymity.

The meaning of an art form may be apparent only to members of a particular subculture. The hair and dress styles of the punk-rock subculture can be seen as art forms; yet they are incomprehensible to many older Euro-Americans. And the meaning of many operatic arias is clear only to opera fans. Observers who are not familiar with the particular subculture, or with a particular aspect of a culture, are often unable to interpret the meaning of the art. The only way to understand the meaning of a particular cultural art form is to study it within the larger context of the culture in which it occurs.

Anthropologists use several approaches to study art. The *thematic* approach looks for content and themes. One theme encountered in the stories of several cultures is that of the trickster figure. In the southeastern U.S. one such trickster is B'rer Rabbit, who always outwits B'rer Fox and B'rer Bear. Another famous figure is the Coyote found in the mythology of Native Americans of the Plains and Plateau culture areas.

The *textual* approach views art as a form of text. Punk-rocker outfits and the three-piece suits of Wall Street brokers are part of the larger text of U.S. clothing, which varies by region, occupation, and social status. The *contextual* approach looks at the relationship of

Figure 15.1 Navajo women weave rugs on upright looms. The spindle-whorl beside the woman contains hand-spun wool for weaving. (Photograph by Harry Teller)

art to other aspects of culture. The gothic cathedrals of Europe are more than magnificent architectural monuments. They also make a statement about religious aspirations, and represent a concentration of economic resources and a will to create which lasted throughout the time needed to complete their construction.

The *functional* approach to the study of art searches for the social and psychological reasons that art exists in a culture. Using this approach, an anthropologist might attempt to analyze why medieval Europeans poured such tremendous resources into the construction of vast cathedrals.

The *stylistic* approach classifies art according to style and genre. For example, one style of music is identified as the genre "opera," and subdivided into Baroque opera, grand or classical opera, and light opera (or operetta).

The *performance-oriented* approach views the whole creative process of art and its culmination in the interaction of art and audience. Using this perspective, one might study the training of Michelangelo, including the influence of his predecessors and contemporaries; his turbulent life and stormy relationships with patrons; and the process of designing and supervising much of the construction of St. Peter's Cathedral in Rome. Finally, one might consider how people have interacted with the cathedral in the centuries since its construction.

Finally, the *synchronic* approach looks at art in a cross-section of time, comparing, for example, the ballet styles in Moscow, London, and New York in the 1980s. The *diachronic* approach, in contrast, traces art through time. A diachronic study of Chinese calligraphy might trace its development from the bronzes of 2000 B.C. through the work of master calligraphers living today.

Art is a vehicle of communication. It manifests emotions and meanings, reflects social behaviors and social structure, and mirrors a world view.

Visual Art

Each culture assigns its own meaning to items of visual art. The eyes painted on the bows of traditional Thai boats are not for decoration; they are a safety device. The Thai believe that these eyes can see dangers ahead, and will protect the boat from harm.

Masks are a form of visual art used in many cultures. Cave paintings in France suggest that gatherer-hunters of 28,000 years ago used masks in ceremonial dances.

The earliest masks seem to have been used in religious ceremonies as a means of drawing down the spirit to ensure a good hunt or to acquire spiritual power. The ceremonial dance masks of the Northwest Coast Indians were carved in secret. The masks represented natural beings and mythological creatures. Thus, the Tlingit dancer who wore the mask of the sea lion took on the power of the sea lion's guardian spirit, a power said to engender wealth.

The Eskimos made three types of masks. Masks of plants and animals gave magical aid in the procurement of resources. Masks depicting the odd features of enemies or other people were worn by performers in humorous plays. And shamans and medical practitioners had special masks associated with their powers. The Eskimo believed that the making and wearing of ritual dancing masks influenced the being represented by the mask. This living immortal being was honored by the dance and in return, brought game to the people.

Wherever masks are worn, they fulfill one or more of three main functions. The mask may disguise or hide identity, as Mardi Gras masks do. It may transform the wearer into another person, or into an animal or spirit, as do the masks of the Tlingit. And a mask may protect the wearer against harm, as does the mask of a hockey goalie or baseball catcher. Masks are used in social and religious ceremonies, secret societies, healing rites, magical rituals, and for

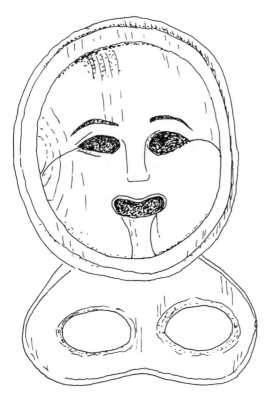

Figure 15.2. Eskimo finger mask (wood)

And among some cultures in Africa and New Guinea, masks of the dead are made. The mourners sing to these masks and feast them; and through them, they ask the dead not to return to bother the living. Destruction of the masks symbolizes the final severance of the dead from the living.

The materials used for the creation of artistic objects can be highly perishable, or durable enough to last for centuries. Masks carved from wood, if properly cared for, can be handed down from generation to generation, as they were on the Northwest Coast. The ancient sculptures of Buddha in India have stood the test of time and are still venerated today. And the Egyptian pyramids have stood for more than 4,000 years, memorials of pharaohs long vanished, and symbols of human aspirations of immortality.

Among the more perishable art forms are the sculptures made by Tibetan monks for the Butter Image Festival; the corn dollies made by the ancient Celts and symbolically burned during the solstice rites; and the special cakes and candles made by the Chinese for the New Year celebration.

Sculptures are often used as religious symbols. In Hinduism the depiction of deities takes various forms, ranging from the detailed sculptures of realistic images such as the dancing Siva, to abstract symbols and folk images which combine elements of realistic and symbolic images (such as a special rock symbolizing a deity). The traditional Hindus believe that ceremonies empower the images as surrogates for the deity, or make them a home for the deity. Once the images have become empowered, they are to be treated with all respect as though they were the deity; because they are the place the deity manifests.

The totem poles of the Northwest Coast Indians were not venerated as the abodes of gods; but rather as historical markers. The totems contained carved symbols of real or mythological events of importance in the life of the owner, clan, tribe, or in the history of

pleasure and fun. Masks are often used in association with dances, costumes, and music and stories.

In the Japanese Noh drama, the mask defines the character, and the costume elaborates that definition. The ritual movements of the performer and the chanting of the narrator-musician chorus recounts the tale, which the audience watches in silence. Noh is a restrained drama, and subtle nuances of movement (such as the movement of a single finger) convey immense meaning.

Masks of the dead serve to preserve the personality of the deceased, and to help the soul on its travels to the hereafter. The Maya and Aztec Indians of Mexico carved elaborate and beautiful masks of stone, or fashioned masks of gold, silver, clay or copper to place on the dead.

his ancestors. Totems were usually raised at potlatches. Totem carvers were paid well for their work and were held in high esteem in the social ranking order. The totem poles were just one of the rich cultural repositories of art.

Architecture also sometimes depicts the divine. Both Buddhism and Hinduism have a symbolism of the divine mountain known as Mt. Meru. Many southeast Asian palaces were built below a hill which served symbolically as Mt. Meru. A famous architectural representation of the mountain is the recently restored monument of Borobudur in Java. Here, a classic masterpiece of art recently brought to the fore the kind of latent conflicts that such a masterpiece can engender; fanatic Moslems hated what they saw as idolatry in the monument, and attempted to destroy it.

Borobudor represents the sacred Mt. Meru. A series of relief sculptures around it depict a human's journey from the depths of difficulty through the stages of religious development, until the top of the hill represents the attainment of release from the cycle of rebirth. On the top of the hill are numerous images of the meditating Buddha. Borobudor is located on the island of Java, in Indonesia, and in the thousand years since its erection, climate had done much damage. An international effort was mounted, through the United Nations, to restore the monument. When this had been completed there was a ceremony at which Indonesian officials and Buddhist clergy were present.

Religious wars often involve destruction of religious art. Moslems have destroyed Hindu temples in the name of erasing idolatry, and Hindus have destroyed Moslem mosques in the name of erasing defilers of the Hindu faith. Nor has Europe been without such destruction. One of the accompaniments of the Protestant Reformation was the destruction of much traditional Catholic art, and the loss of much of the tradition of church music. In Scotland, for example, there was a rich tradition of Celtic church music, but this was lost after the Reformation. The fact that people can feel so threatened by art is a testament to its importance in human expression and symbolization.

Art has been used to decorate the human body. Among the Nuba of the Sudan, cicatrization (scarring) is a form of art and beauty. Traditional raised scar patterns adorn the arms, breasts, stomach, and back. Skin carving begins for the Nuba girl at seven or eight years of age. Her entire body will be covered by the time she has borne all her children. The Nuba men have more symbolic motifs and animal designs incised in deeper cuts on their bodies. Scarification is practiced among many African cultures as part of an initiation ceremony (Oskar Leiz, 1966). In Euro-American culture, women paint their faces to conform to a cultural concept of beauty.

Art is also used to decorate objects used in daily life. Crafts, such as pottery, basketry, quilling, beading, and weaving are expressions of artistic talent and creativity. The exquisite lace-making of Irish women (especially older women) has long been admired around the world, and is an art form that is often passed on from mother to daughter. And Hopi women used to hold pottery "bees" similar to the quilting bees held by early white settlers of North America.

Some cultures use plain utilitarian serving objects, and others may stylize and decorate such objects to the point where they lose most utilitarian value. And sometimes, both types can be found in the same culture. For instance, in the U.S., one can find both plain plastic spoons which are meant to be used once and thrown away, and elaborately embossed "collector's plates" which are intended only for display.

The styles and themes exhibited in works of art can afford a look into the culture itself. Northwest Coast Indians confirmed their social and spiritual order through their art. Items such as totem poles and masks, jewelry, spindle whorls, and painted dance screens declared the owner's lineage, wealth and status. Some objects had mythical or spiritual meanings. For instance, the bear design on a woven Haida spruce root hat is an important family crest. Haida referred to the bear as "elder kinsman," and a bear which had been killed was treated as a high-ranking guest in the chief's house.

It seems that all cultures assign symbolic meanings to colors. Among the Native Americans, colors could represent life or death, war or peace, female or male and night or day. The color blue, for example, had many meanings. The Cherokee interpreted blue as "north," but to the Navajo blue symbolized "women." And the Hopi used the sacred color blue to represent the gods.

Each culture has its own value judgments about art, its own opinions of what is "good" or "bad" art. In Renaissance Europe, "good" art was the realistic portrayal of humans and other animals. But at the same time in Southwest Asia, Islamic art forbade depiction of humans and animals, emphasizing instead geometrical and abstract representations, and detailed depictions of plants. The use of space also differed dramatically. In the art of Renaissance Europe, the entire space of the painting or wall surface was decorated. But in Chinese, Japanese, and Korean painting, empty space in a painting was used with deliberate effect to create a perception of space and distance.

Art often reflects environment as well. Just as the narrow Northwest coastal area was filled with trees and crammed between mountain ranges, the artwork of the inhabitants was also filled with detail. But the artwork of the Plains Indians reflects a wide openness, akin to the vast expanses of open prairie in which they lived.

Music

Ethnomusicologists study music in all its forms throughout the world. Although music is sound, not all sound is music, which is another way to say that one person's music is another person's noise. In American culture of the 1980s the twangy guitar music of country rock may be just irritating noise to a fan of the heavy steel style.

Music can be used as a form of leisure and relaxation, an inducement to trance, or a gateway to the supernatural. St. Basil, Bishop of Caesarea in the 4th century, said, "Could there be anything more blessed than to imitate on earth the ring-dance of the angels, and at dawn to raise our voices in prayer and by hymns and songs to glorify the rising Creator?" (Wosien 1974:29). The *alabanzas*, Mexican Catholic folk hymns, glorify the folk-saint El Niño Fidencio. The *alabanzas* are vehicles of communication which disseminate the historical and ideological messages of the folk religion known as Fidencismo (Craig 1984). The dogma of this cult is conveyed, maintained, and regenerated through the performance of the *alabanzas*. The *alabanzas* have a transformative effect in helping to achieve and maintain the transition from a normative state to a liminal state within the religious and curing rituals. As Wallace has stated in discussing the general use of music in religion, ". . . the participants are consciously aware that musical performance facilitates entry into a desired state of heightened suggestibility or trance in which possession and other ecstatic religious behavior can be expected to occur" (1966:54).

The Native American shamans used song to enhance their power. Warriors owned songs which protected them in battle. Power songs were inherited or were received as divine or ancestral gifts. Songs were considered to be the breath of the spirits; therefore, a person singing would be a source of great power. The Eskimo

Figure 15.3 These Crow drummers and singers at the Crow Fair Pow-Wow, 1988, are wearing Anglo-American dress, but the songs they sing are centuries old, and continue the Crow musical tradition. (Photograph by Dale McGinnis)

fought duels with songs. Whoever sang the most effective and powerful song was judged the winner.

Songs are sung in many cultures as prayers to bring victory, rain or sunshine, fertile crops, and luck in gambling games. Healers sang songs to heal the sick. And mothers world-wide hum their little ones to sleep with a soothing lullaby, while love-sick swains have poured out their hearts' desire in song.

Songs often carry a message. Popular love songs have an open message. Many of the songs of slaves in the United States prior to the Civil War bore clandestine messages. For example the words "Follow the drinking gourd for the old man's awaitin' to carry you to freedom"

were specific, although covert, directions. "Follow the drinking gourd" referred to the Big Dipper constellation which points to the North Star, thus directing slaves to head north to freedom.

Dance

Singing and dancing often go together. Indeed, they form an important part of Greek and Jewish wedding celebrations. Many cultures use dancing as an important form of expression. Anthropologists study the form, meaning, and context of dance in order to gain a fuller understanding of a culture.

Figure 15.4 Dancers perform at the Native American Pow-Wow held annually in conjunction with Ki-Yo Indian Days at the University of Montana in Missoula, Montana. (Photograph by Dale McGinnis)

Dances may be part of initiation rituals. Among the Australian aborigines, men learned certain dances as part of their initiation rites. Some of the dances were precise imitations of the habits of hunted animals, and thus served to teach young men valuable information about their future prey. Other dances brought men into contact with the spirits who could help or hinder them in life.

Dance often accompanies music to facilitate entrance into an ecstatic state leading to possession trance. In voodoo cults, dancing is used to communicate with possessing deities.

The Eskimo held dances for religious festivals and social gatherings. Costume dances often reenacted Eskimo mythology. If the dance pleased the spirits, game would multiply and the people prosper. The Hopi raindance was vital for survival. Though not readily

susceptable to explanation in Euro-American terms, it has been noted more than once that the raindance did bring crop-sustaining rain when the skies promised only drought.

Like music and song, dance is also frequently associated with religion. The Cheyenne and most of the Plains Indians (but not the Crow or Blackfoot) developed an elaborate Ghost Dance in reaction to the white takeover of the region. The Ghost Dancers believed that if they all followed "The Way," the Indians would regain their lost paradise on Earth.

Dancing has always been a natural medium through which humans have expressed a continuum of emotions such as sorrow, joy, anger, ecstasy and devotion. Dance can convey an emotional or cultural theme, and certain dances or styles of dance often receive cultural sanction and approval. This may occur through official or state recognition, such as the Baile Folklorico of Mexico, which travel nationally to share Mexico's regional dances.

A highly skilled dancer may acquire status and prestige, as do top-ranked Soviet ballet dancers. On the other hand, dancers may be looked down upon, as was the case in traditional China. And Puritan England forbade dancing, viewing it as a useless and vain activity displeasing to their God.

But the Dervish mystic sect of Islam uses ritual whirling dance as a path to direct communion with Allah. Many cultures believe that dance has divine sanction. Dance can also serve as a mode for communicating with or about the gods, as it does in India.

Siva, the Supreme Lord of the Dance, is a major Hindu deity. Siva is the source of cosmic harmony and rhythm. Siva's three dances symbolize the three aspects of his being. In the Dance of the Destructive Aspect, ten-armed Siva dances to destroy the chains that hold each soul to the fleeting world of illusion. In the Dance of the Yogic Aspect, two-armed Siva dances his evening dance on Mount Kailasha, the Himalayan Hermitage of the Lord, to grant spiritual bliss and peace to his followers. And in the Dance of the Gift-Giving Aspect, four-armed Siva dances the mystic cosmic dance to stamp out evil, shower grace and offer salvation to those who seek it (Bhavani, 1965).

The classic Hindu treatises on classical dance say that dance itself consists of three main parts: the combination of both dancing and acting; pure dance of movements without any special meaning or mood; and that form of the dance comprised of body, hand and limb movements and facial expressions. The treatises also say that the meaning of dance is conveyed in three ways: by hand gesture and facial expressions; through the song and melody; and by the rhythmic timing, expressed through foot movements. Thus, Indian classical dance is an exact science and art with detailed rules for the performance. Dancers who have mastered the art are able to express their unique individual style through the dance.

The highly structured and formalized dance of India, like European ballet, requires years of specialized training and practice. Other dances, such as impromptu dances of joy, require little or none. But all dances express cultural meaning.

Verbal Art (Folklore)

Oral and written literature are both forms of verbal art. Verbal art includes poetry, myth, storytelling, song, and jokes and riddles. All the categories of art are interrelated and sometimes the boundaries are not easily defined. Song, for instance, can be classified as a genre of either verbal art or of music.

Folklore is verbal art which is usually oral and traditionally has been passed down from generation to generation. It has many functions. It can be entertainment, as in the verses called out in a square dance. It can serve to sanction established sacred and secular beliefs, attitudes and institutions, as in Brunei Malay tales which tell of ancient holy wars of Islam. It can also be a form of education, as in the children's nursery rhyme "one, two, buckle my shoe," which teaches counting.

Myths are a special form of folklore. Often myths are a metaphorical statement made by the people of a particular culture in an attempt to describe and explain the indescribable and the unexplainable. Thus, myths often account for the origins of a cultural group, or explain the beginnings of the universe and the world. Myth has a pragmatic social function in validating the rites and institutions of a society. Most clans, for example, have myths describing their connection to a common ancestor. The Haida of the Northwest Coast have such a myth recounting the descent of the Raven Clan from the bird Raven. Totem poles, songs and dances all buttress the claim of descent from Raven. And a Shinto myth states that the imperial family of Japan is descended from the Clan of the Sun Goddess Amaterasu (*circa* 660–585 B.C.) who sent her grandson down to take charge of Japan. The first emperor of Japan is said to have been Jimmu, the great-grandson of Amaterasu's grandson. Accordingly, each emperor is said to be a descendant of Jimmu.

Myths also have a sociopolitical function. Wars have been started and viciously pursued under the influence of prevailing myths and ideologies. The Crusades, Nazism, and the doctrine of Manifest Destiny are three examples. As Malinowski stated, "Myth, studied alive, is not symbolic but a direct expression of its subject matter . . . Myth fulfills in primitive culture an indispensable function; it expresses, enhances and codifies belief; it safeguards and enforces morality; it vouches for the efficiency and contains practical rules for the guidance of man" (Malinowski, 1926).

Ritual usually accompanies myth. Those who have access to the sacred knowledge of the myths also have access to power and higher status. African elders of the Poro secret society in Sierre Leone are one such group. In traditional India only the highest caste, the Brahmin, could read and recite the myths about the gods. Anthropologists study the "living" myths of people. Ethnographic descriptions of how legends and myths are recited and expressed in ritual allow the anthropologist to use a more holistic approach to studying verbal art's function in culture.

Writing casts verbal art into a fixed form, and preserves it through time. Written religious texts are considered to have a special power. The Bible, Koran and sacred texts of Buddhism, Hinduism, and Taoism are believed to have power in the very sound and writing of their words.

Written literature or writing itself does not have to be connected with religion in order to be prestigious. Educated traditional Chinese valued calligraphy as the ultimate expression of learned taste in art and literature, and as the mark of an educated person. The literati were the men who had studied the classics and memorized a thousand pages and more of classical text. Those who were illiterate valued calligraphy even though they could not understand what it said. Sometimes, magical properties were imputed to it. For the boat people of South China, a strong healing potion was said to be a scrap of writing from a scholar's desk, mixed with water or carbonized and mixed with water.

Those cultures which do not have written texts rely completely on oral tradition.

Art in Culture

Folklore, verbal art, music, visual and performing art are convenient categorizations. But there are other ways to view art. For instance, in East Asia the living of life was considered an art. And traditional arts, studied and practiced sincerely for years, could come to embody the essence of life.

The traditional martial arts were more than a practice or an art; they became life itself. Tai Chi Chuan, a series of slow dance-like movements, is a martial art, a dance of life, and a moving meditation. Practiced properly, it provides strong physical training combined with the mental awakening of deep meditation. When Tai Chi students practice Chinese calligraphy, they find that the movement and spirit of Tai Chi and calligraphy are interrelated. Students often study traditional medicine in order to understand their own body and health, and to be able to help others.

Eventually Tai Chi becomes a part of everything the student does in life, and everything the student does in life becomes a part of Tai Chi. Thus, Tai Chi is life, and life is Tai Chi.

Similarly, the art of tea in Japan, when considered on a deeper level, represents life. The Japanese developed the formal tea ceremony to express life and the purpose of being. The traditional Chinese also have a tea ceremony, although it is less formal. Still, the preparation and consumption of tea, often combined with the appreciation of a scenic view or the composition of poetry, is an aesthetic art much appreciated by the literati. Contrast this with the gulp and guzzle of the American coffee break.

Many cultures limit access to particular forms of artistic expression. In the early Christian church, only those who were baptized were allowed inside the main sanctuary where frescos and other art decorated the walls. In ancient Israel only Jews were allowed past the outer "court of the Gentiles" of the temple into the inner precincts. And only the educated literati of China could read and appreciate many of the classic poems.

Status often limits or determines access to art. Only members of the Chinese emperor's court heard the court music, but they seldom heard the folksongs of peasants. In Renaissance Italy, only the elite of the cities saw the art produced for the rulers. Only those who had access to the Vatican in Rome could see the frescos of the Sistine Chapel painted by Michelangelo. Australian men made rock paintings in caves which only the initiated men were allowed to enter. And in the United States, the wealthy have the means to have private art collections, and money to travel makes prestigious museums more accessible.

Music, dance, and art play a part in producing a full life. Art can be used as a medium for communicating with the spirits, and may be sacred in itself. Art serves as a means of social cohesion and group identity, but also as a way to indicate order. Art expresses cultural emotions and meanings, and provides a form of leisure and relaxation. The comforting joy of Christmas carols and the social event of their being sung or heard in a group shows their social as well as religious aspects. To a Jew, the recitation of the Torah evokes a sense of continuity and unity with others.

Thus, art is essential to human survival as a mode of symbolic communication through which the individual is introduced to other aspects of culture which can lead to a fuller life. The anthropological study of art in all its myriad forms contributes to our holistic understanding of humans as cultural beings.

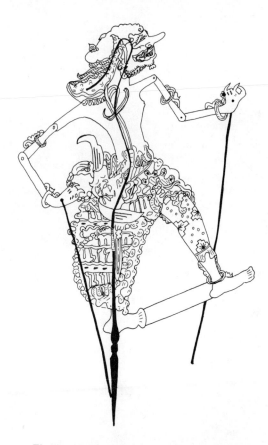

Figure 15.5 Indonesian shadow puppet

SUGGESTED READINGS

Boas, Franz. *Primitive Art*. New York: Dover Publications, 1955.
This work is considered to be a classic in regard to the fundamental components of non-industrial art, music and dance.

Forge, Anthony, ed. *Primitive Art and Society*. London: Oxford University Press, 1973.
This work contains a series of essays on art in its relationship to society.

Kurath, Gertrude K. Panorama of Dance Ethnology. *Current Anthropology*, 1960, pp. 233–254.
This article is a summary of the dance as performed around the world.

Merriam, Alan P. *The Anthropology of Music*. Chicago: Northwestern Universty Press, 1964.
This book examines the social aspect of music from an anthropological viewpoint.

The Lighter Side of Life— Games and Entertainment

16

Play exists in all cultures. Entertainment and games may be mere leisurely past-times, but more often they have important cultural functions.

Play is basically an enjoyable mode of behavior. Through play, individuals can learn to respond to the emotional and social aspects of the world around them (Schwartzman 1980). Games are one aspect of playing, and have several defining features. *Games* are organized play with competition between two or more sides. Further, the competition has accepted rules for playing and for determining the winner of the game. *Entertainment* is any pleasurable way of passing time which does not involve competition. It may include eating, drinking, storytelling, and in many industrial societies, the arts.

The Anthropological Study of Play

Anthropologists look at play because it is an interesting activity to study (sometimes even fun), and also because of the many functions play has in culture. Play often acts as a socialization mechanism. Competitive play is often related to status, as in baseball or football games. Play serves to hone skills through contests involving the dexterity and skill needed for survival activities, such as the hunting games played by !Kung San boys. Play can make labor more pleasurable. Singing rhythmic songs often help physical work go more smoothly. Play can have religious connotations, as in the singing of Christmas carols.

It can reinforce ethnic boundaries and group identity, readily seen in the World Cup soccer finals (Roberts and Sutton-Smith 1962).

Children's Games

Children's play acts as a socialization process, and depends on the cultural setting. Through play children learn the common spoken language and basic social rules of life which are necessary to becoming a full member of the culture and to survive in later life. Yet this serious business of learning how to be social is often dismissed by adults as "just play."

In *imitative play,* children learn by attempting to imitate the behavior of adults or older children. "Playing house" is a common form of imitative play among Euro-American children.

As with any tradition, children's games are often passed on from one generation to another with little or no alteration. Generations of American girls have grown up playing jump rope to the chant, "A tisket, a tasket, a green and yellow basket, I sent a letter to my maid and on the way I lost it, I lost it, eevy ivy over!" At the last words, the rope is spun very fast to "catch" the jumper if possible (Abrahams 1969). Games such as these are both ephemeral and enduring. They are ephemeral because children often forget them as they grow up, and enduring because adults re-encounter them in the games of their own children.

Not all things stand still. The outward game itself may not change over time, but sometimes the verbal forms associated with the games change.

Most cultures have ethnic humor which plays upon prejudice and negative attitudes (Dundes 1971, 1975). Moslem Malays do not eat pork, and place great cultural value on speaking softly and not showing anger. One Malay ethnic joke about Europeans is, "Know how Europeans eat lunch? They fill up on pork and potatoes, turn red in the face, and start shouting for iced drinks."

The study of games gives anthropologists clues to the culture as a whole. For instance, in America, many children play games of "cops and robbers," "army," and "cowboys and Indians," all of which inculcate the child with the values of good and evil, as well as "might is right." These same values can be seen in the games of "soldiers and guerrillas" played in villages in countries where civil war is predominant. Depending on the adult values of the village, children will all want to be either "soldiers" or "guerrillas." The children's choice makes a statement about the political views of the village as a whole.

Play is a form of socialization and as such may be preparation for future specific tasks. Children playing "house" or "doctor" is one example. Among the Crow, daughters of more well-to-do families had miniature teepees and household equipment. When the camp moved to follow the buffalo, the girls packed and moved their own miniature household (Linderman 1932). Children from lower socioeconomic classes of a subordinate culture group may play games that mimic traditional roles. It was not unusual for children of Mexican-Americans who were exposed to traditional roles, such as folk healer or midwife, to play at these roles.

Through playing games, children acquire the skills needed for survival in life. This ranges from children of hunters and gatherers playing at "hunting" or "finding plants" to children in industrial societies playing "pilot" or "big executive." In the United States, computer games serve to provide survival skills for children who will need familiarity with computers to survive as adults.

Competitive Games

Games of chance and strategy are symbolic forms of competition (Roberts and Sutton-Smith 1962). Thus, dice and other gambling games pit individuals against one another and against the anonymous player, "luck." Chess is a game of strategy which requires mental dexterity, logic, and a special type of memory. Some computer games are electronic variants of simplified chess combined with the manual dexterity needed to play pinball machines.

Sports often function as a form of combat or as a socially accepted outlet of potentially destructive aggression. Military organizations play "war games" as combat preparation, and ironically, there are instances in which combat has been seen as a sport.

Medieval European kings saw war as the sport of royalty and nobility, a type of living chess game, to be fought in proper elaborate attire with certain rules of chivalry. Only knights and the royalty were entitled to ride horses. All others had to go on foot (and indeed, could not afford horses in any case).

Headhunting was once a major Trobriand Islands competitive activity. Since headhunting raids were outlawed, the British game of cricket has come to fulfill the same role of competition for men's groups from different villages. The men's groups dress in special finery and parade onto the field with ceremonial dancing and much taunting back and forth. The game then takes place. The victors stage a victory celebration complete with verbal denigration of their opponents, just as they formerly would have denigrated those whose heads they had taken.

Figure 16.1 Cockfighting is a popular sport in much of Southeast Asia. (Photograph by L. A. Kimball)

Lacrosse was a serious game for the Iroquois of the American Northeast. The winners took the lives and possessions of the losers. The lacrosse game served as a substitute for inter-village war and inculcated the attitude of being bold and ignoring looming death. Blows from sticks or hits by flying lacrosse balls killed many competitors. Death on the lacrosse field was an honorable death, as was death in war.

The American game of football is a formalized combat sport. One need only hear giant defensive players talking about how they "love to mash quarterbacks" or a discussion of "aggressive hard-hitting" football to see the combative aspects. However, football can also

Figure 16.2 Riding bucking broncos is an important event in the All Indian Rodeo held annually in conjunction with the Crow Fair and Celebration held at Crow Agency, Montana. (Photograph by Dale McGinnis)

be seen as a model of the traditional route to success in American society: dedication, hard work, and self-sacrifice for the good of others (Arens 1976).

Games as Social/Political Statements

Games may be social or political statements. Nowhere is this more clear than in the politicization of the Olympics. Whole childhoods are devoted solely to preparing for competition in the Olympic Games in the name of national pride.

The traditional Chinese dragon boat races gave expression to fierce clan and guild rivalry. The races originated in the death of the poet Qu Yuan, a statesman of the Chu Kingdom in China. He saw his country decline as kings refused to take his advice, and let themselves be misled by flatterers. Seeing the utter ruin of his country and having no hope for the future, Qu Yuan wrote a final poem and drowned himself. From then until now, on the fifth day of the fifth month of the Chinese calendar, dragon boat races have been held in commemoration. Guild and clan groups traditionally had the boats built and decorated them. There was much pride in the appearance of the boats, and prizes were given for the decorations on them. But the highlight of the day was a race, rowed furiously, in which each boat sought to cover the river course ahead of all the others. In Singapore, Hong Kong, and elsewhere, the dragon boat races are still a major annual event.

A very different type of competition is found among the Malays. The person who can make the best *pantun,* .quatrain verse, is someone looked up to by others. Extended families take pride in having one or more individuals who are good at making the *pantun.*

Joking relationships and insult contests have been reported throughout Africa and Europe (Huizinga 1950). "Playing the dozens" in Black American culture is a form of verbal dueling and is an ethnic identity marker (Abrahams 1970). Playing the dozens is a verbal exchange between two players, a ritual of insults and puns. It functions to help players express aggressive feelings and develop verbal skills. Among boys, it contributes to masculine identification and teaches a youth to control his feelings and temper. An individual who is good at playing the dozens acquires a higher status in the Black community. This is also true in *munafra,* an Arabic version of the dozens, and the *opo,* a singing game of the Ashanti (Schechter 1970).

The very activity of playing a certain game can serve as a status indicator. Golf was long an elite game in Britain and America. Today, membership in the right golf club remains a marker of elite status. Those who aspire to membership in the elite may take up golf as a way of seeking higher status. Playing a round of golf also serves as a pretext for individuals to gather in a non-formal setting to carry on private negotiations which might not be possible in a more formal setting.

Many traditional societies in New Guinea and Melanesia have special men's houses, forbidden to women. Placement of men within the houses reflects social status, with the leading men in one section, the youngest boys in another, and all the other men ranged according to their current social standing. The decision to go on a headhunting raid was made in the men's house. In the Trobriands today, men sit in the men's house to prepare for a cricket match. They prepare the special costumes and plan the pre-match dances. After the cricket match, they discuss minute details of the game, and analyze its outcome, just as they once would have done for headhunting raids.

Leisure time activities can reinforce solidarity within a group. Lounging on the verandah of the village mosque in Brunei provides a form of group solidarity for the men. This verandah is a territory not normally used by women. Lounging on the village dock has a similar function. The lounging men's groups

Figure 16.3 Group identity has many expressions. The Crow Parade held at Crow Fair, 1988, Crow Agency, Montana, provided an opportunity for the Crow to express their identity by parading in traditional attire. (Photograph by Dale McGinnis)

exchange information and gossip, and thus serve a communicative function in the village and provide a way to spread information between villages. Women are less apt to have leisure time for lounging. But old Brunei Malay women frequently visit different houses and lounge in the kitchen area chatting and helping with some task as an expression of solidarity. They also pass on information and gossip, and thus are a significant channel of communication.

Women come together in American society at such places as the YWCA, health fitness centers, schools, local bars, and churches to participate in leisure activities. Making or creating crafts is often a time for women to gossip, have a little fun, and cement the bonds of non-kin relationships. This is a time for both pleasure and relaxation. The Cheyenne Quilling Society, an exclusive women's society, came together leisurely to quill and decorate buffalo robes. Each member sought to quill thirty full buffalo robes, an accomplishment which was believed to ensure the women a long life full of good fortune (Niethammer 1977). Quilting bees are still held in the United States, and give women a chance to make something beautiful and useful, and to gossip. Gossip as a form of information system exists in almost all cultures, among both sexes, and within all classes in a ranked society.

Work into Play

Bringing out the play element in work can be a game. Competition often centers on who can do the task faster or better. "Joshing," casual chatting and socializing add an element of entertainment to the performance of work tasks. Many manual tasks had their associated songs whose rhythm matched that of the work and helped one to continue working systematically and less tiringly. The words of the songs might be humorous, sad, nonsense, or might express wishes and longing. The sea chanties were songs whose cadence matched that of the task at hand, be it hauling up the anchor or pulling on the lines to move the sails.

One survival strategy is to make work into entertainment. This is often done by gathering mutual self-help groups, as in "barn raising." Among the Amish today, a large number of men gather on a certain day to raise the main timbers of a new barn and put the roof on. Often they will complete the entire barn in a day or two. The women prepare large quantities of food for this event. It is a social occasion for men and women, and gets important survival work done. The Amish use horse-traction and must have barns for their horses.

Work itself may have the elements of a "get together." In Brunei, the Kadayans, the traditional rice growers, would dress in their finest clothes and sing as they harvested the rice. This was the time when the young men and women saw each other and often courted in song. It was a happy time for all because food for the year was secure.

Not all tasks are communal. Lone individuals may make games of work. Office workers construct paperclip chains, fishers hum as they repair nets, and farmers "get some good thinking in" as they plow the fields.

Games and Religion

Some play has a religious function. When games are played as part of a religious ceremony, they can be considered sacred. The myths and stories retold in the shadow puppet play of Java remind the hearers how the first people on earth received games as gifts from the gods (Geertz 1960).

Entertainment can take on religious forms in the preparation of a large feast. Such an occasion is both social and religious. In Brunei, the preparation of a wedding feast involves the coordination and working together of many people. The religious aspect lies in the belief that it is the will of Allah that all should marry. Thus the wedding has religious significance as well as the social one of joining two families together.

Traditionally special entertainment marked the Brunei Malay wedding week. Dances, storytelling, and music filled the days and nights. Special quatrain verses recited in bawdy language often gave ribald descriptions of connubial life. Today, rock bands, taped music, and television provide most of the entertainment. The marital couple are symbolically royalty during the time of their wedding and the older festivities mirrored the entertainments presented to royalty in the palace.

Traditional American Thanksgiving and Christmas dinners are partially religious events. Stories are told, acquaintanceships renewed, and kinship bonds strengthened at these feasts. The popping of popcorn and subsequent stringing for garlands on the Christmas tree is a time for fun, laughter, and relaxation.

Dancing as relaxation can be viewed as sacred or profane. The Saturday night dancing at the local club in American culture is a form of courting, social interaction, and play. But in India the art of dancing is seen as being a form of worship. Many Indian classic dances supposedly draw their origin from the gods themselves (Bhavani 1965).

The Lighter Side of Life

Play is an important aspect of culture and the study of play can tell a lot about the values, beliefs, social structure and behavior in a culture. People in the distant past surely talked among themselves, sang in celebration, and had their own games and pleasures. Their children played and imitated the tasks of the adults until

Figure 16.4 Hopi "Raindancer," deer kachina

they learned them and became adults in their turn. Astronauts have taken golfclubs to the moon, and while in space have teased the earthbound. Life is a serious proposition, but humans need levity and play almost as much as they need the means to survive.

Jokes, which may be viewed as both verbal art and play, tell much about a culture. They are culture-specific, and usually unintelligible to members of another culture. Humor may provide a safety valve for unbearable tension. Abraham Lincoln was asked how he could joke when a civil war was going on. He replied that if he did not joke he would cry.

Games, entertainment, and play enliven people's existence in every culture. The English proverb, "All work and no play makes Jack a dull boy," expresses the human need for a lighter side to life. Young children almost always seem able to find some small instant of joy or beauty in every day, unless they are in dire circumstances or in surroundings of terror. Therein lies a hope for humanity.

SUGGESTED READINGS

Culin, Stewart. *Games of the North American Indians*. New York: Dover, 1975.
This book is considered by many to be a classic in the area of North American Indians. The work is based on both museum collections and ethnographic accounts. It is well organized into a readable text.

Lancy, David and Allan Tindall, eds. *Study of Play Problems and Prospects*. New York: Leisure, 1976.
An interesting collection of articles that range from children imitating medicine doctors to surveys of children's games in Africa.

Salter, Michael, ed. *Play: Anthropological Perspectives*. West Point: Leisure, 1978.
A collection of twelve essays dealing with play.

Sutton-Smith, Brian. *The Folk-Games of Children*. Austin: University of Texas Press, 1972.
This book examines games of children from an anthropological as well as folkloric point of view.

Our Place in the Universe and the Dilemma of Today

17

All cultures have their own view of the world, and their own conception of the world as a part of a larger scheme of things. Humans query this place in life and in the universe, and arrive at many different answers.

The Anthropological World View

The anthropological world view emphasizes that all humans are cultural beings. As Tylor (1871:1) said at the inception of anthropology as a formal study, culture is, ". . . that complex whole which includes knowledge, belief, art, morals, law, custom, and any other capabilities and habits acquired by man as a member of society." Or in different words, culture is learned, shared, and transmitted patterned thought and behavior.

Culture is a vast and complex entity. The present book has delineated, defined, and analyzed some of that complexity. Cultural anthropologists analyze cultural systems such as language, family, religion, politics, and economics. Anthropologists also analyze how individuals interpret these systems, interact with them, and modify them. Through understanding cultural systems and how they are interpreted by individuals and groups, anthropologists begin to understand the functions, structure, and symbolism of culture. In broader perspective, the study of anthropology is anthropological semiotics; for all culture is "signs" which have meaning, and semiotics is the study of the production and meaning of signs.

Every culture has a world view, an underlying mental blueprint which conceptualizes how the universe should be structured and ordered in all areas of life. The world view includes many ideologies, such as political and religious, which consist of patterned and shared beliefs and values that are held by members of the social group. Each group specifies what are the proper and improper social behaviors and actions for that group. Beliefs are the expectations, opinions, and value judgments held by a specific cultural group. If a *misionero,* a follower of the Niño Fidencio, believes that certain *curanderas,* folk healers, may act as vessels for the spirit of the Niño Fidencio, then that individual holds the belief in spirit possession as well as other beliefs associated with the religious belief system of Fidencismo.

A belief is something that is interpreted as being true, and often times carries the connotation of absolute "truth." This connotation of absolute truth is also imparted to the ideology, the belief system itself. The Nazi belief in the superiority of the Aryan race fueled Hitler's war against the Jews. Leaders often use ideology as a coercive or persuasive measure. Leaders of totalitarian states, such as North Korea, use their interpretation of an ideology to justify coercion. American leaders use the ideology of patriotism to persuade the American voters to support American presence in other countries because we are the "big brothers" of these small nations.

Anthropologists maintain that each culture is a viable, valid working system for those

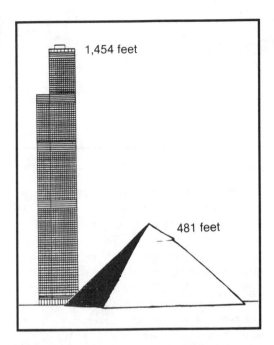

Figure 17.1 Large buildings make a cultural statement. The skyscraper expresses technological hubris; the Ancient Egyptian pyramid expresses a desire to be immortal.

1,454 feet

481 feet

individuals who are members of that system and cultural group. *Cultural relativism* means that the behaviors and customs of a given culture must be understood in terms of that society's culture. Crow culture should be understood in terms of the Crow, not from a biased view based on English, Chinese, !Kung Bushman, or any other culture. To accept cultural relativism does not mean condoning human suffering; accepting cultural relativism means arriving at a true understanding so that help, if needed and wanted, can be better provided.

The reality of the modern world is that hundreds of cultures interact, often at cross-purposes. No generalization about human behavior can be made on the basis of one culture alone. Cultural anthropologists make cross-cultural comparisons of cultures, and of particular aspects of cultures, as a way to better understand human culture.

Cosmologies

All humans have sought to understand their place in the universe. As a road to this understanding, each culture formulates a cosmology. Given the complex and intricate subtlety of human being, it is no surprise that some groups have more than one cosmology.

Cosmologies are the sacred myths and beliefs concerning the original creation of the world and its subsequent structuring and ordering. Drawing on these cosmological belief systems, humankind imbibes meaning for both thought and action, belief and ritual, on all levels and spheres of life—sacred and profane, individual and social, local and national. Cosmologies have an explanatory function and value. They elucidate the proper order and way of life so that balance may be achieved and disequilibrium and chaos may be held at bay. Cosmologies are used as models of and for social structure. As models of social order they may be used to justify economic and political power, sanction polygamous or monogamous marriages, validate land claims, and explain in general why things are done as they are.

Brunei Malay

The traditional Brunei Malays had two main cosmologies in addition to the Koranic one. The first cosmology explained earthquakes. In this cosmology the bovine Gampa stands atop the fish Nun which swims in the Cosmic Sea. The Gampa bovine has 99 pronged horns, and the earth is held in those horns. When the Gampa bovine shakes his head, the earth shakes, quakes. Hence, earthquakes are called *gampa bumi*—the earth being Gampaed.

The other traditional Brunei Malay cosmology explains humans, spirits, the underworld and the upperworld. In this cosmology the earth is flat and has four corners. Somewhere on Earth is Mt. Siguntang, the sacred mountain. At another place, unknown, is the Navel of the World. And somewhere there is the door of the earth which gives access to the underworld. Beneath the earth are seven layers of the underworld. In the first layer, immediately below the earth, is the layer from which came everything that now populates the earth. All the present "contents of the earth" came up from the first level of the underworld onto the earth itself through the door in the earth. The seventh and lowest layer of the underworld is very cold and nothing moves there. Hovering above the earth are clouds. At the bottom of the clouds are the "kingdoms at the foot of the clouds." Above the clouds is the first level of the sky. There is a door of the sky in this layer. The sun sits in the first layer. In the second layer is the moon. Big stars are in the third layer, and small stars are in the fourth layer. Just as each layer of the underworld has a door which provides communication, so too does each layer of the sky have a door which provides communication. In the seventh heaven, the uppermost layer of the sky, is the Throne of the Lord.

Traditional Brunei Malays who are deeply religious and also deeply traditional, do sometimes think about the two different cosmologies. They reconcile the two by saying that when there is too much sin on earth the earth becomes too heavy on one side, so the Gampa bovine shakes its head to even things up, and that causes earthquakes. And besides, they say, "Allah made it all."

Western

As the Brunei Malays have two main cosmologies, so too does Western culture. The scientific paradigm seeks to explain both the present state of the cosmology and the past. The scientific paradigm says that the history of the universe began with the Big Bang, and after that matter spread out through and became the universe. What exists today is the large universe we live in, which is billions of light-years in diameter. Astronomers cannot determine whether or not anything lies beyond this finite universe. The known universe has many interesting features, such as black holes which can gulp matter and compress it into unimaginable densities. Within the astronomical universe are many galaxies of stars. One of the average two-armed galaxies is the Milky Way, in which the Sun is a star with nine satellite planets.

Modern astronomical studies, including interplanetary artificial satellites, have shown that Earth is the only habitable planet within the Solar System. The Earth formed some four billion years ago. Early life arose in the seas. By 400 million years ago plants and animals lived on the land. And 100,000 years or more ago fully modern humans were walking the Earth.

The Earth itself has a complex structure. The mobile outer crust of the Earth forms seabeds and dry land. The biosphere is the region in which life occurs. The biosphere extends from the bottom of the deepest sea, through all the waters of the Earth, over all the land, and up into the lower atmosphere. Within the biosphere humans live in communities and cultures located at various places on the land surface of planet Earth.

Western cosmology forms a grand scenario, but one in many ways daunting to the individual person. Science can ask, "What was there before the Big Bang?", "What is outside or beyond the finite universe we know?" But it cannot answer those questions.

The scientific paradigm has provided many valuable insights, and has done much to better our life, though it has also increasingly provided the means to endanger it. But humans are complex universes in themselves; and deep understanding must come very slowly.

The second cosmology used in Western culture to illuminate the past, order the present, and make plans for the future is the

Figure 17.2 This traditional Navajo clan matron symbolizes the Navajo's continual striving for a harmonious relationship with the universe. (Photograph by Harry Teller)

religious interpretation of creation. One version of this cosmology (Genesis 2) is an abstract and poetic description. The other, better known, is the Judeo-Christian-Islamic cosmology which provides a specific chronology. According to this version God created the world and all that rests upon, in, and above it, including man, in six days and upon the seventh day He rested. God fashioned Adam and Eve, the first man and woman, and made them lords over the dominions of the earth and all the plants, wildlife, aquatic animals, birds, and everything else. Christians and Moslems have conquered peoples, claimed land and re-sources, and established themselves as the "lords" of the masses, all in the name and sanction of their God.

Hopi

Other cultures have their own cosmologies and their own concepts about the interconnectedness of the universe. The members of that culture know that theirs is the true and correct cosmology.

The Hopi view the universe as being dependable and harmoniously constructed. The universe has an inherent duality, for it contains both good and evil in equal amounts. The

Earth is a living entity that contains energy. Humans should utilize and revere this energy. Spirit beings are ubiquitous, they exist in all animate and inanimate objects.

Within the harmonious universe exist the kachina spirits, who reside on the San Francisco Peaks near Flagstaff, Arizona. The kachina have three separate but related aspects. The first aspect is the kachina spirits themselves. The second aspect is the masked kachina-impersonating dancers who appear in many religious ceremonies. The third aspect is the small dolls carved and painted in the likeness of the kachina.

The kachina dolls are made for children but are not toys. Adults expect a Hopi child who receives a kachina doll to study, treasure, and respect this wooden image of a supernatural being. The giving of a kachina doll to a Hopi child is an early stage of the child's religious education.

The kachina spirit's role in the universal scheme is to act as a mediator between the world of mortals and the world of the supernatural. Some kachina beings are good, others are demons (Colton 1959). Kachina are thus expressions of the Hopi dualistic worldview which contains both good and evil.

Hindu

The traditional Hindu cosmology sees an individual's present life as but one in the cycle of lives lived in one rebirth after another. The universe itself passes through stages, of which the present is the Kali Yoga, the era of decline preceeding destruction. But once the present universe has been destroyed, there will be another universe created, just as there was a universe before the present one.

Our Place in the Conceptual World

Cosmologies are perhaps the grandest of human conceptions. The concept of "culture" is also a grand conception, one which has led to deep insights into human life.

I take my seat wherever I go.

Figure 17.3 (Technological dependency has many forms.) (Cartoon by David Flemming)

Anthropological studies and findings have profoundly reshaped the understanding of humans and their place in the universe. Anthropological findings are not clad in the mystique of complex mathematics, but they have greatly altered the course of modern intellectual thought.

The concept of culture and the use of cross-cultural comparisons remain valuable tools for all present and future cultural anthropological research. But the next step is to go beyond the cross-cultural perspective. Anthropology thus far has developed and operated within the Western intellectual conceptual-analytical framework.

Now anthropologists are trying to go beyond the Western scholarly paradigm. One way to do this is to take the intellectual conceptual-analytic perspective of another culture, and apply it to the study of cultures. The following two examples give an idea of this approach.

Yin-Yang

The Chinese yin-yang perspective holds that two elements, yin and yang, are inherent throughout the cosmos, in all things and actions, and in each individual. The yang is the positive, outer, warm, light, energetic, and shallow. The yin is the negative, inner, cool, dark, retiring, and profound. Yin and yang must always go together. There can never be pure yin nor pure yang. As one increases, so does the other.

Looked at from a yin-yang perspective, the yang, the positive aspect of modern industrialized technology makes available to people a great abundance of desired material goods. The yin, the negative aspect, is the increasing pollution, health problems and human social costs. The greater the yang-produced abundance, the greater the yin harmful effects. If the yang production becomes excessive major catastrophe ensues and the industrialized technology becomes yin negative. This happens in run-away motors that self-destruct into yin chaos from extreme yang energy production. Three Mile Island and Chernobyl were instances where over-abundant yang energy suddenly became a yin disaster (Tweddell and Kimball 1985).

Kapunan

Brunei Malays have the concept of *kapunan*. *Kapunan* means "highly vulnerable to illness and accident because of an unfulfilled desire for a food." Brunei Malays say that children who want a particular food, but do not get any to eat, will surely fall ill or have an accident because they are *kapunan*. Brunei Malays say that Americans who are "good" parents indulge their children's food whims within reason, and thus prevent their children from becoming *kapunan*. The Brunei Malays add that American parents have no "logical" explanation for their behavior because they lack the concept of *kapunan*.

The Future

Anthropologists have just begun to use the analytical concepts and perspectives of non-Western cultures in anthropological studies. This newly trodden path of study leads to an exciting future in anthropology.

The Dilemma of Today

People have always worried about the future. Southwest Asian and Central American hunter-gatherers felt doomed by the failing game supplies. But they developed a nascent agriculture which eventually led to modern agriculture. The ancient Egyptians thought the end of the world had come when the Sea Peoples invaded around 1,200 B.C. But the Egyptian empire recovered and lasted another 1,000 years. Thoughtful people of the fourth century A.D. saw the fall of Rome as the end of reason and light, but eventually Europe developed the present Western intellectual tradition. The Black Plague appeared to be the harbinger of the world's end in medieval Europe, but some Europeans survived and life continued on. The Chinese of the late Sung dynasty thought the world was ending as the Mongol invasion ravaged the land, but the world was not ending. The Chinese empire would last for 500 years after the expulsion of the Mongols.

Our present era also seems to be a time of troubles and impending doom. The Four Horsemen of the Apocalypse—famine, plague, natural disaster, and war—still stalk the earth.

The southward spread of the Sahara desert has brought starvation to once-proud pastoral nomads, and to millions of subsistence farmers. War and drought have caused hunger and misery in the African Horn region. The poor in India's slums and rural areas, and in Latin America's slums, go hungry or starve. In the

United States, the "land of plenty," many children and elderly suffer grave malnutrition, and hunger is a growing urban problem nationwide.

Modern sanitation has halted the great pandemic diseases which once swept the globe. But bubonic plague lurks in many wild rodent populations, waiting to pounce if given a chance. Modern jet travel could spread lethal diseases with unprecedented speed, and antibiotic-resistant disease strains are proliferating.

Natural disasters fill the newspapers. Drought besets Africa; volcanic eruption and mudslides kill thousands in South America. Half a million die in an earthquake in China, and floods devastate whole villages in Bangladesh.

Wars beset much of the globe. Some are open armed conflicts, others the terror and retaliatory terror of guerrilla war. The mushroom-shaped cloud of an atomic bomb has become a worldwide symbol of fear, fear for oneself, fear for the future.

The French have a saying, "The more things change, the more they stay the same." Perhaps that also applies to the Four Horsemen of the Apocalypse. Our mushroom cloud may be no more frightening than the Mongol invasions or the Black Plague were.

Paths Toward the Future

Human life has always been a strange mixture of yin and yang, the yang of lives satisfied and fulfilled, the yin of troubled lives haunted by despair. No one has ever been able to see through the impenetrable veil of the future. But a look back through the mists of time shows that many have gone before us, conquered the challenges of life, and left a legacy for the future.

The planet Earth is a precious world, one small habitable sphere set amidst the vastness of the universe. Science fiction and wistful imagination dream of inhabited planets elsewhere in the universe, but none are known. Perhaps we really *are* alone in the universe, one small vibrantly alive place in all the vastness.

Mother Theresa of Calcutta has said that "poverty of the spirit" is the critical problem facing the industrial world. Others have identified the same problem, but given it different names.

The first step toward overcoming "poverty of the spirit" is understanding the richness of humanity living in many and varied cultures upon Earth. Through such understanding we can come to see our own innate worth and dignity, and the innate worth and dignity of others. By removing the constraints of unthinking habit we can develop our own inner selves as individual human beings. We can enrich our inner selves through understanding the varied and vivid tapestry of humanity which covers the globe and reaches far back into time.

Today is the first part of tomorrow. The world has become a global neighborhood which

Figure 17.4 Outboard motors have revolutionized transportation in much of the world. This Borneo boat can complete a journey to town in three hours, by paddling that same journey would have taken a full day. Because of this increased speed of transportation, town is now perceived as being much "closer" than it was before. (Photograph by L. A. Kimball)

can prosper only in harmony. An anthropological perspective and understanding of culture provides a basic tool for building the future.

SUGGESTED READINGS

Henry, Jules. *Culture Against Man.* New York: Random House, 1963.
This book examines American institutions from a Marxist and anthropological perspective.

Rosaldo, Michelle Zimbalist and Louis Lamphere, eds. *Women, Culture, and Society.* Stanford, California: Stanford University Press, 1974.
This is an excellent reader on women in a cross-cultural perspective.

Toffler, Alvin. *Future Shock.* New York: Bantam Books, 1972.
This work has become a classic in regard to technological change and cultural lag.

Glossary of Cultures

Algonkian Native Americans of the Atlantic seaboard live in New England in the Northeast Woodland culture area of North America. The Algonkian were swidden (slash-and-burn) horticulturalists who grew corn, beans and squash. They supplemented their horticulture by hunting and gathering. The Algonkian social organization is patrilineal, divided into clans and moieties, with patrilocal residence.

Alorese live on the Island of Alor, which is located between Flores and Celebes (Sulawesi) Islands in Indonesia. The Alorese are agriculturalists who grow maize, rice, millet, and beans. They have a patrilineal social organization which is divided into clans and moieties, with neolocal residence.

Arunta live in central Australia along the upper Finke River. The Arunta were traditionally hunters and gatherers whose diet included kangaroo, wallaby, and emu (a bird). Arunta social organization is patrilineal, divided into clans and moieties, with patrilocal residence.

Ashanti live in Ghana, on the West Coast of Africa. The Ashanti are horticulturalists who raise plantains, yams, and manioc. They are famed as traders, and obtain fish through trade with coastal groups. Ashanti social organization is matrilineal, with bilocal residence.

Atjehnese live in the province of Atjeh (Aceh), in northernmost Sumatra, Indonesia. The Atjehnese are rice farmers who also hunt and fish. Their social organization is based on the Hawaiian kinship system, with uxorilocal residence.

Balinese live on the Island of Bali in Indonesia. The Balinese are farmers who raise rice, yams, cassava, maize, coconuts, and fruit. The Balinese also have a considerable number of cattle and smaller livestock. The Balinese are famed for their elaborate temple architecture and ceremonial dances.

Bavenda live in the interior of South Africa. The Bavenda are horticulturalists who also raise cattle. Their social organization is patrilineally based, but uses double descent; the shrines of the ancestral cults are those of the matrilineage.

Blackfeet Native Americans live in the Plains Culture area of North America, in Montana. The Blackfeet were nomadic hunters and gatherers whose main foods were buffalo, deer, elk, wild roots and berries. The Blackfoot social organization is Hawaiian kinship based with patrilocal residence.

Brunei Malay live in Brunei Darussalam on the Island of Borneo. The Brunei Malay were traditionally fishermen, craft manufacturers, and traders. The Brunei Malay social organization is cognatic kinship with Islamic patrilineal inheritance.

Bura live in the area between Lake Chad and the Nile River in the eastern Sudan of Africa. The Bura are horticulturalists who grow sorghum, millet, and fonio (a grain). Bura social organization is patrilineal, with neolocal residence.

Cherokee Native Americans originally lived in the Southeastern culture area of North America, in what is now North Carolina, but they were moved onto reservations in Oklahoma, where many now live. The Cherokee are horticulturalists who grow corn, beans and squash, the classic North American triad of crops. Cherokee social organization is matrilineal, divided into clans and moieties, with matrilocal residence.

Cheyenne Native Americans live in southeastern Montana, in the Plains Culture area of North America. The Cheyenne were nomadic hunters and gatherers whose main foods included buffalo, deer, elk, and wild roots and berries. Unlike other Plains Indians, the Cherokee supplemented their diet with fish. Cheyenne social structure is Hawaiian kinship based, with matrilocal residence.

Crow Native Americans live in southeastern Montana, in the Plains Culture area of North America. The Crow were nomadic hunters and gatherers whose main foods included buffalo, deer, elk, and wild roots and berries. Crow social organization is matrilineal, divided into clans and moieties, with patrilocal residence.

Dahomeans live on the Guiana Coast of West Africa. The Dahomeans are horticulturalists who grow cotton, peas, pumpkin, yams, and millet. They also raise cattle. Dahomean social organization is patrilineal, divided into clans and moieties, with patrilocal residence.

Fijians live on Fiji in the South Pacific Ocean. Fijians are farmers who grow rice, corn, tobacco, yams, cacao, pineapple, and taro. Fijian social organization is patrilineal, with bilocal residence. Fijians are famed for their long-distance overseas voyages to trade with Tonga.

Haida Native Americans live on the Queen Charlotte Islands, in the Northwest Coast culture area of North America. The Haida are fishermen whose diet is based on salmon and halibut. They also utilize shellfish, and sea and land mammals. Like other Indians of the northern Northwest Coast, the Haida erect totem poles and give potlatches. Haida social organization is matrilineal, divided into clans and moieties, with avunculocal residence.

Hidatsa Native Americans live along the Missouri River in north central North Dakota, in the Plains Culture area of North America. The Hidatsa were agriculturalists who grow corn, beans, and squash. Hidatsa social organization is matrilineal, divided into clans and moieties, with matrilocal residence. The traditional Hidatsa lived in earth lodges; several centuries ago, one group of the Hidatsa left farming and became horse-borne bison hunters. These were the ancestors of the Crow.

Hatian live on the western third of Hispaniola Island off the southeast coast of Cuba. The Hatian are farmers who grow corn and sweet potatoes.

Hopi Native Americans live in northwestern Arizona, in the Southwest culture area of North America. The Hopi are horticulturalists who grow corn, beans and squash. Their social organization is matrilineal, divided into clans and phratries, with matrilocal residence. The Hopi are famed for their *kachina* dolls which represent beings of the spirit realm.

Iban live in Sarawak, East Malaysia, on the Island of Borneo. The Iban are slash-and-burn rice farmers who traditionally lived in long houses. Hunting, fishing, and gathering supplement the Iban diet. Iban social organization is based on cognatic kinship.

Igbo, also called Ibo, live in southeastern Nigeria in western Africa. The Igbo are farmers who grow yam, cassava, and taro. Igbo social organization is patrilineal, divided into clans and moieties.

Indonesians, see Alorese, Atjehnese, and Balinese.

Inuit, also called Eskimo, live in the sub-Arctic regions of Siberia, Alaska, Canada, and Greenland (groups in each of these areas have specific names). The Inuit are northern nomadic hunters and fishermen. Some coastal groups are noted for whale hunting. Inuit social organization is Eskimo kinship based, with neolocal residence.

Iroquois League is located in New York State, in the Northeast Woodland culture area of North America. Five Native American Indian tribes, the Oneida, Onondaga, Seneca, Mohawk and Cayuga, originally comprised the Iroquois League; the Tuscarora joined the League in the eighteenth century. The Iroquois were horticulturalists who used swidden (slash-and-burn) techniques to raise corn, beans, and squash; they hunted and gathered to supplement their diet. Iroquois social organization was matrilineal, divided into clans and moieties, with matrilocal residence.

Kadayans live in Brunei Darussalam, on the Island of Borneo. The Kadayans are rice farmers who also raise cattle and water-buffalo. The Kadayans are Moslems; their social organization is cognatic kinship with Islamic patrilineal inheritance.

Karamojong live in northeastern Uganda in eastern Africa. The Karamojong are cattle herders who also grow maize, millet, peanuts, and squash. The recent history of the Karamojong has been one of despair. Disease and drought have caused crop failure and famine. The social organization of the Karamojong is patrilineal, divided into clans and moieties, with patrilocal residence.

Kpelle live in Liberia, West Africa. The Kpelle are farmers who raise rice and cattle. Kpelle social organization is patrilineal, divided into clans and moieties, with patrilocal residence.

!Kung Bushmen live in the northern portion of the Kalahari Desert. Traditional !Kung were nomadic hunters and gatherers. !Kung social organization is bilateral descent with bilocal residence.

Kwakiutl Native Americans live on northern Vancouver Island, British Columbia, Canada, in the Northwest Coast culture area of North America. The Kwakiutl are fishermen whose diet is based on salmon and halibut. They also utilize shellfish, and sea and land mammals. The Kwakiutl are famed for their totem poles, and have a tradition of giving potlatches. The Kwakiutl social organization is Hawaiian kinship with parilocal residence.

Melanesians, see Trobriand Islanders.

Masai live in western central Kenya, Africa, in the East African culture area. The Masai are pastoral nomads with a 7,000 year old tradition of herding cows. The Masai often barter their staple beef with neighboring farmers in order to obtain grain. Masai men are noted for their boldness and daring in hunting lions with spears. Masai social organization is patrilineal divided into clans and moieties, with patrilocal residence.

Maya Indians live in Central America and southern Mexico. The Maya are swidden (slash-and-burn) horticulturalists who grow maize, beans, and squash. The Maya supplement their diet by hunting jaguar, deer, monkeys, and large birds. The ancestors of the present-day Maya built pyramids which soared high above the jungle.

Mende live in Liberia, West Africa. The Mende are farmers who raise rice and cattle. Mende social organization is patrilineal, divided into clans and moieties, with patrilocal residence.

Mohawk, see Iroquois League.

Mongols live in Central Asia, on the Mongolian Plateau in the Mongolian People's Republic, and in the Inner Mongolia region of the People's Republic of China. Traditional Mongols were nomadic horsemen who herded cattle, sheep, goats, and who herded cattle in the more arid areas. From the twelfth to the fourteenth century the Mongolian Empire, founded by Ghengis Khan, was a major Eurasian power.

Muruts live in Sabah, East Malaysia, and in Brunei Darussalam, on the Island of Borneo. The Muruts are rice farmers who use slash-and-burn to raise dry (not irrigated) rice. Murut social organization is based on cognatic kinship.

Navajo Native Americans live in the northern two-thirds of Arizona and in northwestern New Mexico in the Southwest culture area of North America. The Navajo are primarily pastoral nomads who herd sheep. Navajo social organization is matrilineal, divided into clans and moieties, with matrilocal residence.

Nayar live in Kerala, on the southwest coast of India. Traditionally, the Nayar were warriors, and many Nayar men today join the Indian military. The Nayar are noted for the fine work of their coppersmiths. Nayar social organization is matrilineal with matrilocal residence, but neolocal residence is becoming more popular.

Nez Perce Native Americans live in northern Idaho and northeastern Washington in the Plateau culture area of North America. The Nez Perce were nomadic hunters, gatherers, and fishermen. Nez Perce social organization is bilateral, with patrilocal residence.

Nuba live in the Sudan Fringe of Africa. The Nuba are horticulturalists who grow sorghum, millet, and yams. The Nuba also raise cattle, sheep, and goats. Nuba social organization is patrilineal, divided into clans and moieties, with patrilocal residence.

Nuer live in western Ethiopia, Africa. The Nuer are famed as pastoral nomads who herd cattle, and who measure much of the beauty and well-being of life in terms of cattle. The Nuer do some horticulture, but consider cattle herding the only worthy way of life. Nuer social organization is patrilineal, with patrilocal residence.

Nyakyusa live in the Mbeye region north of Lake Nyasa in Tanzania, Africa. The Nyakyusa are farmers who raise plantains, maize, millet, and beans. They grow rice and coffee for trade, and cattle are important in their economy. The Nyakyusa are noted for their age-grade villages. Nyakyusa social organization is patrilineal, with patrilocal residence.

Omaha Native Americans live on the southern Plains in the Great Plains culture area of North America. The Omaha were sedentary village dwellers who raised maize, beans and squash, the classic North American triad of crops. The Omaha supplemented their horticulture by hunting and gathering. Omaha social organization was patrilineal, divided into clans and moieties, with patrilocal residence.

Papago Native Americans live in southern Arizona in the Southwest culture area of North America. The Papago are horticulturalists who raise corn, beans, and squash. Papago social organization is bilateral, with patrilocal residence.

Seneca, see Iroquois league.

Sri Lankans live on the island of Sri Lanka (formerly known as Ceylon), Democratic Socialist Republic of Sri Lanka, off the southeast coast of India. The Sri Lankans are agriculturalists who raise wet (irrigated) rice as their staple food. Most Sri Lankans are either Sinhalese or Tamil, and these two groups are at present in serious conflict with one another.

Thai live in Thailand, Southeast Asia. The Thai are Theravada Buddhists who grow rice, maize, cassava, sugarcane, and fruits. Fish provides the main source of protein. The Thai are famed for their beautiful temples.

Tiv live in northern Nigeria, West Africa. The Tiv are horticulturalists. Tiv social organization is patrilineally based, divided into clans and moieties, with virilocal residence.

Tlingit Native Americans live in southeast Alaska in the Northwest Coast culture area of North America. The Tlingit are fishermen whose diet is based on salmon and halibut; they also utilize shellfish, and sea and land mammals. Like other northern Northwest Coast Indians, the Tlingit make totem poles and give potlatches. Tlingit social organization is matrilineal, divided into clans and moieties, with avunculocal residence.

Trobriand Islanders live on Trobriand Island in Melanesia, northeast of Australia. The Trobriand Islanders are horticulturalists and fishermen. Yams and fish are staple foods. Trobriand Islanders are known for the traditional *kula* trading cycle of trade with people on other islands. Trobriand social organization is matrilineal with avunculocal residence.

Trukese live in Micronesia, northeast of Australia. The Truckese are fishermen who obtain a great variety of seafood from the Pacific Ocean. Truckese diet also includes breadfruit, coconuts, and bananas. Trukese social organization is matrilineal, divided into clans and moieties, with matrilocal residence.

Tsimshian Native Americans live at the lower and upper Skeena River and on the Nass River of British Columbia, Canada, in the Northwest Coast culture area of North America. The Tsimshian are fishermen whose diet is based on salmon and land mammals. The Tsimshian built totem poles and give potlatches. Tsimshian social organization is matrilineal, divided into clans and moieties, with avunculocal residence.

Tungus, who are now called the Evenk, live in Soviet Siberia, in northeastern China, and in Mongolia, in the North Asia culture area. The Tungus today are hunters and farmers, but traditionally they were horse and cattle pastoral nomads. After the Russian Revolution, the Tungus were sedentarized. The Tungus were patrilineal, divided into clans and moieties. The Tungus were famed for their shamans.

Tzotozil are a group of Maya who live in Belize, Central America. see Maya

Wichita Native Americans lived on the southern Plains of North America, in the Great Plains culture area. The Wichita were sedentary village dwellers who raised corn, beans and squash, and supplemented their diet by hunting and gathering. The Wichita social organization was patrilineal, divided into clans and moieties, with patrilocal residence.

Zulu live in southeast South Africa. The Zulu are horticulturalists who grow maize, kafir (a grain) and pumpkin. The Zulu also herd cattle, and count a man's wealth in terms of cattle. In the eighteenth century the Zulu Kingdom was a major east African power. Zulu social organization is patrilineal, with patrilocal residence.

References Cited

Abrahams, Roger
  1969. *Dictionary of Jump Rope Rhymes.* University of Texas Press, Austin.
  1970. *Deep Down in the Jungle.* Aldine, Chicago.
Alvarado, Manuel Zacarias
  1980. *Pre-Columbian calendar system in Meso-America,* unpublished M.A. thesis, Western Washington
    University, Bellingham.
Arens, W.
  1976. Professional Football: An American Symbol and Ritual. In *The American Dimension,* W. Arens
    and Susan Montague, eds., pp. 3–14. Alfred, Port Washington.
Bhavani, Enakshi
  1965. *The Dance in India.* D. B. Taraporevala Sons & Co., Bombay.
Bourguignon, Erika
  1976. *Possession.* Chandler and Sharp.
Calder, Nigel
  1983. *Timescale: An Atlas of the Fourth Dimension,* The Viking Press, New York.
Colton, Harold
  1959. *Hope Kachina Dolls.* University of New Mexico Press, Albuquerque.
Craig, Shawna
  1984. *The Living Legendary of Fidencismo.* Master's Report, University of Texas, Austin.
Curtis, Edward S.
  1930. *The North American Indian,* vol. 19, reprinted 1970 by the Johnson Reprint Corporation, New
    York.
Dalton, George
  1967. Primitive Money. In *Tribal and Peasant Economies: Readings in Economic Anthropology,* G.
    Dalton, ed., pp. 254–284. Natural History Press, Garden City, N.Y.
Douglas, Mary
  1966. *Purity and Danger.* Routledge and Kegan Paul, London.
Draper, Patricia
  1975. Kung Women: Contrasts in Sexual Egalitarianism in Foraging and Sedentary Contexts. In *Toward
    an Anthropology of Women,* P. Reiter, ed., pp. 77–109. Monthly Review Press, New York.
DuBois, Cora
  1960. *The People of Alor.* 2 vols. Torchbooks, New York. First published 1944.
Dundes, Alan
  1971. A Study of Ethnic Slurs: The Jew and the Polack in the United States. *Journal of American
    Folklore* 84:186–203.
  1975. Slurs International: Folk Comparisons of Ethnicity and National Character. *Southern Folklore
    Quarterly* 39:15–38.
Dyson-Hudson, Rada and Neville Dyson Hudson
  1969. Subsistence Herding in Uganda. *Scientific American,* February, pp. 76–89.
Eisenstadt, S. N.
  1956. *From Generation to Generation.* Free Press, New York.
Ekvall, Robert
  1968. *Fields on the Hoof: Nexus of Tibetan Nomadic Pastoralism.* Waveland Press, Chicago.

Eliade, Mircea

    1959. *The Sacred and the Profane: The Nature of Religion.* Trans. by Willard Trask. Harcourt Brace Jovanovich, New York.

    1961. *Images and Symbols: Studies in Religious Symbolism.* Trans. by Philip Maniet. Sheed and Ward, New York.

    1964. *Shamanism, Archaic Techniques of Ecstasy.* Trans. by Willard Trask. Bollinger Series 7. Princeton University Press, Princeton, N.J.

    1976. *Myths, Rites, and Symbols.* Beane and Doty, eds., vols. 1 and 2. Harper Colophon Books, New York.

Evans, Pritchard

    1968. *The Nuer.* Oxford University Press, London.

Forde, Daryll

    1963. *Habitat, Economy and Society.* Dutton, New York.

Foster, George

    1967. Introduction: What is a Peasant? In *Peasant Society: A Reader,* J. M. Potter, et al., eds., pp. 2–14. Little, Brown and Co., Boston.

Gardiner, Alan Henderson

    1961. *Egypt of the Pharoahs, An Introduction.* Clarendon Press, Oxford.

Geertz, Clifford

    1960. *The Religion of Java.* Free Press, New York.

    1979. Religion as a Cultural System. In *Reader in Comparative Religion,* Lessa and Vogt, eds., pp. 78–89, 4th ed. Harper and Row, New York.

Gluckman, Max

    1940. The Kingdom of the Zulu in South Africa. In *African Political Systems,* M. Fortes and E. Evans-Pritchard, eds., pp. 25–55. Oxford University Press, London.

    1961. Anthropological Problems Arising from the African Industrial Revolution. In *Social Change in Modern Africa,* A. Southall, ed., pp. 67–82. Oxford University Press, London.

Haviland, William

    1982. *Anthropology.* 3rd edition. Holt, Rinehart and Winston, New York.

Hodge, Frederick Webb, editor

    1936. *The Indians of the United States, the Dominion of Canada, and Alaska,* reprinted by Johnson Reprint Corporation, 1970, New York.

Hoebel, E. A.

    1954. *The Law of Primitive Man.* Harvard University Press, Cambridge, Massachusetts.

    1972. *Anthropology: The Study of Man.* 4th edition. McGraw-Hill, New York.

Hoffer, Carol

    1974. Madam Yoko: Ruler of the Kpa Mende Confederacy. In *Woman, Culture and Society,* M. Rosaldo and L. Lamphere, eds., pp. 173–188. Stanford University Press, Stanford, California.

Huizinga, J.

    1950. *Homo Ludens, A Study of the Play Element in Culture.* Beacon Press, Boston.

Khazanov, A. M.

    1984. *Nomads and the Outside World,* translated by Julia Crookenden, with a foreword by Ernest Gellner, Cambridge University Press, Cambridge.

Kupferer, Harriet

    1965. Couvade, Ritual or Real Illness. *American Anthropology* 67:99–102.

Leis, Nancy

    1974. Women in Groups: Ijaw Women's Associations. In *Woman, Culture and Society,* M. Rosaldo and L. Lamphere, eds., pp. 223–242. Stanford University Press, Stanford, California.

Levine, Nancy E.

    1988. *The Dynamics of Polyandry: Kinship, Domesticity, and Population on the Tibetan Border,* University of Chicago Press, Chicago.

Linderman, Frank

    1932. *Red Mother.* John Day, New York.

Lomnitz, Larissa Adler
 1988. "Informal Exchange Network in Formal Systems: A Theoretical Model," *American Anthropologist,* vol. 90, no. 1, pp. 42–55.
Lowie, Robert H.
 1935. *The Crow Indians.* Farrar and Rinehart, New York.
 1963. *Indians of the Plains.* Natural History Press, Garden City, New York. First published 1954.
Luz, Oskar
 1966. Proud Primitives, the Nuba People. *National Geographic,* vol. 130, no. 5, pp. 673–700.
Malinowski, Bronislaw
 1922. *Argonauts of the Western Pacific.* Dutton, New York.
 1926. *Myths in Primitive Psychology.* Routledge and Kegan Paul, London.
 1927. *Sex and Repression in Savage Society.* Routledge and Kegan Paul, London.
 1929. *The Sexual Life of Savages.* Harcourt Brace and World, New York.
 1948. *Magic, Science and Religion and Other Essays.* Beacon Press, Boston.
Marshack, A.
 1972. *The Roots of Civilization,* McGraw, New York.
McGinnis, Dale K.
 1981. "One Aspect of the Problem of Law Enforcement on the Crow Reservation," in *Selected Papers from the Thirty-Fourth Annual Northwest Anthropological Conference,* Mary F. Ricks, editor, pp. 55–57, Portland State University, Portland.
——— and Floyd W. Sharrock
 1972. *The Crow People,* Indian Tribal Series, Phoenix, Arizona.
Medicine Crow, Joseph
 1939. *The Effects of European Culture Contacts upon the Economic, Social and Religious Life of the Crow Indians,* unpublished M.A. Thesis, University of Southern California, San Diego.
Mencher, Joan
 1965. The Nayars of South Malabar. In *Comparative Family Systems,* M. F. Nimkoff, ed., pp. 162–191. Houghton Mifflin, Boston.
Murdock, G. P. and Caterina Provost
 1973. Factors in the Division of Labor by Sex: A Cross-Cultural Analysis. *Ethnology* 12:203–225.
Murphy, W. P.
 1980. Secret Knowledge as Property and Power in Kpelle Society: Elders Versus Youth. *Africa* 50(2): 193–207.
Nash, Manning
 1967. The Organization of Economic Life. In *Tribal and Peasant Economies: Readings in Economic Anthropology,* G. Dalton, ed., pp. 3–12. Natural History Press, Garden City, New York.
Niethammer, Carolyn
 1977. *Daughters of the Earth.* Macmillan, New York.
O'Laughlin, Bridget
 1974. Mediation in Contradiction: Why Mbum Women Do Not Eat Chicken. In *Women, Culture and Society,* M. Rosaldo and L. Lamphere, eds., pp. 301–320. Stanford University Press, Stanford, California.
Paul, Lois
 1974. The Mastery of Work and the Mystery of Sex in a Guatamalan Village. In *Woman, Culture and Society,* M. Rosaldo and L. Lamphere, eds., pp. 281–300. Stanford University Press, Stanford, California.
Rattray, R. S.
 1923. *Ashanti.* Oxford University Press, London.
 1927. *Ashanti Law and Constitution.* Oxford University Press, London.
Roberts, John and Brian Sutton-Smith
 1962. Child Training and Game Involvement. *Ethnology,* vol. I, pp. 166–185.
Rohrlick-Leavitt, Ruby, Barbara Sykes and Elizabeth Weatherford
 1975. Aboriginal Woman: Male and Female Anthropological Perspectives. In *Toward an Anthropology of Women,* R. Reiter, ed., pp. 110–126. Monthly Review Press, New York.

Rosaldo, Michelle Z.
    1974. Woman, Culture, and Society: A Theoretical Overview. In *Woman, Culture and Society,* M. Rosaldo and L. Lamphere, eds., pp. 17–42. Stanford University Press, Stanford, California.
Sanday, Peggy
    1981. *Female Power and Male Dominance.* Cambridge University Press, New Jersey.
Schechter, W.
    1970. *The History of Negro Humor in America.* Fleet Press, New York.
Schwartzman, Helen, Ed.
    1980. *Play and Culture.* 1978 Proceedings of the Association for the Anthropological Study of Play. Leisure, West Point.
Slocum, Sally
    1975. Woman the Gatherer: Male Bias in Anthropology. In *Toward an Anthropology of Women,* R. Reiter, ed., pp. 36–50. Monthly Review Press, New York.
Smith, Dana Margaret
    1931. *Hopi Girl.* Stanford University Press, Palo Alto, CA.
Smith, M. G.
    1960. *Government in Zazzau.* Oxford Press, London.
Solecki, R. S.
    1975. "Shanidar IV, A Neanderthal Flower Burial in Northern Iraq," *Science,* vol. 190, p. 180.
Spinden, Herbert J.
    1908. *The Nez Perce Indians.* New Era, Lancaster, PA.
Tweddell, Colin E. and Linda Amy Kimball
    1985. *Introduction to Peoples and Cultures of Asia.* Prentice-Hall, Englewood Cliffs, New Jersey.
Tylor, Edward
    1871. *Primitive Culture.* J. Murray, London.
    1979. Animism. In *Reader in Comparative Religion,* Lessa and Vogt, eds., pp. 9–18, 4th edition. Harper and Row, New York.
Van Gennep, Arnold
    1960. *The Rites of Passage.* University of Chicago Press, Chicago.
Vandenbeld, John
    1988. *Nature of Australia: A Portrait of the Island Continent,* Facts on File, New York.
Vogt, Evon Z.
    1970. Human Souls and Animal Spirits in Zinacantan. In *Exchanges et Communications,* J. Pouillon and P. Maranda, eds., pp. 1148–1157. Mouton, The Hague.
Wallace, Anthony F. C.
    1966. *Religion: An Anthropological View.* Random House, New York.
Warner, Oliver
    1958. *Victory; The Life of Lord Nelson.* Little, Brown, Boston.
Washburn, Sherwood and C. Lancaster
    1968. The Evolution of Hunting. In *Man the Hunter,* R. Lee and I. DeVore, eds., Aldine, Chicago.
Weber, Max
    1958. "The Three Types of Legitimate Rule," translated by H. H. Gerth, in *Bekeley Publications in Society and Institutions,* vol. 5, no. 1, pp. 1–12.
Wilson, Monica
    1963. *Good Company: A study of Nyakyusa Age-Villages.* Beacon Press, Boston.
Wolf, Margery
    1974. Chinese Women: Old Skills in a New Context. In *Woman, Culture and Society,* M. Rosaldo and L. Lamphere, eds., pp. 157–172. Stanford University Press, Stanford, California.
Wosien, Maria-Gabriele
    1974. *Sacred Dance.* Avon, New York.

Index

Blackfeet, 165
Boas, Franz, 8, 95, 102
Body language, 79
Bonaparte, Napoleon, 58–59
Borobudor temple mountain, 20, 51, 217
Boundaries, nation-state, 175–176
Braille, 78
Bride price, 121–122
Bronze, 42
Brujo, 203–204
Brunei Malay, 241, cosmologies, 234–235, circumcision, 70, education, 68–69, pregnancy, 63, 65, 66, 67, religion, 181, death, 75, food, 193–195, 196, 210–211, 238, health beliefs, 205, 207, kinship, 146–147, language, 84, 93, leisure, 228–229, marriage, 118, 124, 126, old age, 73, wedding, 79, 112, 230
Buddhism, art, 179, 217, beliefs, 75, 186, history, 17, 45, 49, 51, scriptures, 89
Bulgarian, 99
Bura, 123–124
Bureaucracy, 169–170, 172
Burma, 51
Bushmen, *see* !Kung
Byzantine Empire, 54, 55

Calendars, 30, 36, Muslim, 53
Canada, language, 85
Capture, of bride, 123
Car accidents, 207
Carnac, 93
Caste system of India, 117, 167, 173
Catal Huyuk, 41
Catholicism, 63, 117, 167, 187
Cave paintings, 31, 32–33, 215
Celestialization, 184
Central America, 23, during current era, 47–48, writing in, 93
Central Asia, current era, 50–51
Chanul, 186
Charismatic authority, 171
Charlemagne, 55
Chavin religious cult, 36
Checks and balances, 175
Cherokee, 218
Cheyenne, 123, 165, 220, Quilling Society, 229
Childbirth, 65–67, death in, 75, food taboos, 195
Childhood, 68–69
Children, 129, 232, games, 225–226, play groups, 168
Chin, Emperor, 39, 89
China, 18, bureaucratic hierarchy, 170, 173–174, in current era, 49–50, 60
Chinese culture, 64, 66, 117, 161, 228, 238, language and writing, 89–92, 99, 222, medicine, 205, 208, 209
Chola Kingdom, 53
Christianity, 86, 181, 186, cosmology, 236, history, 15, 17, 55
Christmas, 79, 230
Chronological present, 15

Chu'lel, 186
Cicatrization, 217
Circum-Mediterranean Africa, 21
Circumcision, 68, 70
City-states, rise of, 45
Clan, 110, 145–146
Classificatory relatives, 148
Cognatic kinship, 146–147
Colors, 218
Columbus, Christopher, 57
Common interest groups, 166
Communication, 77–80, through art, 213
Communist Manifesto, 59
Competitive games, 226–228
Complex ranked hierarchies, 173
Computer jargon, 87
Conception, 63
Confucianism, 39, 45
Conjugal-natal family, 129
Consanguineal kin, 130
Constantine, 55
Contraception, 63
Cooborees, 69
Copper, 42
Corporate clans, 146
Corporate lineage, 145
Cosmologies, 234–237
Cousins, 140–142, marriage, 118, 138
Couvade, 66
Cow and plow agriculture, 42–43
Coyotes, 176
Crafts, 217
Cricket, 226, 228
Crop exchanges, 58
Cross-cultural comparison, 2–3
Cross-siblings and other relatives, 140
Crow, 71–72, 165, economics, 109, incest, 117, kinship, 129, 142, 145, 146, 160, life cycle, 65–66, 117, 119, 131, play, 226, politics, 171, religion, 181, 186, 187
Crow kinship system, 151–154
Crusades, 54
Cultural anthropology, 3, 129
Cultural group, 5–6
Cultural relativism, 234
Cultural stress, 205
Culture, 1–2, 5–8, 63, 233, 237, area, 14, and art, 222–223, and economy, 116, and language, 84–86, time, 14–15, shock, 73
Curandera(o), 159–160, 207, 209
Current era, formation of, 45–46
Cyrus the Great, 42

Dahomeans, 165–166
Dalai Lama, 53, 171
Dance, 219–221, in India, 230, sacred, 186
Dao De Jing, 39
Dates, ways of indicating, 27
Death, 74–75, 185–186, food taboos, 195, rate, 116, of spouse, 125
Deforestation of Europe, 43

Visigoths, 55
Visual art, 215–218
Visual communication, 78
Vocabulary stock, 100–101
Voodoo, 191

Wakandaa, 181
Wallace, Anthony, 182
Warfare, food taboos, 195
Waterloo, battle of, 59
Wealth, 109, 112, 115
Western culture, cosmologies, 235–236
Wheel, 25, 36
Whorf, Benjamin Lee, 95, 102
Wichita, 109
Witches, 203–204

Women's groups, 71, 163–165, 229
World War I, 59, 60
World War II, 60
Writing, 87–93, Chinese, 18–19, 39, 89–92, literature, 222, religious texts, 187

Yangshao people, 39
Yankee-Eskimo kinship system, 148–149
Yi Dynasty, 50
Yin-yang, 238
Yuan Dynasty, 49

Zapotec, 36
Zimbabwe, 48
Zoroastrianism, 17, 45
Zulu, 165